The Masonic Pageant

The Scottish Rite Degrees of the Supreme Council, NMJ

D1611998

Frank Conway, Ph.D., *33°*, MSA

Foreword by
Christopher L. Hodapp, *33°*

A Cornerstone Book

The Masonic Pageant
The Scottish Rite Degrees of the Supreme Council, NMJ
by Frank Conway
Foreword by Christopher L. Hodapp

A Cornerstone Book
Published by Cornerstone Book Publishers
An Imprint of Michael Poll Publishing
Copyright © 2017 by Frank Conway

Cornerstone Book Publishers
New Orleans, LA

First Cornerstone Edition - 2017

www.cornerstonepublishers.com

ISBN-10:1-934935-92-1
ISBN-13:978-1-934935-92-7

MADE IN THE USA

Dedicated to
My wife and sweetheart, Kathleen
and to my son, Francis, of whom I'm very proud.

Acknowledgements

Like most authors, I have had a large group of friends and mentors who have supported and encouraged me in the completion of this book. I will list them in the order in which I received their help.

In Lexington, MA, the headquarters of the Scottish Rite, Northern Masonic Jurisdiction, my good friend Richard Burgess, Past Grand Chancellor, has championed the book from the beginning. John W. McNaughton, Past Sovereign Grand Commander offered his encouragement and Gail N. Kemp, Chairman of the Committee for Ritualistic Matters, granted me Masonic clearance to pursue the book's publication.

In my Valley of Southern New Jersey I thank David Herman, Secretary, for supplying me with ritualistic material that I needed to get started. David A. Glattly, Past Deputy for New Jersey and now Sovereign Grand Commander of the Scottish Rite, NMJ, the late Verdon R. Skipper, Past Deputy for New Jersey, Samuel Carlisi, Past Deputy's Representative to the Valley of Central NJ and Steven R. Miller, Past Deputy's Representative to the Valley of Southern NJ all read the first draft of the manuscript and furnished me with valuable critical analysis. The final draft was professionally critiqued by Gene Fricks, the valley's Treasurer and an editor with many years of experience, and Howard Kanowitz, a lawyer who pointed out some features in the manuscript that he suggested could use some revision. I was also encouraged by the support of my friends David Tucker, Paul Schmeck, Pete Saunders, Allan Kline, Brian Read, Joseph Mezzina, Pat Weisgerber, Ray Thorne, and Ron Brining, among many others.

Very special thanks are owed to my true friends and brothers Roger Quintana, Deputy Grand Master of the NJ Grand Lodge, Doug Policastro, Past GM of NJ and David Dorworth, Past GM of NJ for all of their help.

My friend Robert Herd of Colorado Springs, CO, owner/editor of Living Stones Magazine and author of *The Initiatic Experience* has supported this book enthusiastically as has another Colorado friend, Cliff Porter, author of *The Secret Psychology of Freemasonry.*

Of course, I am indebted to my friend Christopher Hodapp for his excellent and thoughtful foreword to the book. As usual Chris has taken time from his busy schedule and outdone himself to help a Masonic brother. A Masonic book is known in the publishing industry as a "niche book" and, as Chris told me, "Frank, your book is a niche (Freemasonry) within a niche (Scottish Rite) within a niche (Northern Masonic Jurisdiction)." In other words, it probably won't outsell Dan Brown's *The DaVinci Code.*

I also thank the Brothers who have contributed complimentary comments (known in the trade as blurbs) for the book's back cover. Please note: On a few pages of the book I have made critical comments concerning the Northern Masonic Jurisdiction's degree system. I must point out that all of these Brothers have read earlier editions of the manuscript and have not seen most of these comments, some of which I added at the last moment before publication, and they are therefore not responsible for the comments nor do their contributions to the book indicate their approval of those particular comments in any way, form or manner. All the responsibility for critical comments regarding any degree in this book is my own.

Thanks are due to S. Brent Morris, Director of Strategic Communications for the Supreme Council, Southern Jurisdiction and author of *The Complete Idiot's Guide to Freemasonry* for his support and valuable advice. Thanks also to Chuck Osborne, a brother from Florida who I met in Chicago.

I am indebted to my brother, James Conway, for introducing me many years ago to the finer points of philosophical logic, a valuable tool for an historian.

I owe special thanks to literary agent Sheree Bykofsky of Sheree Bykofsky Associates, Inc. for her patience and professionalism as she guided me through the maze of the publishing industry and calmed my first-time author jitters.

I am indebted to Michael R. Poll, owner of Cornerstone Book Publishers, a friend, brother and mentor. He graciously accepted *The Masonic Pageant* for publication and has shared his skills and experience with me as we brought the book to life.

As Tolkien points out in his trilogy, *Lord of the Rings*, "Last is the place of honor" so I lastly thank my wife, Kathleen, the person I honor most in my life, who has supported me unstintingly with love, guidance, patience and enthusiasm in my efforts to produce this book and in every other aspect of my life.

Picture Credits

I would like to thank the Valley of Boston, MA, AASR, for granting me permission to reproduce the cover of their brochure announcing their presentation of the 22nd Degree at the Scottish Rite Membership meeting in Chicago on August 20, 2014 and especially Bro. Ken Scott, Valley Secretary, for aiding me in obtaining the Valley's permission.

Most of the illustrations in this book were purchased for legal reproduction from the stock illustration supply company www.istockphoto.com/Stock_Images. Each iStock image is credited as (©iStock).

We have made every effort to secure evidence that the few remaining illustrations used in this book whose provenance we were unable to ascertain are in the public domain and not under any copyright restrictions. If there are any errors or oversights regarding copyrighted material, we apologize and will make suitable acknowledgement in any future editions.

As stated, I purchased most of the images in the book from iStock, a subsidiary of Getty Images. The following are the names or chosen designations of the people who contributed the stock images that I purchased. I list them here in compliance with iStock's conditions of use. If I have misspelled, left out or misattributed a name I apologize and will correct that in the next printing of the book.

Fig. 1, 42 Duncan Walker; Fig. 4, 15, 18, 27, 39, 41 ZU-09; Fig. 5 JonnyJim; Fig. 6 andipanz; Fig 7. siloto; Fig. 8 estt; Fig. 9 xxf; Fig. 11 ivan-96; Fig. 12 OscarEspinosa; Fig. 13 giannimarchetti; Fig. 14, 22 Tony Buggett; Fig. 16, 19, 20, 43, 44, 50, 51, 53 duncan1890; Fig. 17 MarinaMariya; Fig. 21 decade3d; Fig. 23, 52 ilbusca; Fig. 24 xplorer2; Fig. 25 Fierce Abin; Fig. 26 Wilshirelimages; Fig. 28, 47, 48 Traveler1116; Fig. 29 egal; Fig. 31 Andrew_Howe; Fig. 33, 38 benoitb; Fig. 34 compassandcamera; Fig. 35 RLWPhoto; Fig. 36 KenKPhoto; Fig. 37 bauhaus1000; Fig. 40 Grafissimo; Fig. 45 jackmalipan; Fig. 49 wynnter.

Table of Contents

Introduction

Only a few decades ago you could have made a reference to Solomon's temple or Joseph and his brothers in Egypt or the Four Horsemen of the Apocalypse and most people would have understood the implication. Today any Biblical references other than Adam and Eve or David and Goliath will likely get you blank stares in return. The reason is simple: No one reads or discusses the Bible anymore and Biblical subjects by law cannot be taught in public schools. Over the years this phenomenon has been manifesting in Masonic lodges: I could see that many younger newly-raised Masons were quite unfamiliar with the extensive Biblical material upon which almost all Masonic ritual is based. In addition – possibly due to the pressures of political correctness in 21st-century American society – many young Masons were also deficient in their knowledge of secular European and American history, both of which are necessary for an understanding of Masonic history.

Also, there is the misunderstanding that exists in the general public toward Freemasonry. There are people today who call themselves "conspiracy theorists"; they are convinced that conspiracies, world domination and secret societies are different words for the same thing. Among this crowd, the very mention of Freemasonry is sure to get everybody's attention. As the oldest and most well-known of all the world's secret societies, Freemasonry has been accused of everything from being a pagan cult to murdering its own members to doctoring our dollar bill with its symbols. Television documentaries have even hinted that they are behind the UFOs. Many books have been published in the past two decades that purport to expose one or more nefarious aspects of the Craft. Most of these books have two things in common: They are not written by Freemasons and they concentrate entirely on the blue lodge, or Symbolic Masonic Lodge, which is the first Masonic organization that an aspiring Mason joins. It confers the first three degrees of Masonry: Entered Apprentice, Fellowcraft and Master Mason. There is much more to Masonry than this. This book is the result of an effort I have made to counter the conditions mentioned in the two paragraphs above: The lack of Biblical and historical knowledge on the part of younger Masons and the attitudes of the general public toward the Craft.

At the very heart of the Masonic fraternity is the largest, wealthiest and most powerful body of Freemasonry: The Scottish Rite. Each Scottish Rite center (called a "Valley") confers no less than 29 so-called "higher" degrees on its members, ranging from the 4th to the 32nd degrees. These higher degrees present lessons that are intended to build the character of the individual Mason and, through the individual, the character of the community. On a few favored members the Scottish Rite will also confer the famous 33rd degree, featured in the opening of Dan Brown's book, *The Lost Symbol.* Conspiracy theorists are convinced that this is the degree that admits a Mason into the "inner circle" of Masonic conspiracies. So what is this Scottish Rite?

The Scottish Rite is one of the two main systems of Masonry in the United States, the other one being the York Rite. Both confer other, higher-numbered degrees beyond the Third Degree, which is the highest degree conferred in a Blue lodge. Either, or both, of these systems represent the next step for a blue lodge Mason who wants to learn more about Freemasonry's mysteries. In Masonry this is referred to as "gaining more light." Unlike the Scottish Rite, which is a unified whole, the York Rite is made up of three separate bodies, each granting two to four degrees, which have little to do with one other. This book is about the Scottish Rite and does not cover the York Rite degrees.

In the United States, the Scottish Rite is divided into a Northern and a Southern Jurisdiction. The Northern Masonic Jurisdiction (NMJ) is comprised of all 15 states north of the Mason Dixon Line and east of the Mississippi. The Southern Jurisdiction (SJ) is made up of the other 35 states, including Alaska and Hawaii. The headquarters of the NMJ are in Lexington, MA. The SJ's headquarters are in Washington, D.C. For the most part, the degrees of the two jurisdictions are completely different. This book describes both degree systems, but concentrates on the northern degrees because, up to the present, the NJM has had no comprehensive guide book to its degrees while the SJ has several.

The Masonic Pageant is written from a secular point of view and provides historical background material as well as serving as a comprehensive guide for each of the higher degrees of the NMJ. It is intended to be enjoyed by newly entered Scottish Rite Masons, longtime members of the Rite, blue lodge Masons and anyone in the general public who is interested in secret societies and their activities.

The Scottish Rite in both Northern and Southern jurisdictions presents its degrees in the form of one-act stage plays of 30 to 45 minutes duration. Unlike the three Blue lodge degrees, the Scottish Rite degrees are not normally rites of passage; each one is designed to simply teach the initiate a character-building lesson. At the heart of each degree are the moral lessons presented for the candidate's consideration. In addition to these lessons, the Supreme Council in Lexington has formulated several concepts called "Core Values." These are: Reverence for God, Integrity, Justice, Tolerance, Devotion to Country and Service to Humanity. Most of the Scottish Rite degrees are held to represent one or more of these core values. Each candidate for membership in the Scottish Rite must internalize the degree's lessons and reflect on how he might use them to better his life.

The reader, Masonic or not, should be aware from the beginning that I have, as stated above, written this book from a completely secular point of view. This, I believe, insures that no particular religious or philosophical viewpoint is represented at the expense of any other. This method most nearly expresses the original Masonic attitude toward religion, namely that Masonry only supports "That religion in which all men agree, leaving their particular opinions to themselves (from Anderson's Constitutions)."

In dealing with the historical background of Old Testament stories I have presented only what is currently known to scholars of Biblical archeology about the actual religious milieu of Israel in the pre-Exilic period. Recent archeological discoveries have revealed that environment to have been polytheistic and quite different from the one portrayed in the revisionist versions passed down to us in post-Exilic records (i.e., the Old Testament).

Originally, the NMJ had adopted and used many degrees of the Southern Jurisdiction. From the middle of the 20th century there has been a continuing effort in the NMJ to renovate and impart new vigor to its ritual system. The Ritual Committees believed that the Southern degrees had placed too much emphasis on themes of vengeance and retribution following the murder of the character known in Masonry as Hiram Abiff. This renovation project has resulted in the deletion of most of the original Southern degrees and their replacement by freshly written ritual scripts telling new stories.

Each Scottish Rite Valley of the Northern Masonic Jurisdiction is made up of four groups, called "bodies." The bodies are named below; each body oversees its own particular set of degrees:

The Lodge of Perfection (4th to the 14th degrees)
The Council of Princes of Jerusalem (15th and 16th degrees)
The Chapter of Rose Croix (17th and 18th degrees) and
The Consistory (19th to the 32nd degrees).

In recent decades the Ritual Committees of the Northern Jurisdiction have moved every one of the original Consistory degrees with an Old Testament theme from the Consistory into the Lodge of Perfection. The places left vacant in the Consistory by this rearrangement have been filled by newly written degrees, many having to do with American history (the so-called "Americana" degrees). The result is that all Consistory degrees in the NMJ, from the 19th to the 32nd, now feature stories having to do either with American historical figures or with knights and clergymen of the Middle Ages. The Consistory of the NMJ now consists entirely of degrees having a New Testament (Christian) theme set in Europe or North America.

Also, when the Ritual Committees in the NMJ moved the Old Testament-based Consistory degrees into the Lodge of Perfection, they changed many of the original stories in these degrees from themes having to do with the Hiramic Legend to new stories, some of Biblical provenance and some purely works of the imagination with no basis in either scripture or history.

Starting in the 20th century, the NMJ has jettisoned the ceremonial portion of many of its degrees. This is the portion in which the officers choose an actual candidate or "exemplar" (sometimes referred to as a *neophyte*) from the class to join the play's cast and go through the degree with the actors. In addition, the NMJ has deleted almost all of the mystical and esoteric content of its rituals. The Southern Jurisdiction still retains this kind of material, some of it bordering on the occult. The Northern Masonic Jurisdiction, on the other hand, now presents every degree from a familiar, conventional Judeo-Christian viewpoint. There is not one Biblical-themed degree in the NMJ that would raise eyebrows if presented in a small-town American Sunday School performance. One of my readers has remarked that all of our Northern degrees are now "politically correct."

When treating the degrees that derive from Biblical sources I have consulted the works of Biblical scholars and researchers as well as the scriptures themselves. To insure that this book favors no particular belief system or denomination, I have drawn my scriptural sources from Protestant, Roman Catholic and Jewish Bibles. For each degree, Northern and Southern, I have relied upon the latest information from archeology, historical research, biographies, comparative religion and scientific theory to the extent that I could obtain access to such material. Unless otherwise indicated, scriptural quotations in the text are taken from the New American Bible, St. Joseph edition (1970) as these are written in modern, easily understandable prose.

I have not ascribed a supernatural origin to any historic or legendary event, Biblical or secular, leaving such ascription to the belief system of the reader. When citing the opinions of published workers in the fields of Biblical archeology or comparative religion I have included in my citations both their historical and scientific findings as well as any of their cultural or religious speculations that I thought would be of interest. All historic background material that appears to be speculative or unconventional is based on literature research and does not comprise unsupported revisionist theory of my own. The few occasions of personal speculation on my part are clearly indicated as such. My intention has been to provide purely secular historic information free of mythological or dogmatic content. Other than that, any blame for error or perceived misrepresentation of facts must be laid at my doorstep, as they are my responsibility alone.

This book is entirely my own endeavor and is not an official Scottish Rite publication. The Committee for Ritualist Matters of the Supreme Council, Northern Masonic Jurisdiction, has reviewed the book's manuscript and has found no Masonic impediment to its publication. Other than that, the Supreme Council of the Scottish Rite, Northern Masonic Jurisdiction, is not involved in any way with the book's publication and the Council has not been responsible in any way for financial support of the book.

In writing this book I have indeed perched on the shoulders of intellectual giants; luminaries in Freemasonry, history, archeology, Biblical scholarship and comparative religion. These include Joseph Campbell, Barbara Tuchman, Raphael Patai, Isaac Asimov, Jacob Bronowski and Sir James Frazer, among others. To paraphrase C. S. Lewis I would not want the reader to suppose that I were too stupid to appreciate the brilliance of these thinkers or too small-minded to acknowledge my debt to them.

Frank Conway, Ph.D, 33°, MSA
Cherry Hill, NJ
January, 2017

Foreword

The book you are now reading is one that has been needed for a very long time.

The Ancient Accepted Scottish Rite in the United States has had a tumultuous past, and the current division between the Northern Masonic Jurisdiction and the Southern Jurisdiction is far more than just a simple difference in name and geography.

Between 1855 and 1869, Albert Pike took the largely bare rituals of the Scottish Rite that existed in the mid-1800s, and crafted extensive new morality plays and lectures that were ultimately far too complex and extravagant to be presented in a lodge room. These were no mere recitations of simple lodge rituals to be memorized by a couple of lodge officers and performed to an audience of one single candidate. Pike's ceremonies were designed to be acted out in a theatrical setting by large casts of Masons, and watched by dozens, if not hundreds, of candidates. He was the 19th century equivalent of Cecil B. DeMille, and he envisioned a truly inspiring and overwhelming initiatic experience on a grand scale. By doing so, Pike completely transformed the Rite from mere ritual into rich pageantry.

In a span of less than fifty years, the Scottish Rite became the fastest growing and largest fraternal organization in the U.S., apart from Craft Freemasonry itself. Part of this was the simple attraction for middle class American men to become Knights, Pontiffs, and Princes, without the pesky bother of actually having to be born a plump, blue-stockinged, European aristocrat first. This was the Golden Age of American fraternalism, and by 1889, nearly a third of the 21 million adult men in the U.S. belonged to at least one of the more than 300 fraternal organizations that existed in America at the time. But a larger contribution to the Rite's meteoric growth was due, in part, to the incredible popularity of theater during a time before radio and television existed. Even during wartime in the worst of all battlefield settings, soldiers often staged primitive theatrical productions to entertain themselves during this period. The Scottish Rite valleys built large auditoriums and landmark buildings to accommodate these new impressive and complex ceremonies that eventually adopted state of the art lighting, scenery, rigging, sound effects, costumes, and even pipe organs, to provide a totally immersive experience for these Masonic audiences. Often, these facilities were located in parts of the country where such elaborate productions were rarely seen, and the sheer scope of the performances provided an unbeatable allure to eager members. There was also a certain amount of delight in knowing such productions were available solely to this very select group of not just Masons, but *Scottish Rite* Masons.

Ever since the end of the 19th century, the Southern Jurisdiction has made a commitment to providing study material and other resources for their members to more deeply understand the history and meaning of their degrees. This is overwhelmingly due to the fact that Albert Pike was an extremely prolific writer over his long lifetime. He was a true renaissance man, well versed in the subjects of history, literature, language, symbolism, and comparative religion, and he had an enormous private library devoted to these subjects. Pike remains revered in the SJ to this day. His personal library is preserved in their Washington, D.C. headquarters, the House of the Temple, and even his Earthly remains are interred in the landmark building. His collection became the foundation of what is now one of the largest libraries in the world devoted to the study of Freemasonry.

Pike's seminal work, *Morals and Dogma* (1871), was constructed as a guide to the degrees of the Scottish Rite, but it actually strays far afield of that basic mission. It is largely an attempt to place his degrees into an historical and philosophical framework, exploring religion, myth, symbolism, and many other esoteric concepts. He drew upon a wide range of works for inspiration, and in some cases, borrowed heavily from them. The SJ's Grand Archivist and Historian Arturo de Hoyos spent decades researching the origins of Pike's ideas and inspirations, and published a massively annotated, footnoted, illustrated, and indexed edition of the work in 2011.

Pike's tome was the beginning of the Southern Jurisdiction's long history of dedication to educating its members. The book was given to all 32° members of their jurisdiction up until 1974, but its daunting length and Victorian style were off-putting to most modern readers. Still, the SJ did not want to leave their members without some kind of study guide to enlighten and explain their degree rituals. A shorter and more modern book, *A Bridge To Light*, was written by Dr. Rex Hutchens in 1988, and became the adopted textbook for Scottish Rite Masons in their jurisdiction. Since that time, the SJ has founded the Scottish Rite Research Society, issuing both modern works and new editions of long-lost or unpublished books by Pike and other scholars about their degrees and their concepts. They also developed a self-administered education course, the Master Craftsman Program, which relies heavily on another enormous work by de Hoyos, *The Scottish Rite Ritual Monitor & Guide*. Meanwhile, the SJ's degrees have largely retained most of Pike's original intent, structure, and wording. They were updated in 2004 to remove some of the longer processions and more tortured language, but they are still referred to as the *Revised Standard Pike Ritual*.

The Northern Masonic Jurisdiction, on the other hand, has never provided any kind of educational material to assist its members in negotiating the philosophy, history, and symbolism of its ceremonies. While the SJ largely treated Pike's rituals as being inspired *'from God's lips to Pike's ear,'* the NMJ did not. They adopted some of Pike's rituals shortly after he wrote them, but subsequently abandoned them over the years. In a few cases they have modified earlier rituals that existed prior to Pike's revisions, and in others, they have developed entirely new ones, for a variety of reasons. The NMJ has tinkered with or completely rearranged the degrees, especially since the late 1990s. In some cases, ancient or biblical-based originals have been jettisoned in favor of more modern inspirations, and the degrees we see today in the NMJ are very different from what Masonic audiences witnessed in the 1860s.

Many Masons often ask why there is so much difference between the philosophy of the two jurisdictions in the U.S. regarding their rituals. It can best be summarized by the late Melvin Maynard Johnson, the NMJ's former Sovereign Grand Commander, in his *Allocution* from 1943:

> *"If the time ever comes when the Scottish Rite determines to remain static, when its philosophy may not be adjusted to the needs of a changing world, then is the time for its obsequies. Until then, its leaders should never abandon study of the philosophy of its ritualistic teachings that, by recast and revision, it may keep in the van of advancing civilization."*

Regardless of that longstanding institutional philosophy, over the years there were the occasional calls for uniformity of work between the two jurisdictions. In his 2008 history, *The Degree Rituals of The Supreme Council, 33°, AASR for the Northern Masonic Jurisdiction United States of America*, author C. DeForrest Trexler disclosed one interesting episode that illustrates the philosophical gulf between the two groups:

> *"It is of passing interest that in 1960 the Supreme Councils of the Northern and Southern Jurisdictions of the United States agreed to joint meetings of their respective Committees on Rituals for the purpose of promoting greater uniformity in degree work. Before any meetings were held, however, the Southern Jurisdiction withdrew from the venture on the grounds that its ritual, written by Albert Pike, already "was as perfect as humanly possible." Hence, there was no reason to discuss change, notwithstanding that Pike himself had been the greatest innovator of Masonic ritual and, over a period of 30 years to 1884, had revised the initial versions of his own rituals."*

Partially as a result of their continuous ritual revisions, there has never been a true guidebook to the NMJ degrees since *The Book of the Ancient and Accepted Scottish Rite of Freemasonry*, written by Charles McClenachan in 1867, and last updated in 1904. A three-volume guide, *On The Wings of the Double Eagle* by Rev. Jan Beaderstadt was published in 2004, but it was more of a personal commentary than a guide. It suffered from a lack of historical background and was rendered virtually useless almost immediately by the NMJ's massive reordering and revision of the degrees shortly after its publication. Both endeavors were published independently and devoid of official Supreme Council blessings. So, Scottish Rite Masons up North have been left out in the cold in educating themselves about their own degrees, and even the Supreme Council has largely ignored them. Too frequently, new 32° members have thumbed through Pike's *Morals and Dogma*, only to be bewildered by it in their search for anything even remotely resembling the degrees they have witnessed themselves.

Consequently, Dr. Frank Conway has done a great service for Scottish Rite Freemasons with this book. His volume is far more than just a simple, up-to-date guide to the degrees of the Northern Masonic Jurisdiction. Each chapter contains a synopsis of the stage presentation of the degree itself, along with a brief description of its counterpart in the Southern Jurisdiction. But it is in the center of each chapter where you will find the heart and soul of this work. The historic origins, symbols, and myths behind each degree are thoroughly explored, whether it is a story based largely on biblical accounts, medieval sources, or more recent events. Conway draws upon a vast wealth of knowledge, covering more than 2,500 years of history and legends that have gone into the creation of these degrees, and he provides much in the way of background and context. The eager Brother will find much here to enlighten his journey through the degrees.

Almost as important are the two appendices. The first is a history of the formation and development of what became the Scottish Rite, from its early French origins as a six degree system, into what we have in the U.S. today. The second is a history of the evolution of each one of the NMJ degrees, along with the changes in names, order, and design of the individual rituals since the jurisdiction was formed. For students of so-called *high-grade* Freemasonry, this section of the book is invaluable.

Freemasonry is changing, as it always has, to suit the time in which it resides. Today, the NMJ is faced, like all Masonic bodies, with declining numbers, and the large casts and crews required to memorize and stage the degrees of the Rite are getting harder and harder to assemble once or twice a year. Valleys everywhere are feeling the crunch. As a result, the NMJ has taken the controversial step of recording several of the ceremonies on video and showing them to initiates. The immersive experience of witnessing a live performance of the ritual is lost in the process. It is possible that in the future there will be a consolidation of valleys in any given state. Perhaps that will permit their members to join forces and return to properly staging these degrees as they were intended. But at least Scottish Rite Masons in these valleys now have somewhere to turn in their search for more light to illuminate their degrees.

When the first Supreme Council was formed in 1801, its motto was *"Ordo ab Chao"* - *Order from Chaos*. Frank Conway has at long last brought order from the chaos, helping us to more fully understand the twenty-nine degrees worked in the valleys of the Northern

Masonic Jurisdiction of the Scottish Rite. No, he hasn't written another *Morals and Dogma*. He's actually provided something far more accessible and useful for us all - a true guide to the meaning behind the inspiring words they hear pour forth from the stages of their valleys. Untold numbers of Scottish Rite Masons owe him a profound debt of gratitude for at last providing what they have literally hungered for more than a century.

Christopher L. Hodapp, 33°
Indianapolis
January 2017

The Masonic Pageant

How the Degrees are Presented

I have presented the description of each degree in this book in three sections: The Stage Drama, Historical Background and The [same] Degree in the Southern Jurisdiction. They are explained as follows:

THE STAGE DRAMA

This is the scripted drama presented on stage for the assembled candidates to view. In most of the degrees the story is presented in the form of a staged play featuring a cast of Scottish Rite members. The candidates (collectively called a "class") watch the play but do not participate in it. Out of respect for my fraternal obligations I give only a general and capsule synopsis of the degree's story in a few sentences.

I then describe the lessons or morals that the degree is intended to inculcate in the candidate. This information does not represent my opinions but comes directly from publicly available documents approved by the Supreme Council, 33°, of the Northern Masonic Jurisdiction.

HISTORICAL BACKGROUND

This is an examination of the scriptural stories and real-world historical events behind the degree's drama. I try to show how the degree fits into Masonic lore and include any anecdotal or researched information about the degree that might be of interest. I have inserted historical information, sometimes several pages of it, whenever I thought it might be helpful. Again, all my historical documentation is secular in nature and does not support any particular system of religious belief. Occasionally I comment on the way in which witnessing the degree has affected me and other brethren I have interviewed.

Throughout much of its history, the land inhabited by the Hebrews was divided into a northern kingdom (Israel) and a southern kingdom (Judah). In this book I follow Isaac Asimov's example and, most of the time, refer to the entire area under its modern name of Israel. Where the existence of the two kingdoms is essential to a discussion, I refer to either Judah or Israel separately.

The [same] *Degree in the Southern Jurisdiction*

Often a degree in the Southern Jurisdiction is completely different from its northern counterpart. In some instances the two degrees may be similar, but to the best of my knowledge they are never identical. I have not seen any of the Southern degrees performed and have obtained most of my information on them from Dr. Rex R. Hutchens' excellent book, *A Bridge to Light: the Revised Standard Pike Ritual.* I have also researched the Southern Jurisdiction's degrees in Albert Pike's classic and monumental work, *Morals and Dogma,* a collection of lectures in 19th-century prose that Pike wrote to accompany his original versions of the degrees.

ACCESS TO THE COLOR PLATES

Throughout the book I make reference to color plates (Plate 1, Plate 2, etc.). To view these plates, the reader should go to go to *The Masonic Pageant's* Facebook business page (www.facebook.com/highdegrees) and go to the photo album COLOR PLATES. The easiest way to get into the album is to left-click on the color painting of Moses bowing before the burning bush. Then left-click on the right-and left-hand arrows (< >) to move through the album and find the plates you're looking for. All of the color plates in this album are listed as being in the public domain.

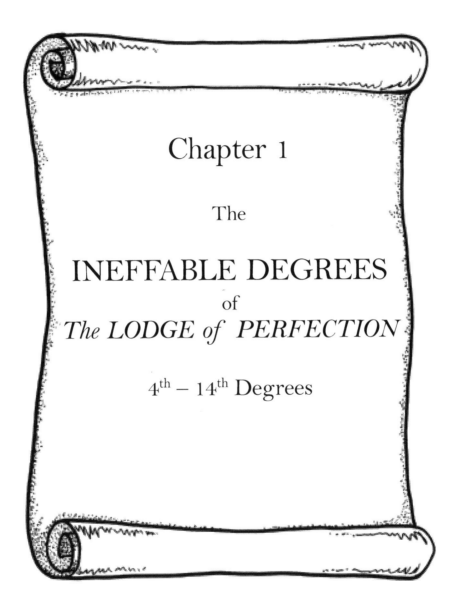

Chapter 1

The

INEFFABLE DEGREES
of
The LODGE of PERFECTION

$4^{th} - 14^{th}$ Degrees

Ineffable means "unspeakable" in a positive sense: that which is too holy to be spoken by the uninitiated. During the Near Eastern Bronze Age (3300 – 1200 B.C.) the "real" names of gods and goddesses were considered so magically powerful that anyone but an initiated priest or priestess feared to speak them out loud. Lay people, when praying to their deities, generally used euphemistic titles like "Lord" or "Lady," which had no magical power. Thus we find titles like *Baal, Ba'alit, Adonai, Adonis* and *Attis*, all of which mean either Lord or Lady.

Incidentally, insisting that the Author of the Universe has a name is as silly as supposing he has a Social Security number. It is probably equally silly to refer to such a being as "he" exclusively since it is generally agreed upon by theologians that the entity we refer to as "God" has no gender. However, most writers on the subject agree that there is no meaningful substitution for masculine pronouns when referring to the patriarchal Hebrew god Yahweh so that is the convention I will follow in this book. I will use feminine pronouns only when I am referring to a goddess.

Today, popular belief holds that, in the religion of the ancient Hebrews, only the High Priest was allowed to speak his deity's personal name out loud, and then only once a year on the Day of Atonement in the Holy of Holies. Further, only the High Priest is supposed to have even known what his deity's "real" name was. All others had to refer to him by the generic title of *Adonai* or "Lord". When the Romans smashed the Jewish revolt of A.D. 70 they killed the High Priest and, according to legend, the exact pronunciation of the Jewish deity's name was lost. Many people think "Yahweh", the name I use in this book, is only a guess.

Actually, Yahweh's name was not really a secret.[1] It was known to most of the Jewish population and the priests spoke it out loud in Temple ceremonies before crowds of worshippers. The name was even known among non-Jewish groups around the Mediterranean before and after the Roman defeat of the Jewish revolt. Physicians commonly used it in magical healing ceremonies along with the names of other gods or goddesses.

The use of a euphemism for a god's "real" name may have come to the Hebrews from Babylonia, where the post-Exilic Yahwist priesthood had probably acquired many civilized refinements. Some Jewish historians date the substitution of "Adonai" for "Yahweh" to the last twenty years of the Babylonian exile.[2]

In the Scottish Rite the Ineffable Degrees, 4°-14° inclusive, are linked historically with the system of 25 higher degrees described in Appendix A. These degrees flourished in France in the 18th century and came to be known as The Rite of Perfection (See Appendix A). In 1740, the first Ecossais (Scottish) Lodge — *Parfaite Harmonie* — was organized in Bordeaux, the oldest and most influential Masonic center in France. Some of these advanced degrees may have had an ancestral source in England and Scotland.

4th Degree:

MASTER TRAVELER
(An introduction to the Scottish Rite)

The Stage Drama

When a man first becomes a Mason, he joins a "blue lodge," which is the usual organization that most people think of when they hear about a "Masonic lodge." The blue lodge is a common building you can find in most American towns; it usually has the familiar Masonic emblem we call the Square & Compasses somewhere on the front of the building along with a notice stating when meetings are held.

It is in this lodge that the candidate will receive the first three degrees of Masonry: the Entered Apprentice, Fellowcraft and Master Mason degrees. But there are other degrees that go on from the third or Master Mason degree and to receive them he must join another Masonic group. In the United States, there are two main Masonic Rites (systems of Masonry) - they are the Scottish Rite and the York Rite. The blue lodges in the U.S. can be categorized by ritual as either York Rite or Scottish Rite. The vast majority of blue lodges in the U.S. belong to the general category of the York Rite (or, a variation of the Preston-Webb ritual). Only a handful of lodges in the U.S. (mostly located in the New Orleans, Louisiana area) work in the actual Scottish Rite blue lodge ritual. These Scottish Rite craft lodges do not work under the jurisdiction of either the Southern Jurisdiction or Northern Jurisdiction. They work under the jurisdiction of the Grand Lodge of Louisiana. For those Master Masons within the Northern Masonic Jurisdiction, they can join a local valley and can be initiated into no less than 29 "higher" degrees, from the 4th (Master Traveler) to the 32nd (Sublime Prince of the Royal Secret).[1]

Unlike the three degrees he receives in the blue lodge, the Scottish Rite degrees, as mentioned in the Introduction, are not rites of passage in which the new member actively participates but are presented in the form of short stage dramas that he witnesses from the audience. The actors in the dramas are Scottish Rite members who dress in period costumes ranging from the time of Moses to soldiers aboard a ship in WW II. The degrees are designed to convey character-building lessons intended to develop the ethical and moral integrity of the recipient.

The stage play's script (called a "ritual" in Scottish Rite Masonry) presents a snapshot of a moment in the history of Western culture. I flesh out that moment and bring it to life in a brief historical essay detailing significant events of the time period featured in each degree's story. I have written the essays from a conventional secular viewpoint and they will sometimes contradict the fanciful, imaginary Masonic "history" portrayed by the degree's author in the play's script.

This degree, the 4th, is an introductory device intended to acquaint the candidates with the nature of the Scottish Rite and the manner in which its degrees are presented. There is no plot. Two principal actors (representing an older, experienced Scottish Rite Mason and a young, newly-initiated member) simply stand off to the side and watch other characters walk across the stage, acting out fragments of several selected degrees of the Scottish Rite. The older man explains to the neophyte what is going on.

The 4th degree is designed to introduce new candidates to the total Scottish Rite experience. The candidates are encouraged to take note of the various moral and ethical issues addressed in the degree fragments represented on stage and internalize them as a basis for further contemplation. The degree's play is intended to whet their appetites for witnessing the full versions of the degrees that the actors have illustrated, as well as the other degrees of the Scottish Rite. The degrees are presented at a day-long Scottish Rite meeting called a "Reunion." (also called a "Convocation" in some areas).

This is a "degree" only in the sense that it represents a necessary step on the path of the candidate; it explains that no one ever sits through all 29 degrees of the Scottish Rite in one day, any more than he would eat breakfast, lunch and dinner at one meal. A candidate will only witness four or five degrees at any one reunion; it would take about six or seven years for a valley to exemplify the entire cycle of 29 degrees (which, today, is not often done). The Scottish Rite is shown to be a center for the individual's moral and ethical improvement as the degrees emphasize the Masonic principles of truth, love, charity and toleration.[2]

Recently the Supreme Council has recorded the 4th degree into a video that a Valley may show to candidates before any other degrees are presented. The degree may still be performed on stage, however.

The 4th Degree of the Southern Jurisdiction:

SECRET MASTER

The Southern Jurisdiction calls this degree SECRET MASTER. It is a direct descendant of the original Henry Francken Ritual of 1783 as modified by Albert Pike around 1855.

Following Hiram Abiff's death, a Lodge of Secret Masters, composed of the Princes of Israel, meets near the Holy of Holies in the unfinished Temple of Solomon. They receive a novice for initiation into their Lodge to fill a vacancy in the temple guards. The Masters instruct the novice in the principal duties of a Temple guard (and, by extension, a Scottish Rite Mason): Silence, Obedience and Fidelity. They lecture him on the different schools of religious mysticism including the Kabala, a favorite magical system of Pike's. The Masters then show the candidate many mystical symbols and explain them. They teach the candidate that he must regard the teachings of Masonry seriously, that wisdom and learning outlast mere monuments of stone and mortar. Also, that the faithful performance of one's duties is a reward in itself, far better than monetary wages.[3]

5th Degree:

PERFECT MASTER
(Two young priests accidentally immolate themselves)

The Stage Drama

The time is about 1250 B.C. The place is the Hebrew encampment in the Sinai Peninsula not far from present-day Jebel Musa ("Mountain of Moses"), the volcano called Mount Sinai in the Old Testament.[1] The degree's drama is a fictionalized version of an enigmatic folk-tale told in Leviticus.[2] According to the story, Aaron's two oldest sons, Nadab and Abihu, "took their censers and, strewing incense on the fire they put in them, they offered up before the Lord profane fire, such as he had not authorized. Fire therefore came forth from the Lord's presence and consumed them so that they died in his presence." Since, to a modern audience, merely kindling the wrong kind of fire on a deity's altar may not seem a sufficiently heinous offense for the god to burn his priests alive, the play's script has the two young men, neither of whom seem very bright, plot some kind of unlikely revolt to replace Moses as leader.

The PERFECT MASTER degree teaches that selfish thoughts and unworthy ambitions will corrupt and destroy a man. If these things are entertained for any length of time in a man's mind, they will poison his personality and he will abandon and forget the duties he owes to God, his family, his country and his neighbor. Honest labor, done with love and devotion by a humble workman, is more acceptable to God than false, vain prayers from the lips of a high-status priest who wears glorious, expensive vestments but whose heart is poisoned by sinful pride. Masons are taught to combine labor (skill), light (knowledge) and love (charity) in all the work they do.

Historical Background

The 5th degree is the first of several Old Testament tales that provide the basis for the stage dramas of the Lodge of Perfection's degrees. These plays dramatically illustrate ethical and moral lessons contained in the degrees of the Scottish Rite. Since many of these degrees have in recent years been moved from their original position in the Consistory into their present location in the Lodge of Perfection there has been, at times, a disconnect between a degree and its title.

The background of this story comes from the journeys of the Hebrew tribes as told in the books of Exodus, Leviticus and Numbers. Another book, the book of Deuteronomy, was later written by Yahwist scribes shortly before the Babylonian Exile and added to these three. The tales in these books describe the wanderings of a confederation of several nomadic Transjordanian tribal groups around the Sinai Peninsula. Their leader, a man named Moses (Egyptian for "Son of") is trying to merge them into a unified nation. Some of these tribes had left the lands bordering Egypt because they had grown tired of having their men conscripted into *corvees* (forced labor gangs) to work on Egyptian monuments.

The tribes were of different, unrelated ethnic clans and worshipped the indigenous gods and goddesses of their home regions. Many of them almost certainly worshiped El, one of the most popular Middle Eastern male deities of the period. At the time the story takes place, Moses (possibly an Indo-European foreigner who had served in the Egyptian army) and his brother Aaron are in the process of introducing a plethora of rules and regulations intended to meld these disparate polytheistic clans into a unified fighting force. Their aim was to invade and plunder the wealthy city-states of nearby Canaan.

One thing that Moses definitely needed was a brand-new god, one that all of these clans could accept with no favoritism shown to any one of them. Unlike the older, more familiar gods and goddesses of the Middle East, the new deity that Moses introduced had no particular gender. It had even manifested itself in the gender-neutral form of a burning bush (Plate 1). When asked its name, Moses said that this apparition had told him that it wished to be called "Yahweh" ("I am who I am"). This could have been an ancient idiom for "None of your business!" [3]

In the days and weeks following the burning bush epiphany, Moses dictated a host of religious rules that he told his people Yahweh had given to him and that the god expected them to observe. The dictation began after Moses came down from the crest of the local volcano (apparently during an eruption!) with a set of ten rules of conduct designed to bring about religious and social cohesion among the tribes. The other rules followed in a series of private epiphanies to Moses over a period of several weeks. Many of the rules Moses introduced, like the sanitary regulations and public health measures, are surprisingly sensible and modern-sounding; they may have been Egyptian army regulations remembered by Moses. Other rules, many given in the form of taboos, had to do with the epiphany of the new god with whom Moses claimed to have spoken.

The story of this degree has to do with an apparent violation of one of the new religious taboos, although the Bible does not specify the exact nature of the taboo.

Fig.1 Moses presenting a bronze idol of an Egyptian theraputic cult called the Nehushtan. See the next degree, **Master of the Brazen Serpent**. *©iStock.*

The footnotes in various Bibles give speculative explanations for the fiery death of the two upstart priests described in the story. These involve lightning strikes, spontaneous combustion and so forth. Here's an idea of my own: The two brothers were out walking in the Sinai Desert when they came across of a patch of naphtha (raw petroleum) that had seeped up onto the desert's surface, not an unusual phenomenon in that part of the world, especially in an era before extensive oil drilling had lowered oil levels. Finding that it could burn, they decide to take some back to the tabernacle tent and impress everybody with this new form of fuel. Back at the tent, they assemble a crowd and hurl a bowl of the thick black liquid onto the fire burning on the altar. When the naphtha, perhaps containing pockets of natural gas, touches the hot altar stones it bursts into a ball of flame, the two brothers' robes catch fire and they burn to death. All the gathered witnesses shake their heads and agree that their new god does not approve of "strange fire" and that they had better stick to the old ways.

Actually, the story needs no scientific explanation. It is a simple reward-and-punishment myth in which humans think they have the powers of a god. These myths were particularly important when one realizes the many different Transjordanian tribal cultures involved in our story. Their religious and cultural differences made it difficult for their new leaders (Moses, Aaron and their chosen supporters, the Levites) to forge a needed ethnic unification. A new god, unique to their group and with no previous tribal connections, suited Moses' purpose perfectly. He needed such unification to raise and train an effective military force to overcome and loot the fortified cities of the urban civilized Canaanites. The hard work of Moses eventually paid off. Soon the nomadic tribes that he controlled accepted the worship of his new god and began to think of themselves as a distinct Semitic nation. They took to calling themselves "Hebrews" (*Hibiri*, "people from the region across [the Jordan river]").

The 5th Degree of the Southern Jurisdiction:

PERFECT MASTER

As with the NMJ, the Southern Jurisdiction also calls this degree PERFECT MASTER. Their ritual is related to the SJ's previous degree in that it has to do with Hiram Abiff's funeral. It describes a yearly memorial service held on the date of Hiram's death in which temple workmen perform a sham burial service to commemorate Hiram's original funeral. A candidate (or cast member portraying a candidate) is initiated as a Perfect Master. The lessons are: Life is uncertain; death can come at any time. The noblest work of humanity is virtue for virtue's sake.[1]

6th Degree:

MASTER OF THE BRAZEN SERPENT
(Moses foils another revolt)

The Stage Drama

The time is, again, about 1250 B.C. The place is another desert encampment of the Hebrew tribes near the Canaanite settlement of Khirbat en Nahas, an area of Edomite copper mines about 25 miles south of the Dead Sea.[1] In this degree's story, Moses faces another revolt designed to replace him as leader. He is saved when the rebels stumble into a nest of poisonous snakes; the mutineers are killed but soon many innocent people are also bitten and are dying. Moses has his metal-smiths make a bronze model of a snake wrapped around a pole (Plate 2). Any snake victims who look at the bronze snake icon are cured of their bites.

This degree teaches that there are trying times ("desert stretches") in the life of every individual person and even in the life of nations. These times can result in a breakdown of faith and discipline. The main point of the degree is to return to faith: faith in ourselves, faith in each other and faith in God.

Historical Background

This degree's story is based on the Biblical events related in Numbers 21:4-9, which, as in the previous degree, take place during the Hebrews' 40-year period of wandering in the Sinai wilderness. The Bible's story relates an attack on the Hebrew camp by a horde of snakes, ostensibly a supernatural punishment for an attempted revolt against Moses.

In the Biblical story, Moses was said to have cured the people whom the snakes had bitten by setting up a tall pole with the bronze image of a snake coiled around it and having the snakebite victims look at it. In religious art of Medieval times the pole had morphed into a tall cross because it had become, in Christian iconography, a graphic foreshadowing of the Crucifixion. This alluded to a popular Medieval legend that people who had gazed upon Christ as he hung on the cross had been healed of their ills (as told in Lew Wallace's novel *Ben Hur*, in which two Jewish women, brought to the scene of the Crucifixion, are cured of Hansen's disease). Some 19th-century artwork shows the top of the pole as an ankh, the Egyptian hieroglyph for "life."

In the Gospel of John we are told that

"Just as Moses lifted up the serpent in the desert,
so must the Son of Man be lifted up that all who believe
may have eternal life in him." (John 3:14-15)

This is one of three references John makes to the "lifting up" of Christ and refers specifically to the Crucifixion. The two other references refer to the Resurrection and the Ascension.

The folk-tale of the bronze serpent ("brazen" is yet another King James mistranslation; brass, an alloy of copper and zinc, was perfected in India around 100 B.C. and would have been unknown to the primitive nomadic tribes of the Transjordan region in the time of Moses) is quite interesting. It may have represented one of the few surviving stories portraying the native religion of some the early Hebrew tribal clans — particularly those that had fled from their homelands on the borders of Egypt. It was edited but not deleted by the Yahwist Scribes. During the Babylonian Exile (586-538 B.C.), they rewrote the compendium of myths, legends and historical events that became the present-day version of the Old Testament, substituting the name of Yahweh for that of whatever other gods mentioned in the stories. This story tells, quite plainly, of the worship of the *Nehushtan*, an Egyptian sacred image in the form of a bronze snake on a pole.

Fig. 2 Carved relief of the Egyptian snake goddesses, Renenutet and Meretseger, possibly the deities that Moses had his artisans portray on the pole. © iStock.

From its description, it sounds like the Nehushtan might have been the icon of an Egyptian therapeutic cult. These cult centered on the worship of certain popular Egyptian snake-goddesses (Renenutet, Meretseger or Wadjet, for instance) who were represented as hooded cobras. Egyptians prayed to these icons as a protection against, or cure for, snake-bite. Anyone raised in snake-infested Egypt or a neighboring region would have been familiar with their worship and would have benefited from the placebo effect furnished by a well-made, impressive idol. Primitive people associated snakes with the renewal of life and health because they shed their skin periodically and appeared to come out shiny and renewed. In later centuries, the icon of a snake wrapped around a staff became the emblem of Asclepius, the Greek god of healing.

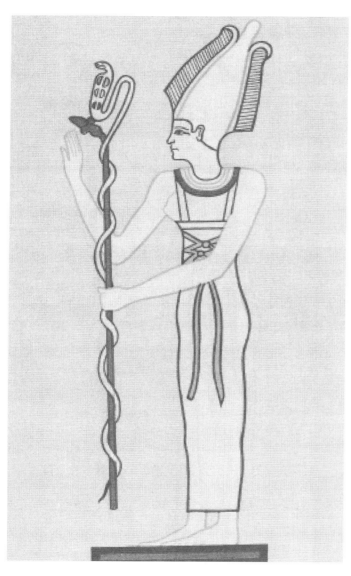

Fig. 3 The Egyptian goddess Nekhebit holding a snake-wrapped papyrus scepter. From E. A. Wallis Budge, "The Gods of the Egyptians."

Also, many of the more important Egyptian goddesses were shown in tomb wall paintings holding a "papyrus scepter" in one hand. This is a five-foot long stalk of flowering papyrus, sometimes with a long serpent coiled around it. The serpent is clearly a hooded cobra (*Naja haje*), possibly the same species that attacked the rebels in Moses' camp. The real form of Moses' idol may have well been that of a snake-wrapped papyrus scepter.

Around 700 B.C., Hezekiah, the 14th ruler (715-686 B.C.) of the southern kingdom of Judah, was looking around for some political public action that would show his Assyrian overlords that he rejected any connection with their hated rival, the Egyptian empire. So he went into Solomon's temple and destroyed the Egyptian Nehushtan as "foreign" idols.[2] Apparently, up until that time, several such snake idols had been housed in the Jerusalem Temple and the common people had been burning incense and praying to the Egyptian goddesses they represented.[3]

The 6th Degree
of the Southern Jurisdiction

INTIMATE SECRETARY

The 6th degree in the Southern Jurisdiction is the same as the Northern Jurisdiction's original INTIMATE ["personal"] SECRETARY degree (see Appendix B: History and Development of the Degrees) except that the eavesdropper is named Zabud. It teaches that zeal and fidelity to one's duty are always rewarded. It says that we are to be zealous, faithful, disinterested (not acting for our own benefit) and benevolent. We are to be peacemakers.[4]

7th Degree:

PROVOST AND JUDGE
(A secret code saves the day)

The Stage Drama

The place is Jerusalem and we are at the building of Solomon's Temple; the time is around 965 B.C. (the exact dates for the building of Solomon's temple are uncertain, as is the existence of Solomon's temple itself)). The story tells of six stonemasons working on the capstones for an arched door in the temple. One of the masons purloins the arch's beautifully finished keystone, the work of another mason, and trouble ensues. They take the matter before seven judges, one of whom had been an Acting Provost (that is, an official or supervisor in charge of the workers) before his promotion to Judge, hence the degree's title. Using a secret method of labeling that was not known to the workmen, the former Provost resolves the matter, the proper mason receives credit for his work and justice is done.

This degree teaches us to righteously judge, and that one law and one custom shall apply to all. Let justice be impartial, tempered with mercy.

"To do justice and judgment is more acceptable to the Lord than sacrifice. Open thy mouth to judge righteously. He that followeth after righteousness and mercy findeth life, righteousness and honor. Blessed are the peacemakers for they shall be called the children of God."

In addition, the degree places a philosophical emphasis upon the task of the Judge as a healer of disputes and the need for Truth, Equity and Justice.

Historical Background

This is a purely Masonic fable and has no real historical or scriptural basis, except for a mention in 1 Chronicles 23:4 of six thousand (!) Levites that Solomon made "officials and judges." In this degree, the stone workers who are building Solomon's temple are said to be both Jews and Freemasons. This is wrong on three counts. The Hebrews of 965 B.C. were not yet "Jews"; they would not take that title until they returned from the Babylonian

Exile. The skilled artisans who worked on the temple were not Hebrews anyway but were Phoenician guest workers, as the Hebrews of Solomon's time knew nothing of monumental building in stone. Also, the form of Grand Lodge Freemasonry described among the workmen would not be around for another 2660 years. Whether Solomon's temple actually had Roman-style arches with keystones is not known for certain but is remotely possible.

Fig. 4 Phoenician workman on the temple of Solomon. These men were all worshippers of the goddess Astarte, the patron deity of their home city, Tyre. ©iStock.

What strikes me most about this story are the attitudes of the supervisor and the judges towards the workers who come before them. In the play, they treat the stonemasons more like slaves or prisoners of war than like skilled craftsmen and respected artisans. The lot of a Master Mason at the building of King Solomon's Temple sounds more like a prison sentence than a life of honorable craftsmanship. All the judges seem to care about is being able to write a report saying that they have handed out some kind of a punishment to someone to show Solomon that they're doing their jobs. One of the degree's lessons should be that government appointees never change.

The 7th Degree
of the Southern Jurisdiction:

PROVOST AND JUDGE

In the Southern Jurisdiction this degree has the same name and number but a different theme altogether. In this version, both "Jews" and Phoenicians are working together on the temple. One of the Jewish laborers, Uriah, thinks the Phoenicians are "unclean" because they're not circumcised (a Jewish custom that did not become commonplace until the return from the Babylonian Exile) and wants his boss, the Provost Naboth, to get rid of them. Naboth doesn't agree. The two men take their quarrel to a judge, Zabud. Both Uriah and Naboth try to corrupt Zabud into favoring their own positions. Zabud throws them both out in disgust. The degree teaches that, since all actions have consequences, we should let justice guide our actions. We should be just in judging others' motives.

The Albert Pike Ritual of 1855-1865 for this degree ends with these questions and answers:

Q . How should Masons always act?
A. With Justice.
Q. How should they deliberate?
A. With Impartiality.

And decide by the rule of Equity. So let us act, deliberate and decide.[1]

8th Degree:

INTENDANT OF THE BUILDING
(Solomon becomes king and breaks up a party)

The Stage Drama

The place is the throne room of David, second king of Israel, in his palace in Jerusalem. His friend, Hiram, king of Tyre, is also present. The time is approximately 970 B.C., the last year of David's reign. The dying king reads his last will and testament. It names his sixth son, Solomon, to be "Intendant of the Building." The "Building" referred to in David's will turns out to be the magnificent temple David had planned to build in Jerusalem (Plate 5).

Hearing this, Adonijah, David's oldest son by his wife Haggith, realizes that David plans to make Solomon, a much younger son, his successor. Infuriated, Adonijah rushes out and proclaims himself king and gives a big party for all his followers to celebrate.[1] David counters this attempted coup d'état by ordering his court prophet, Nathan, to take Solomon to Gihon (a spring outside Jerusalem that was the main source of water for the city) and publicly anoint him king. David orders Nathan to make a great fanfare so that everyone (including Adonijah and his friends) would hear and understand. The counterstrike works; Adonijah creeps back to beg David's forgiveness. David lets Solomon decide his brother's fate. Solomon publicly and piously forgives him for the time being but has him killed a year or so later.[2]

This degree teaches that each new honor that is given to us in life is to be a step toward perfection in our personal moral code. Each honor earned demands attention to a particular duty.

Historical Background

The word *intendant*, as used here, has the same meaning as the modern term *super*intendant: someone in charge of a building. In this story the "building" is the yet-to-be-built Temple of Solomon in Jerusalem. The story relates that David, in his will, designates his young son Solomon to be the person in charge of the planned royal temple. Since the temple will be built after David's death, David is effectively naming Solomon his successor.

At this early period in Israel's history succession to the throne was not fixed by law. Since there was not yet an established royal bloodline (David had been a usurping commoner) there was no right of succession by primogeniture (where the oldest son becomes king). The reigning king could name whomever he pleased as his successor. It would then be up to the new king to defend his throne against any other claimants or pretenders who challenged his right to rule.

The play's writers loosely based the degree's story on the events of 1 Kings, 1. The actual Biblical story mentions neither a reading of David's will to his assembled sons nor the presence of Hiram, King of Tyre. Actually, Hiram did not ascend to the Tyrian throne until 969 B.C., four years after David died and Solomon had become king. His association with Solomon's father David in the Bible is an anachronism probably inserted by post-Exilic Scribes of a later generation. Because Hiram, King of Tyre, was such a famous person for centuries afterwards, these writers thought they were adding luster to David's biography (and providing evidence that he even existed) by linking the two kings. Later generations of Jews held the Phoenician king in such high regard that rabbinic legend tells us that King Hiram, like Elijah and Enoch, did not die but was taken up into Heaven alive. All this for a worshipper of the goddess Astarte!

For the first time we meet David and his son, Solomon (Plate 4). Since so much Masonic lore is built around Solomon and his fabulous temple, we should pause for a moment and review what we actually know about the man.

First, outside of the Bible there is no record of an Israelite king named David who had a son named Solomon. Nor have archeologists found any evidence of a large temple of any kind in Jerusalem around 900 B.C. No artifact that can definitely be attributed to either David's palace or Solomon's temple has yet been found.[3]

In 1993 a disputed archeological discovery was made at a dig called Tel Dan, about 75 miles north of Jerusalem. It was the fragments of an inscribed stone monument called a *stela* that contained the phrase "House of David." The black basalt stela had been inscribed and erected about 100 years after Solomon is supposed to have died in 930 B. C. David was probably a common enough name in Israel around 830 B. C. and most scholars maintain that there is nothing to indicate that the David in the inscription was the legendary Biblical king.[4]

However, as a Mason I accept the existence of both David and Solomon and I will treat Solomon's magnificent Phoenician temple and his glorious reign as if they were undisputed historical facts. If we accept *this* premise, however, we must also accept the premise that Solomon was an actual man of his times and present him and his contemporaries as denizens of a realistic Israel of 1000 B.C. (as revealed by modern archeological discoveries). The resulting picture will be different from that presented by the revisionist histories of the post-Exilic Yahwist scribes. For instance, the religious beliefs of a real king of Israel in Solomon's time would almost certainly not be those we were taught in Sunday school or Bible Study class.

Even with this suspension of critical judgment, we should go one step further and distinguish the Solomon of Masonic lore, a super-pious wise man, from the ruthless and cunning despot described in the First Book of Kings. For instance, Solomon had in his employ a creature known as Benaiah, son of Jehoiada. This character, a Lucca Brazzi type of thug, had "made his bones" in David's army by killing several lions and a spear-wielding Egyptian "of large stature." Armed only with a club, Benaiah had wrested the spear away and then killed the Egyptian with his own weapon. Benaiah was the captain of David's bodyguard and was later made commander-in-chief of the army by Solomon.

Solomon used Benaiah as his personal hit man. He had him kill his, Solomon's, brother Adonijah when that young man was foolish enough to ask permission to marry a woman from the royal harem (which would have constituted a direct challenge to Solomon's authority). Benaiah also killed Joab, David's old army commander who had sided with Adonijah. At Solomon's orders, the ruthless assassin murdered Joab at the very altar where he clung, trembling and shaking, seeking sanctuary. Shimei, a Benjamite relative of Saul who had once cursed and insulted David and later repented, was living in Jerusalem. David's last recorded statement was a plea for Solomon to find some excuse to kill the old man. As H. G. Wells points out in his monumental work *The Outline of History*, David's last recorded word (in King James English translation) is "blood." In a scene that might have been taken from Mario Puzo's novel, *The Godfather*, the dying old king whispers to his son:

> "You also have with you Shimei, son of Gera, the Benjaminite of Bahurim, who cursed me balefully when I was going to Mahanaim. Because he came down to meet me at the Jordan [and apologized], I swore to him by the Lord that I would not put him to the sword. But you must not let him go unpunished. You are a prudent man and will know how to deal with him and send his hoary head down to the grave in blood."

(1 Kings 2: 8 – 9)

Solomon complied and placed Shimei under strict house arrest, under penalty of death if he disobeyed. When he heard that Shimei had left his house to fetch back a couple of straying servants, Solomon sent for Shimei and rebuked him. When he dismissed the trembling Shimei, Benaiah was waiting outside the palace door with orders to kill the old man as soon as he stepped outside. Benaiah, as usual, followed orders.[5]

Solomon's father, David, was said to be "a man of blood." The Solomon portrayed in the Bible was no better. Like father, like son.

For the first time in these stories, a new professional class in Hebrew society – the prophets – makes its appearance. The particular prophet in this story, Nathan, had been the court prophet of Solomon's father, David. He had confronted David with the king's criminal behavior when he had seduced Bathsheba, the wife of Uriah the Hittite, whom David had ordered killed.[6] Unlike most others who dared to oppose David, Nathan survived this episode. Apparently the pin-point accuracy of his accusations caught David off guard and frightened him into submission. Nathan lived on to write histories of David and Solomon and to arrange liturgical music for Temple worship.

Our English word "prophet" is from the Greek, meaning "foreteller," but the original Hebrew word for a member of this class was *nabi*, from a root meaning "to bubble forth," as from a fountain, or "to utter." Apparently a prophet was someone who talked a lot in public. Nathan and most of the other named prophets in the Old Testament were basically licensed public speakers. They enjoyed the freedom (denied to most other citizens) to rant before large public assemblies and, occasionally, to enter the throne room and rant before the king and his *kahal* (court) without fear of reprisal.

The prophets were also licensed pamphleteers allowed to post written diatribes for public view.[7] The topic of their rants and diatribes was usually some form of political demagoguery. It may well be that for every prophet we hear about in the Old Testament, there were probably around 10 others who ranted in the wrong place at the wrong time before the wrong monarch. We've never heard of them because they met a swift and untimely death. The license to rant was probably revocable at the pleasure (or displeasure) of the king.

As a protection against such abrupt and unpleasant career termination, the prophets worked hard to acquire the reputation of being *ro'ehim,* seers or oracles to whom a god speaks directly. Anyone, even a king, who believes that a god is speaking to

Fig. 5 Jeremiah, a 7th century B.C. Hebrew prophet lamenting over the destruction of Jerusalem. ©iStock.

him, will respect the man claiming to be the god's mouthpiece. And he'll think twice before ordering the man struck down in a fit of temper.

Since these prophets claimed that they could hear the voice of either El or Yahweh speaking to them, modern scholars now refer to them as *auditory* prophets. Most of the auditory prophets were educated men from the upper classes who had no trouble mingling with the nobility. Some, like Elisha, the disciple of Elijah, were masters or "fathers" of prophetic schools or "guilds." These were open-air institutions where young men, called *guild prophets*, could receive training in the arts of divination and magic.

Unlike the licensed auditory prophets, the guild prophets or *nebiim* were wandering for-tunetellers, healers, rainmakers and magi-cians. These men probably came from the lower classes and they lived and worked among the peasantry. A prospective client could find and iden-tify a guild prophet by his special costume, his colorful "magic" cloak and, perhaps, an

Fig. 6 David playing his harp before King Saul. Saul appears to be having one of his attacks of depression. ©iStock.

identifying symbol tattooed on his forehead between the eyes.[8] Having no official government sanction, guild prophets relied on charisma and showmanship – including music and wild dancing – to attract clients. To impress their audiences they routinely entered into ecstatic trances and convulsive seizures, either staged or induced by eating toxic mushrooms. No less a figure than Saul, after the auditory prophet Samuel had anointed him king of Israel, fell in with a band of these itinerant shamans as they were writhing on the ground in their ecstasies. Saul, whose mental stability seems to have been marginal at best, immediately fell down and rolled around in the midst of them.[9] Onlookers thought he was crazy.

The 8th Degree
of the Southern Jurisdiction:

INTENDANT OF THE BUILDING

In the Southern Jurisdiction the 8th degree is also called INTENDANT OF THE BUILDING. It takes place after the death of Hiram Abiff and describes the selection, to succeed Hiram, of five exceptionally skilled young artisans whom Hiram had personally mentored in their crafts. They are: 1) Gareb the Hebrew, a worker in gold and silver, 2) Zelec of Gebal, a stone mason, 3) Satolkin, a carpenter, 4) Yehu-Aber, a Phoenician artificer in bronze and 5) Adoniram, a superintendent and administrator. The ritual includes a candidate who is obligated as an Intendant of the Building. The degree teaches that benevolence and charity demand that we correct our own faults as well as those of others. One should transmit his knowledge to the next generation. Labor is honorable if done with sobriety, temperance, punctuality and industry.[10]

9th Degree:

MASTER OF THE TEMPLE
(The quest to find God)

The Stage Drama

The time is 963 B.C. and the place is the outer court of Solomon's new Temple in Jerusalem. Solomon is about to dedicate his temple and has invited an assembly of priests of various Mediterranean religions to witness the occasion. Each of the priests gives a short talk on his particular pantheon of deities; Solomon listens politely. Other guests include Hiram, King of Tyre and Zadoc, Solomon's High Priest. Also present is a man named Hadad from the bordering kingdom of Edom. After the foreign priests make their speeches and Solomon is about to begin the dedication ceremony, Hadad causes trouble. Like Job he has recently suffered an unbelievable number of catastrophes. He delivers a blasphemous tirade against Yahweh and narrowly escapes death at the hands of a mob. He then falls on his knees and is converted to belief in Yahweh by an appearance of the archangel Uriel.

This degree teaches that a mutual belief in a Supreme Power should bind all men together in a worldwide brotherhood. This universal brotherhood is the particular message of the Ninth Degree. All through the ages, men have been seeking God, each in his own way, and have worshiped Him, each in his own tongue. A Master of the Temple is taught that God is best served by those who best serve their fellowmen and who reveal in their own lives the compassion of the Eternal.

Historical Background

The Quest for God

Humanity's quest to know the Great Architect of the Universe began long before the time of the Old Testament, long before recorded history of any kind. 100,000 years before Abraham walked the earth people who we would hardly recognize as human – the Neanderthal family groups of Ice Age Europe – buried their dead painted with red ochre and covered with flowers.[1] They sometimes placed the bodies in the fetal position, facing the east. Perhaps they hoped that the dead would be born again into the morning of a new life.[2]

Around 20,000 years ago, people who looked like us wandered through the European wilderness, following the streams and rivers. They were the clans of Paleolithic ("Old Stone Age") hunters. They found refuge from the Ice Age cold in the caverns of France and Spain. There they painted the walls of their cave homes with images of the game animals, many of them now long extinct, that they hoped to kill and eat.

Fig. 7 A bison painted on a cave wall, Altimira, northern Spain. Circa 15,000 B.C. ©iStock.

In those days a successful hunt could mean the difference between survival and starvation, and the painted cave images indicate the practice of magical ceremonies aimed at bringing home an abundance of fresh meat. The cave dwellers also carved countless tiny statues of women, some of them appearing to be pregnant. These images – of stone, ivory, bone and clay – were frequently tapered at the bottom, as if they were meant to be thrust into the earthen cave floor. These statuettes probably represented goddesses, a logical personification of Deity for such people who lived on the bare edge of survival. They would naturally have looked for support from a cosmic, all-nourishing Mother. They had no need of a bad tempered, thunderbolt-throwing god like Zeus or Thor or Yahweh who would cast horrific punishments on them for the least transgression. The wilderness environment of Ice Age Europe was doing that to them already.

Around 9,600 B.C., the first known organized religion, complete with carved stone temples, came into existence near Göbekli Tepe in the area that is now southern Turkey, near the northern border of Syria. The worshipers who built the temple were Neolithic ("New Stone Age") hunters and gatherers who lived throughout the area in scattered mud-hut villages of several hundred citizens each. They belonged to the period that Archeologists call Pre-pottery Neolithic A (10,000 – 8,500 B.C.).

Fig. 8 A Cro-Magnon hunter painting a bison on the wall of his cave. Circa 20,000 B.C.© iStock.

The deities they worshipped are unknown, as these people left no written records. They had no pottery, no domesticated animals, no agriculture and no metal. They fashioned all their tools or weapons out of flint, bone, antler or wood. With this primitive equipment they managed to excavate, dress and carve stone pillars weighing up to 16 tons. Without draft animals or wheeled vehicles, they transported these huge pillars hundreds of yards from the quarries to the temple area. The pillars are much more expertly smoothed and sculpted than those at Stonehenge, built some 6,000 years later.

These Stone-Age temples consisted of T-shaped stone pillars arranged in tight concentric circles. Many of the pillars were decorated with sophisticated carvings, in bas-relief, of local animals, most of them predators. In the center were two free-standing pillars which may have had offerings of game animals hung on them. The carved animals are thought to have represented guides to the spirit world from whom the worshippers sought help or guidance. The temple complexes, the first in the world so far discovered, appear to have been permanently inhabited only by a handful of priest and priestesses who were supported by the hunting and gathering bands that lived within about a 50-mile radius. Archeological evidence indicates that, several times a year, hundreds of people converged on the temples for some sort of festival or religious ritual. The temples, which have only been partially excavated, were finally abandoned for unknown reasons around 8,200 B.C.[3]

From around 3,500 B.C. to 1200 B.C., as the early Mediterranean civilizations arose, the quest for God led people to envision the Great Architect in human form as a local deity, a god or a goddess. Babylonia had Ishtar. Egypt had Isis, Hathor, Osiris, and Ra. Mycenaean Greece had Zeus, Hera, Poseidon, Athena and Aphrodite.

Fig. 9. Animals sculpted onto a pillar. Archeological dig at the Prepottery Neolithic A temple complex at Gobekli Tepe, Turkey, built around 9,600 B.C. © iStock.

The people of these early religions yearned for gods and goddesses who looked like them, acted like them and enjoyed the same things they enjoyed. These were gods the people could understand, gods they felt comfortable with, gods who could enjoy the meat and drink the priests offered up in sacrifices. They wanted their gods to have goddesses as wives and the goddesses to give birth to other gods. Sometimes they imagined the gods or goddesses to lust after human beings (Genesis 6: 1-4) and give birth to demigods or "heroes" (from the Greek *heros*, possibly "Hera's" or "One who belongs to Hera").

There is no reason for us to look down on the religion of these early people. Nor should we think that they prayed to their conception of Deity with any less devotion than a modern Christian or Jew. Like us, they were trying to walk uprightly before their gods and conduct their lives with integrity and righteousness. They were doing the best they could with the knowledge and wisdom at their disposal.

We should also keep in mind that, while God has not changed, we have. As we have developed, our concept of Deity in the industrialized West has grown from a multitude of gods and goddesses to One God. But we should not allow the hindsight we have inherited from 3000 years of philosophical and religious development to delude us into a feeling of superiority over our ancient ancestors. Contrary to Hollywood and popular opinion, they were not praying to the physical clay or stone images of their gods. They used the images to focus their attention and to induce a feeling of awe and reverence toward Spirit. To people of that time, Spirit could be imagined in either a masculine or a feminine form. Jesus told the Samaritan woman at Jacob's well:

"God is Spirit, and those who worship him must worship in Spirit and truth." [4]

Today many people in the Western World think of the Hebrew desert god Yahweh as the One Universal Spirit, or as God the Father in the Christian Blessed Trinity. In other words, as "God" with a capital G. But when, according to Moses, he first manifested to mankind in the form of a burning acacia bush he would have been regarded by his worshippers as just another god among other gods. This means no disrespect to our current concepts of God. It only means that there was no other way in which Yahweh could have been regarded by the nomadic semi-barbaric tribesmen wandering the Sinai Peninsula around the year 1200 B.C.

With all our modern hindsight, we can no more castigate Solomon for not being a monotheist than we can fault him for not getting flu shots, not fighting his enemies with machine guns or not putting satellites into orbit. Solomon and the other inhabitants of Israel were polytheists because, at that time, there was nothing else for them to be. The monotheism we now find throughout the stories of Solomon and his times was written into the Old Testament centuries later, during the Babylonian Exile.

At that time there was simply no concept of one single transcendent Spirit whose Body was the physical universe and whose Mind sustained all of creation. That would come later. In their book, *New Thought: A Practical American Spirituality*, C. Alan Anderson and Deborah Whitehouse refer to these changes in metaphysical outlooks as *revolutions of understanding* which, in time generate revolutions in ways of living.[5]

The notion of Yahweh as the one True God was most clearly defined in Babylon during the Exile, sometime around 545 B.C. We don't know the name of the prophet who promoted this idea. Today we call him Second Isaiah because scribes had appended his writings (Isaiah 40-55) to the end of the Book of Isaiah.[6]

Second Isaiah formulated his theological arguments to account for the invasion and destruction of Jerusalem, Yahweh's holy city that his people had thought was invulnerable. Before the Exile, Yahweh had been a bad-tempered, ruthless Indo-European war god who lived with his wife, the goddess Asherah,[7] in a small room in the back of a stone temple. Second Isaiah pictured him as a solitary, all-present, all-knowing, all-powerful bachelor deity dwelling in the sky (although a sub-school of medieval Rabbinic lore gave him another wife in the form of the Sumerian owl-goddess Lilith). Second Isaiah preached that the Exile was Yahweh's punishment for the Hebrews' sin of worshipping the other gods and goddesses acknowledged by the people of Israel.

The One True God hypothesis was later refined in Christianity by colonies of Christians in the western Mediterranean. These thinkers incorporated the insights of the Greek philosophical schools into their theology. The later Christian concept of a triune godhead (three persons in one God) would find its culmination in the theological theses of St. Augustine and Thomas Aquinas in the early Middle Ages.

In Judaism the refinements were made by the Jerusalem and Babylonian Talmudic study groups between A.D. 200 and 500. These groups produced a series of essays that formed two texts: the *Mishnah* or summation of the Oral Law and the *Gemara*, in which the Oral Law is related to parts of the Tanakh (Holy Scriptures, including the Pentateuch and the Prophets). These refinements have formed the basis of much modern Rabbinic Law.

The people of Solomon's time had none of the advantages we now enjoy from the 3000 subsequent years of religious study and contemplation that is our intellectual heritage. As stated above, it is important to recognize that God himself does not change; it is we who are discovering, one revolution in understanding after another, to this very day, more and more about his nature and his works. The latest advance in religious understanding, described beautifully in Anderson and Whitehouse's book, is called process theology. This view envisions God as an ever-growing, ever-improving Cosmic Presence, the Ultimate Experiencer in whom we all live and have our being.

The story of this degree tells of an ecumenical council in which Solomon brings priests of several religions together at the dedication of his Temple. So this would be a good time to review what is known about the pre-Exilic Hebrew religion and the various forms under which the people living in Canaan during Solomon's time worshipped Deity. Here are the principal gods and goddesses of Canaan, circa 1000 B.C.

El (אל) was the prehistoric high god of Canaan. In the Hebraic version of the Babylonian-Sumerian creation myth, he enjoyed walking in the Garden of Eden during the cool evening hours. He was almost certainly the god of Abraham, Isaac and Jacob, a position later claimed by post-Exilic scribes for Yahweh. He was a laid-back, friendly god who assumed a human form when he walked and chatted with the patriarchs. He dropped in and had dinner with Abraham [8] and later engaged in some friendly tussling with Jacob and gave him a new name.[9]

After that all-night wrestling match, El gave Jacob a new name: Israel (either "He has striven with El" or "Let El show his strength!"). Following a dream while spending the night camped outside the shrine of Bethel ("House of El," an ancient shrine of El) Jacob exclaimed "Truly El is in this place, although I did not know it!" (Genesis 28: 16). The most exalted title used by El's worshippers was Elohim (אלהים, possibly "El, greatest of gods!", now translated simply as the plural noun "gods.").

Asherah of the Sea was a Sumerian mother goddess, the wife of El (and, up until Josiah's reforms, the wife of Yahweh as well) and the mother of all the other gods. Her tiny idols, found by archeologists throughout Israel, flare out at the bottom so her worshippers could easily carry them about and set up them up anywhere on the clay floors of their houses.[10] In her temples she sometimes appeared as the statue of a seated woman holding a basin of water (representing the sea), symbolizing her powers of creation, on her lap. As a fertility goddess she was represented by phallic wooden poles (called Asherahs) set up on hills ("high places") alongside the altars of El, Baal or Yahweh. These poles represented the divine Tree of Nourishment by which Asherah (and, in Egypt, Hathor and Isis,) nourished the royal family and, by extension, all their subjects. The two bronze pillars on the porch of Solomon's Temple (Plate 5) were symbols of her presence, as was the huge bronze basin called the "Sea."

Fig. 10 The Canaanite goddess Astarte, shown here in an Egyptian image riding on a lioness. She holds the ring of royal authority in her left hand and bestows a blessing with her right hand. ©iStock.

Asherah's worship was universal throughout Israel from the time of the Judges until the reign of Josiah (638–608 B.C.). The principal city dedicated to her was Sidon, a Phoenician city on the Mediterranean seacoast, north of Tyre. Ahab, king of the northern Kingdom of Israel (875 B.C.), married a Sidonian princess, Jezebel. She was a devout worshiper of both Baal and Asherah; Ahab set up a temple to Baal and a large, elaborate statue of Asherah in Samaria, his capitol city (1 Kings 16: 32). It was said that 450 prophets of Baal and 400 prophets of Asherah ate at Jezebel's table (1 Kings 18: 19). Either the queen had the largest table in the Middle East or else she arranged the prophets into more manageable groups of, say, 40. That way one group could eat breakfast on Tuesday, another group have lunch on Thursday, and so on. After he became king, Solomon also married a Sidonian princess and adopted Asherah as the patron deity of the royal family.[11]

Astarte, also called Anat or Anatha, was the daughter of Asherah. She was, like her mother, a fertility goddess and also a deity of war and childbirth (Plate 3). Until Josiah's Yahwist reformation (620 B.C. and onwards) she was the principal female deity worshipped by the common people, both men and women, throughout Israel. She was one of the

31

personal household deities of Solomon and up until recently many scholars have assumed that his Phoenician-style temple was dedicated mainly to her worship, with only a tiny back room (the Holy of Holies as it was later called) set aside for Yahweh. Her effigies, ceramic or metal plaques showing a smiling naked woman holding lilies or snakes in each hand, have been found by the hundreds throughout Israel.[12] More about this important goddess later.

Baal-Habad was the son of El and the brother of Astarte. The first part of his name means "Lord"; like his father, he was easy-going, friendly and quite popular with the rural country people of Israel, who considered him to be even more approachable than El. His altars dotted the countryside, usually flanked by the wooden poles of his mother, Asherah, and the bronze plaques of his sister, Astarte.

Baal was just one of many versions of the dying-and-resurrecting grain god of the Mediterranean region. This god had many names: Adonis, Attis, Tammuz, and Osiris, among others. Every spring, just before planting time, he would die and descend into the underworld. For three days and three nights the women of the community would join in public mourning rites for him as if he were an actual relative of theirs who had died. Then, at dawn on the fourth day, he would rise again from the dead and everyone knew that the rains would come and the crops would grow. As late as 590 B.C., during the Babylonian Exile centuries after the reign of Solomon, the priest Ezekiel complained about the Hebrew women he had seen weeping for Tammuz (a local version of Baal) in the Jerusalem temple during the reign of King Zedekiah.[13] Baal, Tammuz and similar agricultural dying-and-rising grain gods were very popular with the farmers in Israel.

The cult of Baal persisted in North African Phoenician colonies until its reputed connection with human sacrifice caused Rome to suppress it in the 2nd century A.D.

Yahweh (יהוה) first appears in a burning bush to an Egyptian military officer of uncertain ethnic ancestry named Moses. When Moses asks the god what his name is, the voice replies "I am who I am." This could have been idiomatic Hebrew for "None of your business." The voice then takes pains to maintain that it was he, not El, who was really the god of the legendary patriarchs Abraham, Isaac and Jacob. When Moses (who seems to have almost unrestricted, daily face-to-face access to this deity) doesn't appear to be getting anywhere with the stubborn Pharaoh, he complains to the god and implies that maybe Yahweh isn't really the god of the Patriarchs as he claims to be. Yahweh replies with a brief résumé, in which he makes it clear that El was merely an earlier version of him.

> "Yahweh also said to Moses, 'I am Yahweh. As Elohim I appeared to
> Abraham, Isaac and Jacob, but my real name, Yahweh, I did not make

known to them. I also established my covenant with them, to give them the land of Canaan, the land in which they were living as aliens."

(Exodus 6: 2-4)

From that point on, Moses, speaking in Yahweh's name, declares that Yahweh is superior to all of the other Canaanite gods and that he is to receive the largest share of the people's worship. Moses forbids the people to worship any new foreign ("strange") gods and goddesses that they will encounter in their travels.

From his depiction in the Bible, Yahweh appears somewhat different from the other Canaanite gods. His theological attributes may have been colored by foreign influence.

Between 1500 and 700 B.C. the Middle East suffered a series of invasions. The invaders were tall, light-skinned, blue-eyed, fair-haired tribes of migrating Indo-European peoples from northern Europe. Scholars now think that they originally came from the steppes of central Asia north of the Black Sea. These war-like barbarians worshipped a trinity of gods that included a fierce, hammer-wielding thunder god who would become the Northern European god Thor, the lightning bolt-thrower Zeus, and the Indian Shiva.

Coming from the steppes of Eurasia, the newcomers introduced a new kind of warfare into the Middle East: cavalry. The tactical advantage of organized, mobile and maneuverable sword-wielding warriors who rode into battle on horseback soon reduced the once-dreaded Egyptian wicker chariot manned by archers to a second-rate weapon.

Until they encountered the wine-producing grapes of southern Europe the northern invaders drank mead (fermented honey) or *soma*, a ritual drink made from the narcotic herb ephedra. They buried their dead, accompanied by their personal treasures and weapons, in narrow hill-graves called barrows. The tribes travelled in horse-drawn wagons and drove herds of cattle along with them. They lived in organized clans, each clan headed by a warlord who derived his power from the consent of the clan's elders.

Two Indo-European peoples who invaded and settled in Canaan and its surrounding areas were the Hittites (2200 B.C.) and, farther west, the Scythians (700 B.C.). Although the "Peoples of the Sea" have sometimes been lumped in with these invaders, their alternate name of *Caphtorim* or "People of Crete" (Deuteronomy 2: 23) indicates a likely Mediterranean origin for them. Amorites have sometimes been labeled as Indo-Europeans but the use of the name "Amorite" to indicate almost any Transjordanian people clouds the issue.

Some of these invading tribes settled in the area of steppe and desert east of the Jordan River now known as the Transjordanian region. Hardened by the plundering inter-clan warfare of their Eurasian homeland, they harassed Egypt with border raids and laid siege to some of the Canaanite cities. Their influence, mannerisms and theological views spread throughout the Transjordan region.

The religious mindset of the Indo-European invaders could have influenced some of Yahweh's early attributes. As warriors, they worshipped fierce, bloodthirsty war gods in the mold of Ares (the Roman god Mars), a god who slew his tribe's enemies with pestilence or thunderbolts. The more civilized Canaanites, on the other hand, favored a calm, urbanized trading god, a law-giver who expected his people to live up to the agreements they made with him.

The Indo-Europeans, on the other hand, admired aggressive gods who favored one particular people over all others. In their mythological tales their gods (like Zeus and Odin) cheated on their wives and forced themselves on every woman or goddess they came across. The native Canaanites preferred their gods to be family men, husbands and fathers who knew their own children. Moses and his people may have mixed certain foreign perceptions of deity to complete their early concept of Yahweh. Yahweh's lack of womanizing was probably due to the patriarchal Hebrews' reluctance to allow women to get near enough to their god to gain any influence over him whatsoever or to receive power-giving gifts from him.

Yahweh's cult did not really catch on for centuries, until the returnees from the Babylonian Exile, all Yahwists, made his worship the official state religion of Judah. The triumph of Yahwism had already gained considerable momentum before the Exile in the religious reformations of the Yahwist King Josiah (620 B.C.) but it would not completely succeed until the armies of Nebuchadnezzar had decimated the old, native polytheistic population of Israel.

The ninth degree is another Masonic fable with no Scriptural backing. Many of the characters are imaginary, as is Solomon's invitation to priests of the various Mediterranean religions to be present at the dedication of the Temple. Biblical scholars and Near East historians believe that rank-and-file Hebrews in Solomon's time were *henotheists*, which means that while they believed in the existence of foreign gods, they were quite nationalistic and tolerated only the worship of their native Canaanite deities on the soil of Israel. Members of the powerful priestly party were the least tolerant of all and would have balked at Solomon holding a council that included the followers of any gods other than Yahweh, El (the original god of the patriarchs), Asherah (the goddess of the royal family) or Astarte (the common folks' Queen of Heaven) in the dedication ceremony. All of the upper class Hebrews looked down on the dying-and-rising Baal as a low-class farmers' deity worshipped only by the local hayseeds. Besides, his worship was popular with the hated Philistines, which made him *deus non grata* around the royal court.

The play's script has the Phoenician priest referring to Astarte, the Great Goddess of Biblos and Tyre, as "Ashtoreth." He would more likely have called her either Astarte or Anath, her proper Phoenician names. Her temples (including the one built by Solomon) were staffed by priestesses who practiced sacred prostitution. Most scholars believe that, because of this practice, the later Yahwist post-Exilic writers combined her name, Astarte, with the Hebrew word *boshet* ("shame") and came up with "Ashtoreth." On the other hand, Ashtoreth may have been her legitimate name in Hebrew.

Actually, sacred prostitutes were well-regarded, powerful women of high status. Hosea, an auditory prophet from the northern kingdom of Israel, married one named Gomer (Hosea 1: 3). Mathew begins his Gospel with a genealogy of Jesus (Mathew 1: 1 – 17) and among Jesus' ancestors he lists two Old Testament prostitutes: Rahab and Tamar.

Rahab (Joshua 2: 1) was a sacred prostitute in Jericho who sheltered the two spies sent by Joshua to reconnoiter the city. Tamar was a widow (Genesis 38: 15) who disguised herself as a sacred temple prostitute in order to seduce her reluctant fiancé, her father-in-law Judah, into having roadside sex with her. The law of levirate marriage required Judah to marry his widowed daughter-in-law and father a child by her. He would then have to raise the child as his dead son's heir. He dragged his feet on the matter until Tamar's successful ruse worked; she became pregnant and could provide proof that Judah was the father. The later Yahwist Jews came to refer to these temple women as "harlots," which was, in some sense, correct. Their original Hebrew title had been *qedesha* ("consecrated holy women").

Most modern Biblical scholars acknowledge that the religious worldview of Israelites in Solomon's time was very different from that pictured in scriptures written during the Babylonian Exile, the post-Exilic scriptures that have come down to us. At the time of Solomon, the religion of Hebrews living in Israel was probably not very different from that of any of the other peoples of the Near East. As stated before, they were almost certainly henotheists; that is, they acknowledged the existence of many gods, but maintained only that their own indigenous gods were superior. They were also quite nationalistic and felt strongly that citizens should not worship foreign gods publically on the soil of Israel.

We should certainly recognize that, in the time of Solomon, the worship of Yahweh had not yet gained the ascendancy it would achieve after the Babylonian Exile. The later Deuteronomist scribes and editors who, during the Exile (around 560 B.C., centuries after Solomon's time), wrote the now-accepted revisionist history of Israel, were all Yahwists. They inserted their own theological views into the biographies of people who had lived in a widely different culture 400 or more years earlier. For instance, they would have us believe that Hebrews had always worshipped Yahweh as their one and only god (that is, as Universal God) from the time of Abraham. During Solomon's time, the cult of Yahweh was probably popular only within the Levite priesthood headed by Zadoc, the High Priest. The prophetic party headed by Nathan was most likely composed of men who prophesied in the names both of Yahweh and of the Canaanite high god, El. El is thought to have been the god the patriarchs of the book of Genesis worshipped[14] and was probably the most widely worshipped male deity in Israel in Solomon's time.

Solomon, a politically shrewd monarch in his early years on the throne, acknowledged several deities. He publicly worshipped El, Asherah, Yahweh and Astarte but privately favored Asherah. She was the Canaanite version of the ancient Sumerian love-and-war goddess Ishtar who was known and adored by both men and women over the entire Eastern Mediterranean region. Her son, Baal, was the dying-and-resurrecting god of the crop cycle. Solomon had modeled his Phoenician-style temple in Jerusalem on similar temples of Asherah in Sidon and Tyre. He dedicated his temple to her worship, along with the worship of Astarte (complete, at times, with sacred prostitution), El, Yahweh, Baal-Tammuz, the snake-goddesses of Moses' Egyptian Nehushtan and perhaps, to please his Egyptian wives, Isis and Hathor.

The Jewish historical scholar, Raphael Patai, maintains in his book *The Hebrew Goddess* that Asherah was Solomon's principal deity from the beginning of his reign. She became the chief deity of the Jerusalem Temple after her statue and rituals were installed in the Temple by Solomon's son Rehoboam following Solomon's death. Patai points out that for two-thirds of the entire time (236 out of 370 years) that Solomon's Temple is supposed to have stood in Jerusalem, Asherah's cult statue (either a seated woman holding a basin of water or a standing naked woman holding her own breasts) stood in the Temple. For all that time she was worshipped enthusiastically by the king, the court, and the priesthood with little or no Yahwist opposition.[15]

Some modern Biblical scholars even maintain that Asherah, not Astarte, was the deity referred to by the derogatory epithet "Ashtoreth." They believe that the Hebrew letters of *boshet* ("shame") were mixed in with the letters of Asherah's, not Astarte's, name, to produce Ashtoreth's name.

Whatever the case, archeological finds of the last few decades indicate that, outside of the royal palace, Astarte was the most widely worshipped goddess in Israel during Solomon's reign. The finds referred to are the large number of Astarte plaques that have turned up in Israel. If this were the case, then Solomon's inclusion of her in his pantheon would have been understandable and politically astute. However, we should consider that the present-day preponderance of Astarte plaques might be because artisans made them of long-lasting, fire-resistant ceramic, gold or bronze. Worshippers of Asherah, on the other hand, usually carved her images from wood. Consequently, they were subject to fire and decay, which may account for their paucity.[17] They were also the favorite targets of Yahwist mobs during the frequent religious persecutions unleashed by reformist kings.

Like her mother Asherah, Astarte was yet another avatar of the Sumerian goddess Ishtar, patron of love, fertility and war. The misogynistic Hebrew men feared the greater status and freedom that women enjoyed in the more sophisticated goddess-worshipping civilizations of Mesopotamia, a marked contrast to women's lowly status in the cultural backwater of Solomon's Israel. The formerly nomadic Hebrews were still extremely patriarchal and regarded women as little more than chattel slaves, the property of their fathers and husbands. Many male Hebrews of the ruling class felt their men-only theocratic rule threatened by the power and influence that women exercised in the great empires of Babylonia and Egypt and the nearby city-states of the coastal Phoenicians. They distrusted the Great Goddess and feared her cultural influence. They confined their worship, directed by prevailing political winds, to El or Yahweh.

The common women of Israel, on the other hand, prayed to Astarte for both fertility and protection in childbirth. Astarte was an astral deity and her symbol was a six-pointed star, representing the planet Venus. The women baked little star-shaped cakes as offerings at her shrines, with the full support of both their husbands and their local municipal governments.[18] These were the cakes that the Yahwist prophet Jeremiah complained about. He saw women baking them when he visited Hebrew enclaves in Egypt where refugees who had fled across the border to escape the Babylonian invasion lived.

> "…from all the women who were present in the immense crowd … Jeremiah received this answer: 'We will not listen to what you say in the name of Yahweh. Rather… we will burn incense to the Queen of Heaven [Astarte] and pour out libations to her, as we and our fathers, our kings and princes have done in the cities of Judah and the streets of Jerusalem."
>
> (Jeremiah, 44: 15 – 19)

They then lamented that the Babylonians had sacked Jerusalem and the Hebrews had suffered exile because the people had neglected the worship of Astarte (Plate 4), not Yahweh.

> "Then we had enough food to eat and we were well off; we suffered no misfortune. But since we stopped burning incense to the Queen of Heaven and pouring out libations to her, we are in need of everything and are being destroyed by the sword and by hunger. And when we burned incense to the Queen of Heaven and poured out libations to her, was it without our husbands' consent that we baked for her cakes in her image [six-pointed stars] and poured out libations to her?"
>
> (Jeremiah, 44: 17 – 18)

The cult of Astarte among the Hebrews outlasted that of her mother, Asherah. Asherah's worship was suppressed by King Josiah in 621 B.C. and it never recovered. Astarte's worship even outlasted the return of Zerubbabel from Babylon with his band of monotheistic Yahwist exiles. On the island of Elephantine in the Nile River, near the southern border of Egypt just south of the first cataract, there was a garrison of mercenary Hebrew soldiers and their families. The Pharaoh Psamtik II had established the garrison sometime after 592 B.C. to guard against raiding parties coming up from Ethiopia. According to Patai, records from 420 B.C. indicate that the Hebrews on Elephantine were worshipping three gods in their temple: Yaho (Yahweh), Ishum (a Sumerian fire god noted for his mastery of weapons – a soldier's god) and Anath (Astarte, both a martial deity and a protector of women in childbirth).[19] This was 100 years after Zerubbabel had taken over leadership of the returned Jewish exiles from Babylonia in 520 B.C. and had established the monotheistic worship of Yahweh as Judah's state religion.[20] The Hebrew soldiers and their families had to abandon their temple when the Egyptians evicted them from Elephantine around 407 B.C.

In the degree's drama, Solomon would have done himself a favor if he had allowed the mob to kill Hadad. This Hadad was an Edomite noble. He had fled to Egypt to escape the slaughter of the Edomite royal family that Joab had carried out under David's orders. Following David's death Hadad had returned to Edom where he raised a guerilla band that harassed Solomon's eastern border for years (1 Kings 11:14-22). His presence as a guest at Solomon's court was as unlikely as Woodrow Wilson inviting Pancho Villa to dinner at the White House.

It is another interesting anachronism that it is the archangel Uriel who enlightens the unbelieving Hadad. None of the angels ("messengers") alluded to in the pre-Exilic Hebrew Scriptures had proper names. Rabbi Simeon ben Lakish (died A.D. 270) taught that all angelic proper names were brought back to Jerusalem by Jews returning from the Babylonian Exile and many modern rabbinic scholars agree. Even in post-Exilic writings, only three angels, Gabriel, Michael and Raphael, are specifically named.

The first mention of Uriel is in the Jewish apocalyptic Book of 2 Esdras, written about 30 or 40 years after the Romans destroyed the Temple in A.D. 70. Here the Old Testament prophet Ezra asks God a number of questions and God sends an archangel named Uriel to instruct him. The name Uriel means "Fire of El". In Leonardo Da Vinci's painting "The Virgin of the Rocks" (Plate 8) Uriel is the beautiful archangel on the right, supporting the infant John the Baptist who is pointing to the Christ child.

The 9th Degree
of the Southern Jurisdiction:

ELU OF THE NINE

In the Southern Jurisdiction this degree retains Pike's original theme of vengeance for Hiram's murder. "Elu" is from an old French word meaning "one who is elected" and refers to the nine knights Solomon elected (chose) to hunt down the assassin. One of the nine, guided by a star, finds the cave where the assassin is sleeping and butchers him with a dagger. Solomon is at first angered that the knight has not brought the assassin back alive but eventually pardons him. The moral lesson centers on the virtues taught in the degree: generosity, disinterestedness, courtesy, devotion, firmness, self-denial, heroism and patriotism.[21]

10th Degree:

MASTER ELECT
(Solomon gets bad news from upstairs)

The Stage Drama

The time is around 940 B.C. and the place is an outer porch in front of Solomon's royal court. Zadok the High Priest, Nathan the king's court prophet and Benaiah, Solomon's ruthless hit man, are standing around talking in front of a detachment of troops in the palace guard. The guard detail consists of two units, one made up of men called Cherethites, the other made up of Pelethites. They are chatting about Solomon's many wives and his foreign goddesses. One of the guards makes fun of the aging Solomon's cavorting with young concubines and foreign women like the famous Queen of Sheba (Plate 4). Another guard defends Solomon's sexual proclivities and the two almost come to blows. Zadok, Nathan and Benaiah break up the fight; they have their own problems to worry about. They talk about an unpleasant duty that awaits them. The three of them have to confront King Solomon and chide him for building temples to foreign deities on Israelite soil (violating the henotheistic principle that only the native gods and goddesses of Israel should be worshipped publicly in the land).

As they had feared, Solomon is not amused. He becomes furious and Zadoc must plead for their lives. Later, when alone, Solomon is told by a vengeful Yahweh (an off-stage voice) that his kingdom will soon be torn asunder. This degree teaches that a violator of his obligations and commitments will not go unpunished. Further, excuses, rationalizations and other evidences of a lack of repentance will likely increase the severity of the penalties.

This is one of the new degrees that has been written from scratch to replace an older degree. In this degree's story, characters living at the time of Solomon talk about "Masonic brotherhood" as if they were speculative Masons of some 2,700 years in their future. The story itself has no scriptural basis in any of the Bibles I have consulted, although it may exist in traditional Rabbinical folklore.

Historical Background

The two contingents of palace guards referred to in the play, the Cherethites and the Pelethites, represent two foreign ethnic contingents of mercenaries that Solomon had inherited from his father David (2 Samuel 8: 18). David had perhaps imported them into Israel as exotic and colorful enhancements to the royal court, much as the Babylonian emperor Nebuchadnezzar had employed Greek mercenaries with their shining bronze armor for his bodyguard.

Solomon's guardsmen may have been Minoans from Crete, Philistines from the Negev or bowmen and slingers from one of the tribal territories on the fringes of the Egyptian empire. They composed an elite corps of tough fighting men and it is unlikely that any of them would have cared how many wives Solomon had or which gods and goddesses he worshipped. They were also present as bodyguards of Solomon when he went to Gihon to foil Adonijah's attempted coup[1].In this degree's story, the author gives most of them Hebrew names.

The 10th Degree of the Southern Jurisdiction:

ELU OF THE FIFTEEN

The Southern Jurisdiction still retains all of the many Pike rituals that tell of the hunt for Hiram's murderers and their eventual capture and execution. This is a very important degree in the Southern Scottish Rite; the ritual is long and the setting is elaborate. Many symbols from the Jewish Kabbalah are seen decorating the audience chamber of King Solomon. A shepherd named Pharos has discovered the hiding place of the three assassins. Two of the nine brethren from the previous degree (the two degrees are considered two parts of a whole story and are usually conferred together) stumble on the cave and kill one of the ruffians. Soon they find the other two ruffians and both are executed in Jerusalem. The ritual is loaded with political and religious symbolism and the degree is one of the last to treat the Hiramic allegory. The degree teaches that ignorance is the principal enemy of human freedom and – something that would have had the original Solomon scratching his head – that a free press is essential to true liberty. Remorse and guilt are God's punishment for sin and are more severe than any human punishment. The lessons are that tyranny and despotism are the products of ambition and that fanaticism brings about intolerance and persecution.[2]

11th Degree:

SUBLIME MASTER ELECTED
(Death and taxes in the time of Solomon)

The Stage Drama

The story takes place during the reign of King Solomon, shortly after the completion of the Temple, around 961 B.C. The story tells of the misdeeds and fate of three avaricious tax collectors working for Solomon: Abinadab, Abijah and their boss, Nadab, the Chief Tax Collector. They viciously extort money from the poor people of Capernaum, a town on the northern tip of the Sea of Galilee, about 75 miles north of Jerusalem. There's also a love interest in the drama: Nadab has his eye on the beautiful Tamar, the young daughter of Zibeon, a citizen of Capernaum. Nadab offers Zibeon a tax break in exchange for his daughter's hand. Zibeon thinks it over. He's a good father but, in the Israel of 961 B.C., women are regarded as family property and his daughter is a tradable commodity, an asset that Zibeon could use to his advantage. Tamar is really in love with Jonathan, a poor but honest young man who is said to be a member of "the Craft."

In one scene in Capernaum's market place Nadab and his two toadies interrupt a religious service that a local religious leader named Joshua is conducting and loudly demand more tax money from everyone. It is Shavuot or the Feast of Weeks (the modern Christian Pentecost), a harvest celebration held 50 days after Passover.

Another scene has Abinadab and Abijah laboriously hauling a heavy, unguarded cart laden with gold all the way from Capernaum to Jerusalem (75 miles!). There is some pseudo-Shakespearian slap-stick involving the two men getting drunk. At the play's end Solomon and his ever-present friend Hiram, King of Tyre, straighten everything out, punish the evil tax collectors and reward the story's young hero, Jonathan.

The moral lesson of this degree is the virtue of good citizenship. Evil deeds should be punished. Honesty and respect for others should be rewarded. A Scottish Rite Mason should be earnest, honest and sincere; the lesson of the Eleventh Degree is that the true and faithful brother sooner or later will receive his just reward.

The Degree encourages the practice of being a responsible citizen. It emphasizes that the true and faithful Mason should not condone or excuse dishonesty or corruption by public officials. If chosen to public service himself, the Mason should consider his office a sacred trust to be administered with humility and in the true interests of all the people. When confronted by corrupt, tyrannical, or illegal behavior on the part of a person in authority, the Mason should remain loyal and courageous in the conviction that right eventually will prevail.

Fig. 11 The parable of the rich man and the poor man paying their taxes in the temple. ©iStock.

Historical Background

This is another apocryphal Masonic fable with no scriptural basis. It may have stemmed from 19th-century American social concerns regarding the relationship of the common citizen to the heads of government as well as the problem of corruption in government administration. The egregiously corrupt administration of Ulysses S. Grant (1869 – 1877) and the arrogant behavior of Northern government officials in the South during the Reconstruction period following the Civil War may have influenced the development of the degree's theme (the duty of a responsible citizen to stand up to a corrupt government administration) under the pen of the ex-Confederate officer Albert Pike, who wrote the current degree.

Pike's script keeps closely to the 19th-century version of Francken's original ritual. While lengthy, it is well-enough written to keep the attention of the audience and the moral lessons are clearly illustrated. It adheres closely enough to Biblical history so as not to present any obvious inaccuracies. (But why is King Hiram always hanging around

Solomon's court? Doesn't he ever go home? He spends more time in Jerusalem than he does in Tyre.)

The Joshua who led the prayer service that Nadab and his friends interrupted, was not, of course, the military leader, Joshua ben Nun, who had led the Hebrew tribes in their conquest of Canaan six or seven centuries earlier. Nor was he a priest (*kohanim*) or a licensed auditory prophet. He was an early form of rabbi, a local neighborhood spiritual teacher distinguished by his knowledge of the scriptures. His congregation thought such a person to be possessed of the *bat qol* ("Daughter of the Voice").[1] This was the spirit of wisdom – usually heard as a female voice from an invisible source in the dark – that people thought enabled a spiritual director to interpret the Mosaic Law.[2] Joshua could preach to the people only on the holy festivals or *Kallaben* days, as during the Feast of Weeks in this story.

The 11th Degree
of the Southern Jurisdiction:

ELU OF THE TWELVE OR PRINCE AMETH

In the Southern Jurisdiction, we are dealing yet again with the aftermath of Hiram Abiff's assassination and the punishment of his killers. Solomon's deputies haul the three culprits into the Audience Chamber of King Solomon where a judge named Zabud and fifteen men called Elus (who had been appointed in the previous degree) await them. They convict and execute the ruffians. Solomon is told of the trial and he approves. Then the king hears complaints regarding his tax collectors: they are extorting more money than necessary and keeping the surplus for themselves. Solomon appoints twelve of the fifteen Elus to govern each of the twelve provinces in Israel. The twelve Elus are promoted to the rank of Princes *Ameth* (a Hebrew word meaning a man who is true to his word). A Prince Ameth is supposed to be an advocate for the people and to protect them from corrupt government agents.

The lesson of this degree is that life is a school and Masonry is work. Be earnest, true and reliable. One should strive to be a champion of the people.[2]

12th Degree:

MASTER OF MERCY
(Joseph and his brothers in Egypt)

The Stage Drama

The story of Joseph (Genesis 37-50) begins on the plain of Dothan, a region of wheat and barley fields and level grazing grounds about 45 miles north of Jerusalem. The time is around 1729 B.C. Joseph is about 12 years old; his older brothers are jealous of his favored treatment and sell the young boy into slavery (Plate 9). He winds up in Egypt and works his way up to the position of vizier, or prime minister. A great famine (foreseen by Joseph) breaks out and his brothers come to Egypt to beg for grain, which the Egyptians had providentially stored during times of plenty. The brothers find that they must deal with the country's prime minister. They don't recognize the 40-year old Joseph and he toys with them. He finally uses his position to relieve his family and reconciles with his estranged brothers. Joseph's forgiveness and generosity reunites the family.

The purpose of the Twelfth Degree is to teach the quality of forgiveness. Forgiveness means a spirit of compassion and a tenderness of heart that dispose a person not just to overlook the opportunity for revenge, but to cease to feel enmity or resentment toward an offender. In this degree, the quality of mercy disposes us to overlook injuries and treat an offender better than he deserves.

Historical Background

The playwright based the script on the story of Joseph, son of Jacob.[1] To anyone familiar with the story there are no surprises here as the ritual follows the Biblical account pretty closely except that, in the Bible, the brothers dip Joseph's multicolored coat in goat's blood and present it to their father Jacob, telling him that Joseph has been killed by a wild beast. In the following play, the brothers sell his coat to the same caravan leader to whom they sell Joseph (Plate 7).

In the drama, Joseph claims his brothers sold him to the traders in the valley of Shechem. But by the time he caught up with them the brothers had left Shechem and were grazing their sheep 17 miles farther north on the plain of Dothan. There is some controversy among Biblical scholars as to whether Joseph was sold to Ishmaelite traders or to Midianites, as the Bible mentions both in connection with his abduction.

The Midianites were descendents of Midian, the fourth son of Abraham by his concubine Keturah. He had married Keturah after the death of his wife Sarah (when he had to have been at least 137 years old!). The Midianites had settled in the territory east of the Jordan and throughout much of the area east of the Dead Sea.

Ishmaelites were descendents of Ishmael, the son that Abraham's Egyptian maid servant, Hagar, bore to him. Ishmael is traditionally regarded as the ancestor of all non-Jewish Semites, such as the Arabs. *Ishmaelites* is a generic term frequently used in the Bible to refer to any nomadic tribe of the Arabian peninsula.

The Bible does not name the pharaoh who honors Joseph and there is no historical record of a Canaanite named Joseph achieving high rank in the Egyptian government of 1710 B.C. We know that Sobekhotep V, an Egyptian pharaoh of the 13th dynasty, was on the throne about the year 1730 B.C., when Joseph was supposed to have been sold into slavery. By my calculations, Joseph would have confronted his brothers about 1704 B.C., during the reign of Merneferre Ay, the 13th-dynasty ruler who ruled from 1714 - 1691 B.C.

Assigning exact dates to events in Genesis is problematic and can give rise to disagreements, even among experts in the field. Some scholars maintain that the famine in Egypt did not start until 1697 B.C., years later than the dates I have given here. One birth date given for Joseph is 1734 B.C., which would make him ten years younger during the time period I have outlined.

The early pre-literate tribes of the Transjordanian grazing lands were nomadic herdsmen, mercenaries and raiders who lived in awe of the near-by glamorous Egyptian Empire. They probably loved to spin yarns in which one of their numbers had managed to become a nobleman or high-level functionary in the superpower that was Egypt. As in the tale of Joseph, the yarns would be sure to include a reference to the virility of the captive nomad man and the lust his manhood inspired in upper class Egyptian women. These legends were written in their present-day versions following a long series of revisions beginning in the Deuteronomic reform of King Josiah, a confirmed Yahwist, around 630 B.C. In these revised versions Yahweh's name replaces all references to El or any other gods actually worshipped by the people in the tales.

The 12th Degree
of the Southern Jurisdiction:

MASTER ARCHITECT

In the Southern Jurisdiction this degree is called MASTER ARCHITECT and tells of Adoniram, the murdered Hiram Abiff's special protégée who had demonstrated superior knowledge and skill and, subsequent to Hiram's death, was appointed Chief Architect of the Temple. He was to be the successor of Hiram and oversee the other men who had been made Intendants of the Building. Here, Hiram represents the executive head of a free government. The degree teaches that wisdom is a gift from God and should be preferred over riches. Also, wisdom and knowledge bring honor, discretion and understanding.[2]

13th Degree

MASTER OF THE NINTH ARCH
(A treasure found in a nine-story underground temple)

The Stage Drama

The time is an unspecified year during Solomon's reign (roughly 971 – 931 B.C.) Workmen come across what appears to be a series of underground crypts (here called "arches"), one under the other. They go digging in the buried ruins and, finding some interesting artifacts, they run to tell King Solomon. The king and his good friend Hiram, king of Tyre (who, in the rituals, spends so much time hanging around Solomon's court that he must have become a naturalized citizen of Israel), are sitting in Solomon's throne room. Solomon is interested and sends the men back to see what more they can recover from the dig.

While they wait, Solomon tells Hiram of an ancient antediluvian hero named Enoch. The god El had whisked him up to a mountaintop (an appropriate action for Enoch's god, El Shaddiah, sometimes translated as "El of the Mountain") and taught him many valuable things. Solomon thinks that the ruins the workmen stumbled upon are the remains of Enoch's fabled nine story-deep underground temple and he hopes they will uncover some of the patriarch's valuable secrets. The men finally dig down to the ninth crypt and find a name engraved on a gold plate. They bring it back to Solomon who, with Hiram's help, interprets their find.

This degree teaches that difficulties and dangers, however great, should not deter the true and faithful brother from progressing onward to perfection. It teaches the great truth that the finest things in life come only as the result of constant and often painful effort. Our Masonic teachings and obligations help us to carry out our daily duties and responsibilities. Some of these require courage and determination.

Freemasonry is a continuing journey. Let us remember that on this road of life we are striving toward Perfection.

Historical Background

For the first time we have a degree's drama based on a genuine Masonic legend. The legend predates both the creation of the Scottish Rite degrees in France and establishment of Grand Lodge masonry in 1717. Researchers trace the incorporation of the ancient legend of the patriarch Enoch into speculative Freemasonry to two 17th-century Masonic manuscripts. These are the Inigo Jones Manuscript (1607) and the *Old Charges and History of the Craft* by J. Whytestones (1610).

Reminiscent of the Atlantis legend, these documents tell of great achievements in science and agriculture attributed to the generations of men before Noah's Flood. Legends say that these ancient people particularly excelled in the Seven Liberal Arts: Grammar, Rhetoric, Logic, Arithmetic, Geometry, Music and Astronomy. These old Masonic manuscripts claim that, shortly before the Great Flood, angels warned the patriarch Enoch of the coming catastrophe. Accordingly, he attempted to preserve his civilization's knowledge and wisdom by secreting documents in the hollow interiors of two stone pillars, proof against both conflagrations (fire) and inundations (flood).

The documents say that, after the flood, early Egyptians discovered Enoch's hollow stone pillars and derived their arts and sciences from the rolls and records contained within them. A later version of the story says that the Egyptians found one pillar and the Hebrews of Solomon's time found the other. In some versions of the legend, Enoch engraved the information on the outer surface of the pillars.

Fig. 12 An engraved Egyptian pillar. ©iStock.

Following the Grand Lodge "Revival" of 1717, ritualists discarded the story of Enoch in favor of the more abundant material dealing with King Solomon. They wrote new blue lodge rituals that conflated Enoch's two stone pillars with the two bronze Phoenician-style pillars on the porch of King Solomon's Temple. The ritualists retained the legend that the two pillars on the temple porch were hollow and contained esoteric and technological Masonic documents in their interiors although, with no flood coming, there was no longer any logical reason why they should.

Who was this Enoch? He pops up all over the place, from the Old Testament to post-Exilic Apocryphal books. His name appears in rabbinical folklore, Elizabethan mysticism and 17th-century Masonic legend. Nowadays his name even figures in New Age magic. Since his legend has played such an important role in early Masonic lore, he's worth looking at in some depth.

Barely present in the Bible,[1] just mentions Enoch as an antediluvian patriarch (that is, a prehistoric tribal chieftain who lived in the time before Noah's flood). A descendant of Adam by Adam's son Seth, he was the father of Methuselah and a great-grandfather of Noah. He was born seven generations after Adam and lived to the ripe old age of 365 years. At the end of his time on Earth he did not die but was taken directly up into Heaven alive.[2]

The apocryphal Book of Enoch (which no present-day version of the Bible includes) was written sometime between the Old and New Testaments, probably between 150 and 80 B.C. Workers have found copies of it among the Dead Sea scrolls so we now know its contents in some detail.

The main storyline of the book tells of the descent of certain rebellious angels to earth because they lusted after the more attractive daughters of men. The book says these amorous angels (called the "Watchers") taught mankind many useful things such as metalwork and agriculture, as well as many evil things, notably warfare and slavery. In later Jewish folklore Enoch is said to rule over all of these angels and it was actually *his* knowledge and wisdom, not El's, that the angels imparted to men.

In the New Testament the disciple Jude, brother of Jesus and James, quotes a line from the Book of Enoch in his epistle.[3] In the Book of Sirach (written around 190 B.C. and recognized as canonical in the Roman Catholic Bible), another Jesus – Jesus ben Eleazar, son of Sirach – says:

"Few on earth have been made the equal of Enoch, for he was taken up bodily." (Sirach 49: 14)

In rabbinical legends of the Talmudic period, Enoch meets 'Anpiel ("Branch of El"), an angel who presides over seventy gates in the Sixth Heaven. 'Anpiel carries Enoch up to the Seventh Heaven to remove him from the sinfulness and degeneracy of the antediluvian world. Rabbi Ishmael wrote that Enoch had personally told him (in a vision, perhaps) that he, Enoch, was supposed to witness to all mankind that Yahweh (a later substitution for El) was not a cruel deity in spite of the Deluge he was about to unleash. Once in the Seventh Heaven, Enoch, under the tutelage of angels, was given knowledge and understanding of the entire universe, past, present and future.

Then Yahweh transformed Enoch into a fantastic creature called *Metatron*. Metatron was described in Rabbinical literature as being as large as the world, with 365,000 eyes (1000 eyes for each day of the year?) and thirty six wings. El (or Yahweh) gave him a crown decorated with forty-nine jewels and the Hebrew letters spelling out the phrases that the god uttered at the creation of the world. All the angels in Heaven bowed down before him and he glowed and emitted rays like the sun.

From this description we can see that Enoch is a thinly disguised deity of some kind. Note that his years of life equal the number of days that the earth takes to travel once around the sun. His legend may have originated in the dim remembrance of a Babylonian sun god with a similar-sounding name that the Hebrews had heard about during the Captivity. The Scribes in Babylon who were rewriting and revising the ancient myths and legends of their people may have written him into Genesis as an exceptionally pious super-patriarch. They probably intended to give both Adam and Noah additional prestige by their relationship to him.

The Enoch of 17th-century Masonic mythology is different; a mysterious ancient wise man but not divine. Sometime during the sinful days before the Flood, God told him to build a subterranean temple, which he carried out with the help of his young son Methuselah, who did most of the work. The temple consisted of nine brick vaults, one directly under the other, connected by a vertical shaft running through the center of each vault. In architecture a vault is an arch that has been rotated 360 degrees to form a domed ceiling or roof. An underground vault is called a crypt.

The legend says that Enoch made a triangular gold plate that he encrusted with jewels and fastened to a triangular agate stone. He engraved a word on it and placed the stone with its attached plate on a white marble pedestal in the ninth, or lowest, crypt. Modern Masonic lore declares that the word was Yahweh's name, the Tetragrammaton ("four-lettered word"), although Yahweh did not make himself and his name known to Moses until centuries after Enoch. He finally made, directly over the uppermost vault, a stone trapdoor fitted with an iron ring by which it could be raised. He then concealed the door. God permitted Enoch to enter this temple only once a year, like the High Priest in the Jerusalem Temple, who could enter the Holy of Holies only a few times during the High Holy days of autumn.

The 13th Degree
of the Southern Jurisdiction:

ROYAL ARCH OF SOLOMON

In the Southern Jurisdiction this degree, ROYAL ARCH OF SOLOMON, is very similar to the Northern Jurisdiction's version. Again, three workmen lower themselves into a newly-discovered tunnel going down into the ruins of Enoch's ancient temple. They take their finds back to Solomon who rewards them for their discovery. This is one of the few cases where a SJ degree is very like its NMJ counterpart. The lesson of the degree is that moral character is a habit, not formed in a moment. The great law of retribution acts in our memory as remorse at the final judgment.

14th Degree

GRAND ELECT MASON
(The ceremonial degree of the Lodge of Perfection)

The Stage Drama

This is the ceremonial degree of the Lodge of Perfection. Since this is not a play but a Masonic initiation ceremony, I will respect my Masonic obligations and will not describe the drama's story in any detail as I have done with the previous degrees. The stage setting represents a chamber in King Solomon's Temple. The time is the present. The characters in the drama are the current officers of the valley's Lodge of Perfection. The exemplar (the candidate who represents the entire class) is presented with a gold ring (which he returns at the degree's end).

The 14th degree is considered to be the summit of Ancient Craft (i.e., blue lodge) Masonry. As the crowning degree of the Lodge of Perfection, its essence is the holiness of God and reverence for His Holy name. God will not hold him guiltless who takes his name in vain.

Historical Background

This is the last degree in the Lodge of Perfection and is its "ceremonial" degree, the first degree of this kind that we encounter in this book. That means that, in some cases, an actual candidate would be selected from the audience, invested with the degree's regalia and becomes a part of the ritual. There may be as many as twenty to fifty candidates taking the degrees at any given Scottish Rite reunion. One of them, called an *exemplar*, is chosen to go through the ceremony and represent the class. The entire class, however, receives the degree.

The 14th Degree
of the Southern Jurisdiction:

PERFECT ELU

In the Southern Jurisdiction this degree, called PERFECT ELU, is also known as the DEGREE OF PERFECTION because, as in the NMJ, it is considered the perfection or completion of the Scottish Rite portion of the blue lodge teachings. Again, the ritual is similar to that of the NJM. As we have seen before, *Elu* here means a person who has been elected or chosen for some honor or high office.[1]

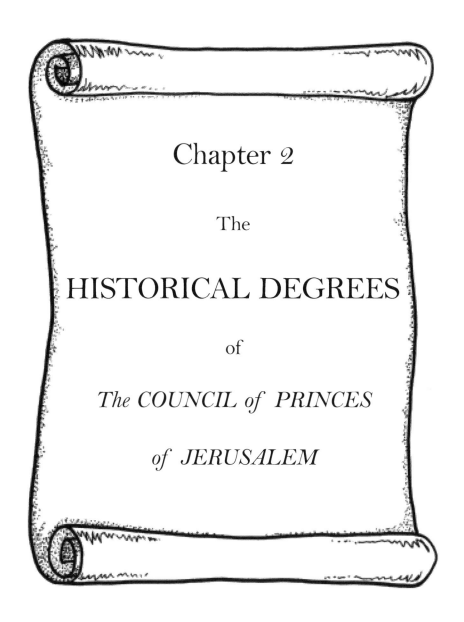

Chapter 2

The

HISTORICAL DEGREES

of

The COUNCIL of PRINCES

of JERUSALEM

Fig. 13 Cyrus the Great, King of Persia, , returning the treasures looted from the Hebrew temple to the Jews who are preparing to return to Jerusalem. Circa 538 B.C. ©iStock

Historical Background

A Council of Princes of Jerusalem is responsible for two degrees: The Fifteenth and the Sixteenth. Once we leave Solomon and his fabulous reign behind us, we leave the realm of Biblical folk tales, mythology and legends and enter the confines of real history. That's the reason these degrees are called "Historical," because they relate actual, verifiable historical events. The events deal with the end of Israel's Babylonian captivity, the return of the Jewish exiles to Jerusalem, and the rebuilding of Solomon's Temple that the Babylonians had destroyed during the sack of Jerusalem 49 years earlier. These two degrees cover the period from 538 to 516 B.C.

In 587 B.C. the army of Nebuchadnezzar, King of Babylon, invaded and sacked Jerusalem. Nebuzaradan, commanding officer of Nebuchadnezzar's invasion forces, spared thousands of the more prominent, upper-class Hebrew citizens from the general massacre. In accordance with the Babylonian policy of forced relocation, in 586 B.C. he deported them from Canaan. He settled them in various parts of Babylonia and in the city of Babylon itself. There they remained for 48 years (not the 70 years of the Bible) until Cyrus the Great conquered Babylonia in 538 B.C. and founded the Persian Empire. He immediately issued a decree permitting all of his captive peoples to return to their homelands and to rebuild their shrines and temples to their native deities. Cyrus' successor, Darius I, continued this generous policy and gave substantial aid to the returning exiles.

Masonic tradition in the Northern Masonic Jurisdiction holds that both Cyrus and Darius were followers of Zoroaster. As such, their religious beliefs were supposedly similar to the monotheistic faith of the post-Exilic Jews. Could these beliefs have motivated their considerate attitude and generous policy toward their captive peoples? In fact, only Darius was a Zoroastrian and neither of them were what we today would call strict monotheists. Nor, for that matter, does a belief in monotheism necessarily imply a high-minded attitude toward helpless captives. Hitler, Himmler and Stalin were all born and raised Christian monotheists. So were the British soldiers who confined thousands of innocent women and children in concentration camps during the Boer War (1899 – 1902) where hundreds of them died from malnutrition and brutal treatment. Nevertheless, both Cyrus and Darius, however many gods and goddesses they worshipped, favored the policy of allowing captive peoples to return to their native lands.

This policy included, of course, the captive Hebrews. By this time most of the Hebrew captives in Babylon who yearned to return home were Yahwists. They wished to go back to Jerusalem and build a new, monotheistic Temple of Yahweh to replace the old, ritually polluted, polytheistic temple of Solomon's time.

The Babylon of the sixth century before Christ was, sociologically and culturally, the most advanced city that the western world had ever seen. Even slaves, like the captive Hebrews, could learn a trade, conduct a business, earn money, and get an education. Elaborate written legal codes stemming from the time of Hammurabi protected their rights and property. Coming from the theocratic, temple-centered society of Jerusalem, the Hebrew captives had been like a group of Amish farm families suddenly transported to 21st-century Manhattan. The city boasted libraries and other public buildings that anyone, slave or free, could enter and enjoy.

Babylon (Plate 11) was at the crossroads of the Middle Eastern Iron Age. The streets teemed with people of every nationality, ethnicity and religion. Although a militaristic society, Babylonia nevertheless depended on a peaceful infrastructure of trade and commerce to provide the needed cash flow that sustained its luxurious culture. An elite class of shrewd Aramean traders and merchants provided this infrastructure. These traders, because of their extensive record keeping and accounting practices, were the custodians of Babylonia's written language. Consequently, everyone in Babylonia and its colonies spoke the Aramean language, Aramaic, and used the 10-based Aramaic counting system (much more useful than the unwieldy 12-based Babylonian system) to keep track of time and the movements of the heavenly bodies.[1] This last detail was important in a time when the agricultural planting cycle was synchronized with the rising of certain stars and planets.

Scattered throughout Babylon were temples, called *ziggurats*, giant stepped towers built to resemble artificial mountains.[2] They were surfaced with shining glazed bricks in brilliant colors; torches and candles illuminated them at night. Some ziggurats were more than 270 feet high; they must have lit up the darkness like enormous Christmas trees and made a fairyland of the nighttime city. The Hebrews were so impressed by these stunning edifices that they wrote them into their folklore. The Hebrews' half-century long sojourn among the ziggurats very likely inspired the myth of the Tower of Babel ("The Babylonian Tower").

Why did so few non-Yahwists join the returnees to Jerusalem? Because by the time Cyrus issued his decree permitting his captives to return in 538 B.C., the non-Yahwist Hebrew captives had, for all purposes, become Babylonians. Most had been born in Babylon, were making a good living there and had come to enjoy the upscale conditions in the city. Their parents had been polytheists back in Israel and they were now perfectly content to pray to the Babylonian gods and goddesses in their glamorous temples. These people intermarried with other ethnic groups in Babylon and happily ate the ritualistically "unclean" food of their captors.[3] All of them probably dressed in the finest Babylonian styles that they could afford. These Hebrews elected to remain behind and, over the years, they assimilated into Babylonian society and disappeared from Jewish history.

Some monotheistic Yahwists also stayed behind in Babylon. Scholars among them founded academies of Jewish learning that would become famous for centuries afterwards. By about A.D. 500 the Babylonian Academies had produced the *Talmud Bavli*, or Babylonian Talmud, which is much more extensively studied and quoted than the *Talmud Yerushalmi* , or Jerusalem Talmud. Written in the eastern Aramaic dialect, it contains the results of 300 years of study-group analysis of the Mishnah (the early oral Hebrew traditions) and the Gemara (collected rabbinic commentaries on the Mishnah). The result of years of careful editing, it today fills about 20 bound volumes. Many of the stay-behind Yahwists had become wealthy and were able to send financial aid to the leader of the return from Babylon, Zerubbabel, and his fellow returnees in Jerusalem.

Inspired by such leaders as Zerubbabel and Ezra, groups of Yahwist Jews endured the hardships of the long journey back to Israel. The second Temple (sometimes called the temple of Zerubbabel) was finally completed and dedicated to the exclusive service of Yahweh in 515 B.C.

15th Degree:

KNIGHT OF THE EAST
(From the splitting of Israel to the Babylonian Exile)

The Stage Drama

The place is Babylon, in the throne room of Cyrus, King of Persia and the time is 538 B.C. Cryus is obviously melancholy over something and his courtiers are understandably upset. The king has absolute power of life and death over them and the Persian method of execution – impalement – was particularly unpleasant. The victim would first have the sharp tip of a long pole thrust up into his rectum. The executioners would then hoist the pole upright and stand it in a hole. Onlookers would watch the victim wriggle and die, a process that could take hours or, given a skillful executioner, even a day or two. The mere possibility of receiving such a sentence would have made anyone nervous.

For instance, almost a century later in 444 B.C., the Yahwist eunuch Nehemiah, cupbearer to the Persian king Artaxerxes, approached the king with an exceptionally bold request. Nehemiah was "seized with great fear" and "prayed to Yahweh in heaven" before he dared to speak.[1] And Nehemiah was supposed to have been the king's good friend! In that case, Nehemiah had good reason for his near panic. He wanted to ask permission to rebuild, not the temple, but the walls and gates of Jerusalem. The Persian government considered walling a city to be a military act and the king could easily have interpreted Nehemiah's request as a prelude to rebellion.

In this degree's story Cyrus assures his nervous courtiers that he isn't angry with anybody; he's just depressed over a bad dream he's had the previous night. The 80-year old Hebrew, Daniel, enters and, when asked, ingeniously interprets the dream to mean that Cyrus should free the Hebrew captives and let them go back home. Cyrus remains undecided until another Hebrew captive, a young man named Zerubbabel who had been born in Babylon, enters. Zerubbabel, dressed in fake manacles to show how he feels about the Exile, also wants Cyrus to let his people go. The king, apparently for the amusement of his courtiers, puts Zerubbabel through of series of temptations and threats, which Zerubbabel resists. Cyrus finally relents and says the captives can go home and rebuild their temple.

This degree teaches the important lessons of loyalty to our beliefs, devotion to Truth and fidelity to our duty and to an obligation.

Historical Background

After the death of Solomon, around 933 B.C., his kingdom split into two separate states. The northern half became the kingdom of Israel with Samaria as its capital and the southern half became the kingdom of Judah whose capital was Jerusalem. The northern kingdom soon became a vassal state to the mighty Assyrian empire and had to pay tribute to its rulers.

Assyria was the cruelest, most vicious empire the Western world had yet seen. It contributed little to the culture of the Ancient Middle East and it practiced massacre, torture and genocide on a scale never before seen. Some modern historians have likened it to a forerunner of Hitler's Nazi Germany.

While the infantry comprised the main strike force of the Assyrian army, it had large numbers of chariots and a substantial cavalry force to back up the foot soldiers. The Assyrian Empire maintained its army by conscription of the peasant class. These men were obliged to fight during the hot summer months but were allowed to return home to harvest the crops and maintain the food supply. Archers supported the charging chariot using compound bows and armor-piercing arrows. The valuable, highly-trained archers were protected from enemy arrows and spears by a bulwark of small oblong shields held in place by conscripted peasants, each of whom carried a spear. All Assyrian warriors wore conical helmets and ankle-length hauberks of leather reinforced by vertical strips of bronze sewn onto the leather.[2]

One Assyrian ruler, Tiglath-pileser III, invented a new form of degradation to inflict on his conquered peoples: forced mass deportation. He would first massacre as many people of a newly conquered nation as he could; he would then round up the survivors and force them to march hundreds of miles away.[3] Then he would relocate them in a foreign land with a strange language, a strange culture, and – most disturbing to people of that time – strange gods. Most people of that period were, like the Hebrews, henotheists; that is, they believed that their own gods had power only in their native land. In a distant land, these people believed that they must identify and worship the local deities or they would suffer even more misfortune.

Around 722 B.C. King Hoshea of Israel, egged on by Egypt, attempted a doomed rebellion against his overlord, the Assyrian King Sargon II. Assyrian armies promptly overran and destroyed Hoshea's northern kingdom. The Assyrians massacred as many of its people, comprising 10 of the original 12 Hebrew tribes, as they could and marched more than 27,000 survivors away into exile. Sargon's government relocated them in Babylonia and other distant city-states under Assyrian rule. The captive Hebrews assimilated into the

Fig. 14 Assyrian soldiers. Note the spear-wielding peasants holding long shields to protect the highly-trained and valuable archer. (©iStock)

local populations and disappeared from history. This was the first major exilic event in the Hebrew's history and the disappearance of the "Ten Lost Tribes of Israel" became the first of many great disasters to befall the Hebrew people.

To repopulate the devastated areas of Israel, Sargon II transported other conquered populations from their native countries into Israel. He relocated them around Samaria, the former capital of the devastated land. They intermarried with those remaining Hebrews who had escaped deportation and formed a new ethnic group called Samaritans. The newcomers asked around to find out which gods and goddesses had power over their new land and the proper ways to worship them.

The Hebrews who had remained in Samaria had copies of a primitive, unedited four-book version of what would later be called the *Pentateuch*. Pentateuch means "A collection of five books," but the fifth book, *Deuteronomy* ("The Second Law"), would not be written for another 100 years. Then it would be "found" in the temple at Jerusalem by the high priest Hilkiah who wanted to curry favor with the young Yahwist King Josiah.[4]

The native Hebrews taught their provincial version of Yahwism to their new husbands and wives. The foreign-born transportees were happy to learn the ways of their new land's god and gradually evolved a composite quasi-Jewish religion called Samaritanism, still practiced today by their descendents.

The Samaritans have always claimed, correctly, that their religion predates the temple-based worship of conventional Jews. They also maintain that the true holy site of Yahweh's worship is not Jerusalem but Mt. Gerizim, in the present-day West Bank area. It is on this mountain that, even today, they offer animal sacrifices on their holy days. Jews have always considered Samaritans to be second-class citizens and when Jesus spoke with a Samaritan woman on Mt. Gerizim at Jacob's well, she was amazed that a Jewish man would even speak to her and said:

> "I can see you are a prophet. Our ancestors worshipped on this mountain, but you people claim that Jerusalem is the place where men ought to worship God."
> Jesus told her, "Believe me, woman, an hour is coming when you will worship the Father neither on this mountain nor in Jerusalem."
>
> (John 4:19)

Twenty years later, in 701 B.C., the Judean king Hezekiah, again encouraged by Egyptian agents, balked at paying tribute to Assyria. So the Assyrian king Sennacherib invaded Judah and laid siege to Jerusalem. Sennacherib boasted that he had shut Hezekiah up in Jerusalem "like a bird in a cage."[5] He wasn't able to breach the city's walls but he destroyed 46 of Hezekiah's smaller fortified cities and transported more than 200,000 Hebrews to distant lands. These people, too, assimilated into foreign cultures and were never heard from again. This was the second great deportation event.

One hundred years went by. The Hebrews were ready for another disaster.

Judah, the southern kingdom, had fallen under the rule of the Babylonian Empire. Zedekiah, son of Josiah, was a puppet ruler who the Babylonian emperor Nebuchadnezzar II had placed on the throne of Judah in 598 B.C. to replace the disgraced Jehoiachin. His original name was Mattanyahu ("Gift of Yahweh"), but he changed his name to Zedekiah when he took the throne.[6] At his coronation, Nebuchadnezzar made his Hebrew puppet king swear an oath of loyalty to Babylon.[7]

Throughout his entire reign, Zedekiah faced continual political unrest from Judah's nationalists, the Egyptian Party (to use Isaac Asimov's terminology). These men and women wanted him to break his allegiance to Babylon and seek vassalage under the once-mighty but now weak Egyptian Empire. They respected and identified with Egyptian culture and thought Egypt had Judah's best interests at heart. Many Hebrew customs such as circumcision and the abhorrence of pig's flesh had come to them through contact with the older and influential Egyptian civilization. These customs were dying out by this time and were only occasionally observed by the rural population, rarely by the urban upper classes.

On the other side of the political fence was the licensed auditory prophet Jeremiah. He had traveled widely and had personally seen both Egypt's weakness and Babylonia's overwhelming military might. He represented the Babylonian Party and urged his king to remain loyal to Nebuchadnezzar.

To dramatize his point, Jeremiah made a light yoke that he wore around his neck. He told people that it symbolized the beneficial, easily-worn yoke of Babylonian rule that Judah should wear to ensure its national survival. Most of the guild prophets belonged to the Egyptian Party; they took the opposite view and denounced Jeremiah for his pro-Babylonian diatribes. Jeremiah's chief adversary was a guild prophet named Henaniah, an early proponent of the power of positive thinking. Henaniah tore Jeremiah's paper yoke off in a rage when the two of them were debating in the Temple. Henaniah claimed that all anyone had to do was think good thoughts about Yahweh and Nebuchadnezzar's army would just melt away and Egypt would return in all its former glory. Finally, feelings ran so high that even Jeremiah had to feign acquiescence to avoid anti-Babylonian mobs that threatened to lynch him. When the mobs dispersed, Jeremiah felt safe enough to curse Henaniah as a false prophet and predict his imminent death, which occurred two months later.

In 589 B.C., the ninth year of his reign in Jerusalem, Zedekiah foolishly caved in to the pressure of popular pro-Egyptian sentiment. Defying Jeremiah's warnings, he declared open revolt against Nebuchadnezzar. The next year, 588, the Chaldean (Babylonian) army under the command of Nebuzaraden, Nebuchadnezzar's field commander, besieged Jerusalem.

For years before this, agents of the Egyptian pharaohs had been stirring things up in Jerusalem. One pharaoh, Psamtik II, had sent letters to Zedekiah urging him to revolt. So the Egyptian Party in Jerusalem was encouraged when Psamtik's successor, Pharaoh Hophra, sent troops to engage the Chaldeans. This caused a brief lifting of the siege while the Chaldeans left and, without much effort, wiped out the Egyptians. Then they returned and renewed the siege.

Throughout the two-year siege, Jeremiah kept exhorting the citizens of Jerusalem to surrender the city and trust to the mercy of the Chaldean general, Nebuzaraden. This so enraged the pro-Egyptian mobs that they forced Zedekiah to throw Jeremiah into prison.

At first he was confined in a relatively comfortable environment, under house arrest in the compound where the palace guards were quartered. But four powerful members of the Egyptian Party became aware that he was secretly getting word out to the people and continuing to preach his doctrine of surrender to the Babylonians. They went to the king and demanding that he put Jeremiah to death. The weak-willed king caved in to their demands and told them that Jeremiah was theirs; they could do whatever they wished with him.

To avoid shedding the blood of a licensed prophet they took Jeremiah to an empty, abandoned cistern near the guards' quarters and lowered him in with ropes. The mud at the bottom of the cistern was so soft and deep that Jeremiah sank up to his knees in it. Then they left him there to starve to death.

But a servant of Zedekiah told the king of Jeremiah's predicament and pleaded for the prophet's life. Zedekiah, with no wish to have the martyrdom of a well-known prophet on his hands, acquiesced and directed the servant to round up a small rescue party, pull Jeremiah out and restore him to his previous state of house arrest in the guards' quarters.

Fig. 15 Zerubbabel directing the rebuilding of the Jerusalem temple. Circa 517 B.C. ©iStock.

Also, he ordered the servant to make sure that Jeremiah received one loaf of bread a day to eat; the same ration that every citizen in the besieged city was getting.

This is where the prophet spent most of his time for the next year. Finally, Jerusalem fell in 587 B.C. King Nebuchadnezzar, who had been told by his spies of Jeremiah's pro-Babylonian tirades, had given his field general, Nebuzaraden, strict orders to treat the prophet well and to let him do as he pleased when he was released. Because of the king's refusal to surrender, as Jeremiah had forewarned, Nebuzaraden sacked the city and burned it and its temple to the ground. Its poorer, lower-class urban citizens who were useless to Babylonian relocation policies, were massacred while many of the peasants in the countryside, experienced farmers and viniculturists, were spared and even given plots of land and vineyards in accordance with Nebuchadnezzar's enlightened policies of reconstruction. The Babylonians forced Zedekiah to watch while they slaughtered his sons. Then they put his eyes out (with their thumbs) and carried him to Babylon where he died in blindness and poverty.

The Babylonians set up a local puppet government with its capital at the now-vanished city of Mizpah, thought to have been located a few miles to the north-west of Jerusalem. They appointed a high-born Hebrew noble, Gedaliah, as the regional governor. Gedaliah tried to reestablish the routine life of the peasantry on their farms and vineyards and reassured them that the rule of Babylonia would be benign and beneficial. But he was soon murdered by a treacherous Hebrew army general named Ishmael who had been egged on by the Ammonite king Baalis. Ishmael intended to supplant Gedaliah as ruler of Judah and he slaughtered many of the Babylonian soldiers that Nebuzaraden had left behind to keep order in the land. Soon he was himself hunted down by other Judahian army officers and fled to find refuge with his Ammonite supporters, accompanied by just eight men.

Then the army officers who had defeated Ishmael began to fear that they themselves would be blamed for the attempted revolt and would be punished when the expected Babylonian reprisals materialized. They wanted to flee to Egypt and they consulted Jeremiah about their plan. He warned them to stay put and explain matters to the Babylonian army when it arrived but they would have none of it. They gathered up the noblewomen whom the Babylonians had left behind and forced Jeremiah to go with them on their flight into Egypt. There the Yahwist Jeremiah spent his last years in the fortified Egyptian town of Tahpanhes, on the eastern edge of the Nile Delta near the sea coast, where he died in an expatriate community of Hebrews whose women baked little star-shaped cookies that they offered to the goddess Astarte, their Queen of Heaven. They mocked Jeremiah's sermons about Yahweh and pointed out that everything had been fine until they neglected their duties to Astarte.[8]

After the Babylonian army had invaded Jerusalem and burned Solomon's temple most of the wealthy upper-class urban Hebrews who had been spared from the general massacre were forced to relocate to Babylon. There they remained for 48 years until the Persian Empire overthrew and replaced the Chaldean rulers of Babylonia. Then Cyrus, king of Persia, came to sit on the throne of Babylon. He took pity on the captive peoples that he had inherited and decided to restore all of them to their homelands. He also financed the rebuilding of temples to their native gods and goddesses.

The story of this degree is a fictionalized account of King Cyrus' decision in the year 538 B.C. to repatriate the Hebrews that Nebuchadnezzar had taken captive.

When Cyrus made his decision to free his captive peoples, there is no record of either Daniel (of lions' den fame) or Zerubbabel being present. Cyrus' action was a political and a humanitarian one based on his own enlightened policies towards the treatment of conquered people and the administration of his empire. Cryus' policies heralded those of the later Roman Empire and, as a result, his Persian Empire was a similar administrative success. The Jews were only one of the many captive groups that Cyrus returned to their original countries and Yahweh was only one of many foreign gods with a brand-new temple financed by Persian money. Every time Cyrus freed a captive group of people he always said that their particular gods or goddesses had "charged" him to rebuild their temples. A good polytheist, he covered all his bets.

Some Masonic authors have stated that both Cyrus and Darius were Zoroastrians and worshipped only one god. Darius was probably a Zoroastrian but Cyrus was a polytheist. Among other gods and goddesses, he worshipped Marduk, the chief deity of his native Persia, whom he was careful to thank publicly for his victory. But even if Cyrus *had* been a Zoroastrian and a worshiper of Ahura-Mazda, he still would not have believed in just one god. Like all Zoroastrians, he would also have acknowledged a few other gods in his pantheon.

Zoroaster (c. 1500 -1200 B.C.) started his career as a *zoatar*, a priest of an ancient Persian religion. While he was drinking from the Daitya River, a *jinn* (a demon or an angel, depending on how you look at it) appeared to him and preached a new doctrine that went something like this:

The god Zurvan Akarana ("infinite time") was sad because he had no son. He offered a sacrifice to the Great Goddess who gave him twins. The first to be born was Ahura-Mazda, ("truth and light"), the second was a hostile creature named Ahriman, ("destructive thought"). À la Abel and Cain, the two divine brothers represented good and evil, respectively. Zoroastrians honored and prayed to Ahura-Mazda as the creator of the universal laws of order they called *asha*. They ignored or denigrated the evil Ahriman, much as modern Christians acknowledge the existence of Satan as the powerful, crafty ruler of the underworld but do not address prayers to him. This system of acknowledgement/

denigration of a chthonic (underworld) god is what scholars of comparative religion call *negative worship*.

There were also Zoroastrian gods of wind, of water and of fire. The Zoroastrians even had a beautiful and noble goddess, Anahita, who distributed a hallucinogenic potion that made men and women fall in love.[9]

Manichaeism, an offshoot of Zoroastrianism, offers a similar theology. The prophet Mani founded Manichaeism in Persia around A.D. 240, some 830 years after the time of Cyrus. This religion teaches that the world we live in is a battleground between a god of light and a god of darkness. Although the dark god created the human race and the individual is dark at birth, he can perfect himself through spiritual exercises. Then, at his death, the god of light will take him up to heaven.

This religion still exists today and has about 200,000 worshippers. Manichaeism is thought to have had a great influence on the early development of Christianity. It certainly influenced the development of Catharism, a variant of Christianity that was wiped out by the Albigensian Crusade (1209–1229), preached by Pope Innocent III to eliminate something that the Church considered a dangerous heresy. One result is present-day Christianity's enormous compendium of literature and folklore dealing with an eternal conflict between God and Satan.

The 15th Degree
of the Southern Jurisdiction:

KNIGHT OF THE EAST, OF THE SWORD OR OF THE EAGLE

In the Southern Jurisdiction the 15th degree is the first degree in the Chapter of Rose Croix. Here it is called by the ponderous title THE KNIGHT OF THE EAST, OF THE SWORD OR OF THE EAGLE, as if the Ritual Committee couldn't make up its mind. Zerubbabel returns to Jerusalem to inspect the ruins of the temple. Then he comes back to Babylon and goes through the same temptations and threats as in the Northern Jurisdiction degree. Cyrus tells the court about his dream which is interpreted by Daniel. Zerubbabel reminds Cyrus that the Emperor has made an oath to his god, Mithras, that he will let the Jews return to their homeland. Cyrus allows Zerubbabel to return with his friends and rebuild the temple. On the way back, a fight at a bridge with Syrian bandits occurs. Zerubbabel returns to Jerusalem, institutes the degree of KNIGHT OF THE EAST… etc. and begins work on the second temple.[10]

16th Degree:

PRINCE OF JERUSALEM
(Wine, women or the king?)

The Stage Drama

The drama opens in a camp near the ruins of Solomon's Temple in Jerusalem. The time is around 520 B.C., about 18 years after Cyrus had proclaimed that the Hebrew captives in Babylon could return home and rebuild their temple in Jerusalem. The priest Joshua is scolding the Jewish governor of the area, Zerubbabel (whose name means "Child of Babylon" or "Born at Babylon"), about the lack of progress on the temple. Work on the temple is going nowhere due to the continued resistance of the local people, the Samaritans. Joshua persuades Zerubbabel to return to Babylon and talk to their friend Darius, nephew of the late Cyrus and new Emperor of Persia. Zerubbabel makes the journey and arrives at Darius' palace on an evening the Emperor is presiding over a debate on the respective power of wine, women or the king. Zerubbabel wins the debate by citing truth as the most powerful motivator and Darius grants his request (Plate 12). Darius also issues orders that prohibit the Samaritans from interfering with work on the temple.

In the Allegories of the Fifteenth and Sixteenth degrees, we are taught, by the example of Zerubbabel, the important lessons of loyalty to conviction, fidelity to duty and devotion to truth.

Historical Background

The Persian Emperor Cyrus died in 530 B.C., just eight years after issuing his proclamation allowing the captive peoples to return home. He was succeeded by his son Cambyses, a practical but unsentimental man who, to forestall any rival claimants for the throne, immediately executed his brother, Smerdis, and married his sisters. Cambyses' first project was to invade and conquer Egypt, the last country still independent of Persian control. He won his battle and took Egypt, but while he was away on campaign, problems arose back home. A Zoroastrian priest tried to usurp the throne, claiming to be Cambyses' murdered brother, Smerdis. In 521 B.C., while rushing back from Egypt to attend to this upstart, Cambyses died (perhaps by assassination). While his name is known to historians, he is not mentioned in the Bible.

The usurping priest managed to take over control of the empire for a few months until he was overthrown and killed by a group of noblemen. Their leader was a young member of the royal family named Darayavaush, better known to history as Darius. Darius proved to be an able ruler and, following the pattern of government set by Cyrus, organized his empire into provinces called *satrapies*, each ruled by a *satrap* (governor). He reigned for 35 years, building roads and canals and improving the state of affairs for all his subjects.

Fig. 16 The Hebrew captives in Babylon were protected by a comprehensive code of laws formulated by Hammurabi, an early king of Babylon. Here, on the stone stela on which his law code is inscribed, Hammurabi (on the left, standing with his hand over his mouth in an attitude of reverence) is depicted receiving the articles of royal rule from the sun god Shamash. Currently on display in the Louvre.

Meanwhile, the captive Jews who Cyrus had allowed to return to rebuild Jerusalem and the Temple were having problems.

When Zerubbabel and his party arrived in Jerusalem, soon followed by larger numbers of other returning Babylonian Jews, they found a strange new group of people waiting for them: the Samaritans. The Samaritans regarded the returnees with suspicion. The returnees looked, talked and acted like Babylonians but claimed to be *Jews*. Jews? What were Jews? Where had they come from and why did they seem to think that they owned the place? Who had put these oddballs in charge, anyway? The Samaritans offered to help with the rebuilding project but Zerubbabel curtly and undiplomatically dismissed them. Samaritan suspicion soon turned to dislike. Who did these high-handed newcomers think they were?

The parents and grandparents of the returning Babylonian exiles had already been wealthy, urban aristocrats before Nebuchadnezzar sent them into exile. Most of the returnees had been born in Babylon and had grown up exposed to the most advanced civilization of the time. This only heightened their sense of social and ethnic superiority. They now spoke Aramaic, the lingua franca of the Persian Empire, while the Samaritans spoke a rustic form of Hebrew, heavily influenced by the foreign tongues of the other conquered peoples who had been exiled there. The returning Jewish exiles dressed in rich Babylonian style and lived in beautiful encampments of colorful Persian army tents, while the local Samaritans dressed in crudely-woven woolen tunics and lived in rustic brick huts. It wasn't very long before each side came to regard the people on the other side as foreigners, religious apostates and unwelcome intruders.

The exiles returning from Babylon looked down on the Samaritans as an illiterate, backward bunch of hayseeds. They saw the Samaritans practicing a primitive religion that only superficially resembled the newly defined Yahwist belief system that the Babylonian Jews were now calling "Judaism." (Implying that it was now the *only* religion of their homeland, Judah). Also, the native Hebrews whom Nebuchadnezzar had left behind had, from necessity, intermarried extensively with newly-arrived foreign ethnic groups who, under Babylonian policy, had been forcibly relocated from their homelands to Israel. So, after two centuries of isolation and intermarriage, the Samaritans did not look, act or speak like the returning Babylonian Jews.

And, most damning of all, they had no use for a temple located in Jerusalem. In fact, they had no use for Jerusalem at all, considering it an unholy, pagan place founded by the sinful, usurping adventurer, David. They also knew the handed-down legends of Solomon's Temple. They knew it was an idolatrous house of polytheistic worship for most of its existence and saw no reason to perpetuate it by building another temple in the same place.

While captive in Babylon, the Hebrews had kept their ethnic and religious identity intact by closing their ranks against outsiders. As a means to this end, they had taken to adopting several spottily observed Egyptian and Mesopotamian customs they remembered. These customs had been current throughout most of the cultures and city-states in Canaan but were not popular in the sophisticated culture of Babylon. The Hebrew exiles gave them mystical or religious significance and, for the purpose of ethnic identity, adopted them as uniquely Jewish rituals.

One of these customs was the practice of male circumcision. Circumcision began in Egypt during the Sixth Dynasty (2345 – 2181 B.C.), as an initiation ceremony marking the passage from adolescence into manhood. The Egyptians considered a bloody bodily alteration to be an appropriate prerequisite to initiation into the mysteries of Isis and Osiris. In the Egyptian Book of the Dead, the supreme god Ra performed circumcision on himself and then created two more gods from his sacred blood. The oldest written record of circumcision is in an Egyptian papyrus from around 2300 B.C. in which Uha, an Egyptian initiate, tells of the mass circumcision of 120 men.[1] He boasts that he alone showed no

Fig. 17 A captive Hebew scribe in a Babylonian library, writing a part of the Old Testament, using stories from Babylonian mythology. ©iStock.

sign of pain or discomfort, in contrast to other men who had to be held in case they fainted.

Such was the prestige of Egyptian civilization in the Bronze Age of the Middle East that most of Egypt's neighboring nations adopted this means of initiation. This included the wandering Hebrew tribes, who even applied it to newborn infants. By the time of the Babylonian Exile, as Egypt's prestige waned, the practice of circumcision had been dying out, even among the Hebrews. The Babylonians, to whom Egypt was a hated rival, considered it barbaric and did not practice it at all. So the Judean exiles revived it and made it into a religious ceremony that would serve to set them apart.

Another Egyptian custom was a strict prohibition against eating pig's flesh. There was a good reason for this. Only the wealthy Egyptians could afford the expensive process of mummification and burial in a stone tomb; most other people were simply put to rest in shallow graves in the loose, sandy soil of the desert. Feral pigs, smelling the bodies, would root down into the graves and devour the corpses. Knowing this, no Egyptian would touch pork and despised anyone who did. It was said that an Egyptian would not even kiss a Greek because the Greeks were known to eat pig meat.[2]

During the time Moses and his people were wandering in the Sinai, other groups of people from areas around Egypt were leaving their homelands and moving into the desert. They were fleeing conscription into the forced-labor corvées that the Egyptian pharaohs levied on foreigners living on Egyptian soil. In the Sinai Peninsula many of these refugees were swept up into the wandering confederation of tribes that had taken to calling themselves Hebrews. Short-legged pigs are impossible to herd and drive for long distances so the Hebrew nomads had never developed a taste for pork anyway. The anti-pork taboo of the fleeing Egyptianized newcomers had no trouble becoming an established custom. But by the Babylonian invasion of Jerusalem the stigma against pig flesh was a thing of the past and most upper-class urban Hebrews were eating pretty much whatever they wanted. So the practice had to be revived with a religious rationale.

The Akkadian Empire reached the peak of its influence in the three centuries between 2500 and 2200 B.C. By the time of the Babylonian Exile its famous founder, Sargon of Akkad (2334–2279 BC), had become a legendary icon of power and wisdom in the Middle East. The Semitic Akkadians had held a monthly feast of the full moon they called the *Shabattu*. Akkadians came to observe it as a day of rest and enjoyment for the citizens throughout the empire.

The Akkadians' fellow Semites, the early Hebrews, had held similar *Shabattu* feasts. There are many references in the Old Testament to new moon festivals. These refer to the ancient Hebrew observance of *Rosh Chodesh*, ("Head of the Month"). This feast took place at the beginning of each Hebrew month (a night of a new moon), and everyone was supposed to abstain from business and work and enjoy themselves; in fact, they *had* to – it was forbidden to work, mourn or fast on that day.

The Babylonians, for their part, celebrated every seventh day in their lunar 28-day months as a special day on which the law prohibited citizens from performing everyday activities. Among the Hebrews, the last day of each lunar month had been an official "day of rest." The Jewish scholar Raphael Patai believes that, during the Exile, the Jews imitated their Babylonian masters and modified their once-a-month new moon *Shabattu* observance into a once-a-week seventh day *Shabbat* or Sabbath.[3] This proved so popular that they wrote it into the Ten Commandments and, when the Jews returned to their homeland, the Sabbath observance served as yet another badge of distinction from their neighbors.

Finally, during the Exile, sometime around 540 B.C., an unnamed prophet arose within the expatriate Hebrew community in Babylon. Today we know him only as Second Isaiah because scribes appended his writings (thought to be Isaiah 40-55) to the end of the Book of Isaiah.[4] This prophet preached an entirely new doctrine regarding the nature of Yahweh. Previous Hebrew prophets, including Isaiah himself, were *heno*theists, that is, they were polytheists who believed other gods existed but who considered their own god or gods to be superior. They had maintained that Yahweh was *better* than all the other gods of the Middle Eastern nations. They claimed he was more powerful than they were, a better fertility god than Baal Hadad, a surer guarantee of victory in war than Astarte, a divinity whose power eclipsed even that of mighty Isis, the Egyptian Great Goddess. When planning his temple, Solomon, as a sop to the Yahwists in his court, had declared:

> And the house I intend to build must be large, for our god [Yahweh] is greater than all the other gods.

> (2 Chronicles 2: 4)

But if that were true, the exiles wondered, why had Nebuchadnezzar's army been able to swoop down and sack Jerusalem with such ease? The Yahwist groups in the exiled community were starting to have their doubts. How could Yahweh have allowed foreigners to loot and desecrate his temple? Why were Yahweh's chosen people languishing as prisoners in a strange country? Were the gods and goddesses of Babylon more powerful than the god of Judah?

So Second Isaiah preached a revival of Yahwism, fortified by a new twist: the declaration that now no other gods even existed. Anyone who prayed to an idol was wasting his time. Second Isaiah said, à la Nietzsche, "All the other gods are dead!" The people should now regard Yahweh as the One True Living God, who would soon smash the Babylonian Empire and free the Jews from captivity.[5]

In pre-Exile times people had sometimes worshipped Yahweh under the effigy of a mighty bronze bull.[6] This idol had been an icon of his predecessor, El and his rival, Baal.[7] Solomon had ordered Hiram Abiff to cast 12 bronze bull Yahweh idols (Plate 5) to support the 12,000 gallon "sea" of Solomon's personal goddess, Asherah of the Sea.[8] He is even thought to have used a bull effigy as a decoration on his throne.

Second Isaiah's new version of Yahweh was different. This god was invisible and lived far away, all alone up in the sky with no wife or consort, remote from mankind and fearful to contemplate. He wanted no more images made of himself. The Babylonian gods had not bested him – they didn't even exist. No, it was Yahweh himself who had been responsible for the Babylonian Exile. It was a punishment, said Second Isaiah, for the sinfulness of the Judean people. If the people repented, Yahweh might consider setting them free. But the Jews must understand that there would be no more idolatry, human sacrifice[9] or temple prostitution[10] in Judah. Yahweh's new prophet, Second Isaiah, predicts with glee the inevitable destruction of all idolatry. He envisions a new, ideal Jewish state with a state-imposed religion that acknowledges the divinity of Yahweh alone. This was the theocratic ideology taken back to Judah by the Hebrew returnees, one that has been resurrected in the present-day state of Israel.

This was the second known experiment with strict monotheism in the Western world. The first had occurred 500 years earlier in Egypt under the pharaoh Akhenaten when he repudiated the traditional pantheon of Egyptian gods and goddesses and substituted the worship of the sun god, Aten. Previous to this, Aten had been a minor solar deity, subject to the more powerful sun god, Ra-Horakhty. But as long as Akhenaten reigned, all Egyptians had to acknowledge Aten as the one true God and all had to give him worship. Originally named Amenhotep ("Amun is satisfied") he changed his name to Akhenaten ("Servant of Aten") and shut down the temples of the other gods throughout Egypt. As soon as he died in 1336 B.C. the worship of Atun ceased and the worship of the traditional Egyptian pantheon returned.

The famous Jewish psychoanalyst, Sigmund Freud, wrote a book in 1939 called *Moses and Monotheism* in which he argued that Moses was not a Hebrew but a native Egyptian. Freud further hypothesized that Moses was a priest of Aten who had to flee Egypt after Akhenaten's death and who carried the Egyptian doctrine of monotheism with him. He eventually joined a wandering tribe of Hebrew sheep herders who accepted his preaching about one deity but, when he became too overbearing with them, murdered him. That tribe, in turn, joined another tribe of desert dwellers in the Sinai Peninsula who worshipped a volcano god they called Yahweh. Moses' followers, to make themselves look important, made up the story about the burning bush; the volcano worshippers were so impressed that they accepted it as true and a new religion was born. Needless to say, Freud's fellow Jews were infuriated and his reputation among them suffered.

So, the returning strangers from Babylon high-handedly told the Samaritans that everyone who wanted to call himself by the new-fangled title of "Jew" had to acknowledge Yahweh to be God with a capital "G," the only deity that existed. The Samaritans were still mainly henotheists and didn't think they needed to be preached to by the returnees.

Also, the revised and heavily edited scriptures that the repatriated Babylonian Jews had brought back with them, interlaced with Babylonian myths, were radically different from anything the Samaritans had ever seen. While the Hebrew captives had been living in Babylon, they had evolved a new social class: the Scribes.

These Scribes had discovered the luxurious, well-stocked libraries of Babylon. There they spent their time copying, rewriting and organizing the early versions of writings they had salvaged from the sack of Jerusalem. These salvaged documents had coalesced over centuries from folk tales and myths and patched-together scraps of remembered history. They represented the collected cultural folklore of Israel. Some myths dated back to the nomadic period of the early multi-ethnic, polytheistic Transjordanian tribes of Moses' day.

The Hebrew Scribes were all members of the now-dominant Yahwist cult. Every time they came across the name of a deity other than Yahweh whom the early Hebrews had acknowledged, the Scribes substituted the name of Yahweh or, following a new custom they had picked up from the Babylonians, the term *Adonai*, or "Lord." They even inserted a whole new book, Deuteronomy ("The Second Law"). Written by Yahwist priests during or shortly before the reign of King Josiah, the Scribes added it to what became the *Pentateuch* that they credited to Moses. In effect, they used the literary resources of the advanced Babylonian civilization to embellish and complete the "Deuteronomic" reform of Josiah that had begun before the exile.

The Scribes ended up by writing a revisionist history, in Aramaic as well as Hebrew, of the Jewish people. They had spruced up their revision with stories taken from Babylonian mythology (the two creation stories and Noah's flood, for example). In every myth the Scribes substituted the name of Yahweh for the original Babylonian or Sumerian deity in the story. Take, for instance, the famous story of Noah's Flood. This was almost certainly based on the *Chaldean Flood Tablets* from the city of Ur in what is now Southern Iraq. These tablets, available to the Scribes in the Babylonian libraries, describe how the Sumerian god Enlil had decided to eliminate humans and other land animals with a great flood that was to become "the end of all flesh."[11]

The character that the Jewish Scribes renamed Noah was originally a Sumerian hero named Ut-Napishtim. He is featured in the Epic of Gilgamesh, the earliest adventure story known to history. In the story, Ut-Napishtim survives Ea's disastrous flood by building a large cubicle ark and taking his family and many pairs of animals on board. When the flood subsides his ark is stranded on a mountaintop and he sends a dove (or, in some versions, a raven) out to find dry land. The dove returns with an olive branch and Ut-Napishtim and his family leave the ark. They plant vineyards, offer sacrifices to their Babylonian gods and goddesses and repopulate the earth. By the time Gilgamesh finds him and listens to his tale, Ut-Napishtim is either a god or a very old man, indeed.

Another useful Babylonian legend the scribes found in the libraries of Babylonia was the famous birth legend of Sargon the Great, king of Akkad. He had ruled the world's first recorded empire, a vast domain that included all of Mesopotamia, from about 2270 to 2215 B.C. The legend records that Sargon's mother was a high-ranking sacred prostitute in the temple of the Great Goddess, Ishtar, and that in the performance of her duties she became pregnant. As was the custom in such cases, she abandoned her child to the will of the goddess. She placed the infant Sargon in a reed basket sealed with bitumen and set him adrift on the Euphrates River. An irrigation farmer named Aqqi, a worshipper of Ishtar, found the drifting basket among the bulrush reeds and drew it from the river. He adopted the infant as his own son and raised him to be a gardener. As he grew up and practiced his step-father's trade, Sargon came to believe that Ishtar favored him and planned a great destiny for him, an intuition that turned out to be correct.

The Jewish Scribes realized that this legend, at that time famous throughout the civilized Western world, would make a perfect model for the biography of their folk-hero, Moses, about whose early life they knew almost nothing. The story they wrote would have the double advantage of making Moses a high-ranking Egyptian official (for prestige) and a biological Hebrew (for nationalistic identity, necessary for acceptance by the increasingly xenophobic Jews). They modified the Sargon birth legend to suit Jewish tastes and added it to their folklore collection.

The Scribes went farther. In their revisionist scriptures, they represented all of the legendary Hebrew patriarchs as being Yahwists like themselves. They did the same for quasi-historical figures like Moses and Solomon. These anachronisms bring to mind the many Renaissance paintings of Biblical events in which the painters portrayed soldiers and citizens at the time of Moses or Jesus in the armor and clothing of 16th- or 17th-century Europeans, dressed as people of the

Fig. 18 The finding of Moses (originaly Sargon the Great?) by Pharaoh's daughter on the banks of the Nile. ©iStock.

painter's own time (Plate 10). Art historians call this process "updating." The Babylonian Scribes practiced ideological, genealogical and theological updating in their rewriting of the Old Testament scriptures.

According to most modern Biblical scholars, Yahwism was not well established in the time of Solomon. It was just one of many sects in Israel that competed with the worship of other Canaanite gods and goddesses. The revised, updated Yahwist scriptures from the Babylonian Captivity presented the situation differently. Whenever the early Hebrews were recorded as worshiping any other god or goddess the Babylonian Scribes said they were "doing evil" in the sight of Yahweh. In the stories, he usually punishes them severely. This was all based on the premise of Second Isaiah: that Yahweh was the one and only God and had brought the Exile upon his people as a punishment for their transgressions.

The captives taken by Nebuchadnezzar had left Israel as provincial polytheistic Canaanite Hebrews and returned as civilized Babylonian Jews. They brought back a newly revised history and a new religion that acknowledged one God and one God only. In the words of H. G. Wells:

"The Jews who returned, after an interval of more than two generations, to Jerusalem [presupposing a 70-year captivity] from Babylonia in the time of Cyrus were a very different people from the warring Baal worshippers… of the kingdoms of Israel and Judah. The plain fact of the Bible narrative is that the Jews went to Babylon barbarians and came back civilized."[12]

The returning Jews looked down on their Samaritan neighbors as heretics and mongrels who looked funny, talked funny and didn't know how to dress. This did not make for harmonious relations between the long-separated ethnic groups. The 16th degree's story recounts a result of the friction that arose between the two sides.

There is an interesting fable connected to this degree. The fable is taken from an apocryphal work called the Book of Esdras, which has never been included in either the Catholic, Protestant or Jewish canonical versions of the Scriptures. In the story, Darius has gone to sleep after a big feast and three of his palace guards wile away the time by arguing over which particular entity is most powerful in the affairs of men. One argues for wine, the second for the king himself and the third holds out for women. The third guardsman, named Zorobabel (Zerubbabel), then goes on to say:

> The third wrote, Women are strongest: but above all things Truth beareth away the victory.
>
> (1 Esdras 3:12)

Darius finds out about the debate and gets an idea. As an amusing diversion for that evening's entertainment, he makes each guardsman defend his choice before the entire court. After the other two have spoken, the third guardsman makes his argument:

> Then the third, who had spoken of women, and of the truth, (this was Zorobabel) began to speak. …Blessed be the god of truth …And all the people then shouted, and said, Great is Truth, and mighty above all things.
>
> (1 Esdras 4:13-41)

Darius declares Zerubbabel the winner and offers to grant him anything he wishes. Zerubbabel asks Darius to reaffirm and restore Cyrus' support for the building of the Temple in Jerusalem; Darius grants his wish. The Masonic version of this fable follows the Apocryphal Biblical version closely.

At the time of the degree's drama Cyrus was long dead and Darius was sitting on the throne of Persia. For years before the events of the story had occurred, the Samaritans had been sending emissaries to Babylonia with false documents to convince the ruler, Cyrus' son, Cambyses, that the returned Jews were up to no good (Ezra 4: 1-24). The Samaritans said that, instead of rebuilding the temple, the Jews were actually planning to build a wall around Jerusalem. In those days, building a wall around a city showed anticipation of military activity and was considered a defensive prelude to a revolt. This would be tantamount to declaring open rebellion against the Persian rulers. Consequently, Cambyses had withdrawn support for the repatriated Jews and had allowed the temple project to languish. When Darius took over the rule of Persia, he continued Cambyses' policies and did not reinstate support for the temple. Hence the need for Zerubbabel's return to the Persian court.

The apocryphal story about the after-dinner debate appears to have been knocking around our fraternity for a long time. According to Laurence Gardner, in his book *The Shadow of Solomon*, over a lintel in the south aisle of Rosslyn Chapel near Edinburgh is an inscription in Vulgate Latin:

Forte est vinu; fortier est Rex; fortiores
sunt mulieres' sup on vincit veritas.

Wine is strong; the king is stronger;
women are even stronger, but above all truth conquers.[13]

Personally, I think that the guardsman who argued for the King's ultimate power had the best argument. Rulers of nations have usually had the most influence over their subject populations and even over neighboring countries (if they decide to invade them). As for power over individual men, it is probably a toss-up between women and ethyl alcohol, with the advantage going to women. If truth has ever had any influence on human behavior and the shaping of human destiny, it certainly isn't evident from a study of history. Very much the opposite. In most imperial courts, whether in Babylon, Rome or China, a habit of making truthful comments would more likely get you hoisted up on a sharp stake than getting your requests granted.

The 16th Degree
of the Southern Jurisdiction:

PRINCE OF JERUSALEM

In the Southern jurisdiction most of the drama's action takes place in Jerusalem. Zerubbabel makes the journey to Babylon, talks Darius into supporting the rebuilding of the temple and returns to Jerusalem. In this ritual, Albert Pike tells us that Zerubbabel's Hebrew name was Sasbatzer, which Pike translates as "Keeper of the Fire." There is no mention of the debate over wine, the king, women and truth. Pike pays more attention to the sorry condition of the people living in Jerusalem. He describes how they are aided and reinvigorated by the kind and just actions of Zerubbabel and another character named Kadmiel ("Standing before El"; i.e., "El's Servant"). Kadmiel was either a Levite or a Syrian prince (Hutchens' description is vague) who had accompanied Zerubbabel when he returned from the Babylonian captivity (Nehemiah 9:4, 10:9, 12:8). Whatever his ethnic identity, Kadmiel is made out to be some sort of warrior prince, similar to the Irish hero, Cú Chulainn.[14]

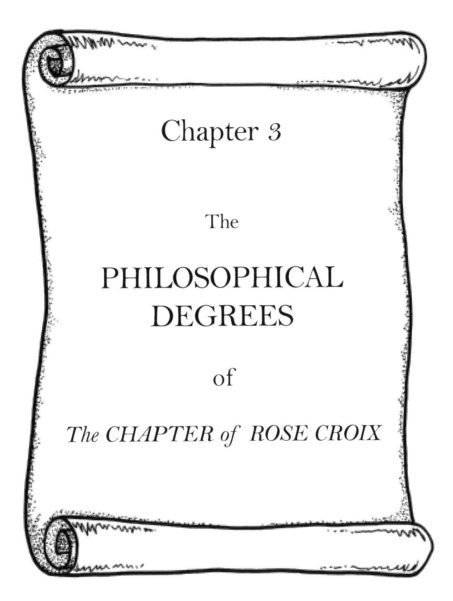

Chapter 3

The

PHILOSOPHICAL DEGREES

of

The CHAPTER of ROSE CROIX

Both of the two Rose Croix degrees deal with events of the Christian era. While providing a gateway from the Old to the New Testament, the Rose Croix degree is meant to be universal in its philosophy. It is basically a pivot upon which our attention turns from the old Jewish law to the teachings of Jesus of Nazareth.

17th Degree:

Knight of the East and West
(The political wisdom of Herod the Great)

The Stage Drama

The time is a few years before the birth of Christ; the place is the courtyard in front of the main gate of Herod's Temple in Jerusalem. Three groups of religious Jews – Essenes, Sadducees and Pharisees – are arguing over what to do about the huge bronze Roman eagle Herod has placed over the Temple's entrance gate, an idol and abomination in the eyes of the city's Jewish citizens. The Pharisees settle the matter by tearing it down and then beating a hasty retreat. Herod, who is ill and close to death, arrives and is infuriated; he vows death to the vandals. He even orders his own son's execution, returns to his palace and dies.

The Sadducees and Essenes commiserate with each other and debate their options. The Sadducees decide to pray about the matter. The Essenes prudently take off for a new hidden refuge, a system of caves on the shores of the Dead Sea, where they will write and then conceal a collection of documents now known as the Dead Sea Scrolls. The scrolls comprise many hundreds of documents in Aramaic, Hebrew and Greek that were discovered between 1947 and 1956. These writings, and other so-called Lost Gospels, shed much new light on the life of Jesus of Nazareth including (according to the interpretations of some scholars) a possible romantic relationship with Mary Magdalene and a hitherto unsuspected friendship and collusion with Judas Iscariot.

The lessons of this degree are that man will fail in all efforts that are based on power, greed and envy; and that divine guidance is needed to keep us from repeating the errors of history. This degree also teaches that we must seek truth in our way of life, and that we should learn from, and avoid repeating, the errors of the past.

Historical Background

After Alexander the Great died leaving no male heirs, his generals divided up his empire among them. One general, Ptolemy, took control of Egypt while another, Seleucus, ruled western Asia. Their descendants, the Ptolemies and the Seleucids, took turns conquering and ruling Judah. In 134 B.C., the Seleucids were in power and a Jewish puppet king, John Hyrcanus, sat on the throne of Judah with the support of his master, Antiochus Sidetes, the reigning Seleucid king.

Hyrcanus was an able ruler and his Judean armies, with the help of their Seleucid allies, conquered the surrounding regions of Samaria, Galilee and Idumea. Idumea was a small region to the south of Judah on the border of Egypt. The Idumeans, much like the original Hebrews, were a mixture of northern Egyptians and nomadic desert herdsmen. They probably worshipped the Egyptian goddess Hathor and the Arabian moon goddess Sin, both patron deities of the Sinai Peninsula. After he overcame them, Hyrcanus forced them to abandon their goddesses and accept Judaism, which most of them reluctantly did. The Judeans, who by then had become quite xenophobic and rabidly nationalistic, never regarded the Idumeans as "real" Jews. Most Judeans thought they were indifferent in their practice and looked down upon Idumean men and women as ethnically foreign.

John Hyrcanus died in 104 B.C. His younger son, Alexander Jannaeus, succeeded him and appointed his own son, John Hyrcanus II, as high priest. After the death of his father, John Hyrcanus II led a revolt to make himself king. He had as a friend and ally a man named Antipater the Idumean, a former governor of Idumea who was Jewish by adopted religion but Idumean by ethnicity.

While this Judean civil war was going on, the shadow of Rome fell across the land. The Roman general Pompey invaded the area and took Jerusalem after a three-month siege. He strolled into the Holy of Holies just to see what was in there but did not damage it. He decided to put Antipater the Idumean, not the upstart John Hyrcanus II, on the throne of Judah as his puppet king. Then, a few years later, the forces of another upstart, Julius Caesar, killed Pompey. Antipater was careful to make friends with Caesar and so stayed on the throne.

However, in 44 B.C., a group of senators, including Caesar's trusted friend Marcus Junius Brutus, stabbed Caesar to death as he entered the Senate and Rome was in turmoil again. In the following year, 43 B.C., an agent of some ultra-nationalistic Jewish group poisoned Antipater. Three years after this, while Rome was occupied with its own civil war, the Parthians (the people who at that time ruled Babylonia) invaded Judah and placed a man named Antigonus Mattathias on the throne. They carried John Hyrcanus II to Babylon and cut off his ears so, as a mutilated person, he could never again be high priest. Everything finally settled down in Judah.

But Antipater the Idumean had fathered a son named Herod by an Arab woman, Kypros. So Herod was Arabian by blood and ethnicity but Jewish by religion. Under cover of darkness the young Herod escaped from Jerusalem and an almost certain assassination. He managed to get to Rome and persuaded the current ruler, Mark Antony, to support him in a takeover of the Judean kingship.

Hedging his bets as always, he walked the white stone paths of Rome's Forum between Mark Antony and Antony's rival for the Roman throne, Octavian, arm in arm with both of them. To show his solidarity with Rome, he took his two new best friends to the Temple of Jupiter, the holiest site in Rome, and offered sacrifice to the Roman gods. Herod then returned to Judah and, with the help of his Roman cohorts, had no trouble throwing the Parthians out, executing Antigonus Mattathias and declaring himself king by fiat (Plate 7) in 37 B.C.[1]

The Judean people distrusted Herod as a pseudo-Jew and a foreigner but he now had the full support of Rome to back him up and there was nothing they could do about it. To cement his kingship, he divorced his Idumean wife Doris and married a Jewish noblewoman named Mariamne. He would eventually marry ten women, one after the other. Paranoid to the point of psychosis, over the next several years he had almost everyone associated with him, including Mariamne (whom he had drowned in her bath) and most of his sons, executed or murdered. The Roman Emperor Augustus (Herod's old Forum buddy, the former Octavian), who was familiar with Jewish dietary laws, laughingly said it was "safer to be Herod's pig than his son!"

Herod spent enormous sums of public money on a project he hoped would endear himself to the Jewish people. He restored and enlarged the dilapidated 500-year old temple of Zerubbabel and lavishly embellished it at tremendous expense (Plate 6). He knew that the office of High Priest was a favorite bone of contention within the Sanhedrin (the rabbinical court, made up of the Jewish priestly caste) and that it would generate a lot of time-wasting squabbling. To forestall this he had 46 members of the Sanhedrin executed. Then, as Henry II of England would do centuries later with Thomas à Becket, Herod appointed his own High Priest, a man loyal to him.

He also, as this degree's story relates, placed a gigantic Roman eagle over the temple's gate to show his Italian bosses where his loyalties lay. A group of nationalistic rabbinical students either tore the eagle down and smashed it or else publicly threatened to do so. Herod was not amused. He rounded the students up, dragged them in chains to his palace in Jericho and, to show everyone how he took care of dissenters, had them burned alive. Herod may have lacked people skills but he knew how to make a point.

While all this political unrest was going on, two new sects in Judaism had emerged and become influential in the lives of Judeans. One sect was quite sympathetic to the Hellenism (Greek culture) that had prevailed in the Middle East following the conquests of Alexander the Great. They called themselves the *Zadokim* ("Followers of Zadok," the High Priest at the time of Solomon). In English this name has become "Sadducees." They were mainly intellectuals drawn from the educated urban upper classes; they spoke Greek and were familiar with Greek philosophy and customs. The Sadducees followed only the written letter of the Jewish law and rejected all folkloric belief in angels, spirits and demons. They did not believe in an afterlife or in the general resurrection of the dead. As a group, they were wealthy and politically powerful. As individuals, they were probably stuck-up, condescending and unpleasant to the common citizens. They were all Roman collaborators.

The other sect called themselves *Hasidim* ("pious ones"). They were mostly from the rural, poorer classes. The Hasidim had split into two sub-groups: the *Essenes* ("Healers") and the *Perishaiya* ("Those who keep themselves apart"). In English the word Perishaiya has become "Pharisees."

The Essenes, the smaller of the sub-groups, were ascetics who lived in monastic communities on the northwestern shores of the Dead Sea. They were a secretive sect and not much is known about them. Their doctrines seemed to have been apocalyptic; that is, they thought that the end of the world was right around the corner. Researchers believe they are the people who recorded and hid the Dead Sea scrolls, including the forty or so Lost Gospels.

The Pharisees lived throughout the land among the people and were less strict in their observance of *Halakha*, Jewish law and tradition, than the Sadducees. They practiced a milder, traditional religious system that can best be summarized by the teachings of Hillel, a contemporary of the young Jesus who also made his living as a carpenter. One day, while Hillel was building a house, a heckler approached with a crowd and shouted: "Rabbi, give a summation of the Law that a man can recite in the time he can stand on one foot." Hillel replied "What is hateful to you, do not do to your fellow man. This is the whole of the Law; the rest is commentary. Go and learn the commentary." He then chased the heckler away with a carpenter's yardstick. Today we call this teaching "The Golden Rule." It became very popular among the people and was quoted by many rabbinical teachers, including Jesus.[2]

The story line in this degree is not taken directly from the Bible but is a well-researched piece of fiction detailing some of the problems the puppet king Herod the Great faced. He had to practice a political balancing act to placate both his Roman masters and the many fanatical sects of religious zealots and rabid nationalists that were abroad in the land. These political activists and hotheads recklessly taunted the overwhelming military might of Rome. They were constantly fomenting and encouraging rebellion among the citizens of Judah.

Herod, who had lived in Rome and hobnobbed with Roman leaders, knew first-hand of Rome's power and the temperament of its Senate. The constant show of dissent in Jerusalem eventually resulted, as Herod feared it would, in a disastrous war. In A.D. 70 Roman legions under Flavius Titus, son of the emperor Vespasian, sacked Jerusalem and destroyed Herod's magnificent temple. The rest of Palestine was largely untouched by the Romans and peace returned to the land.

Fig. 19 Roman eagle, symbol of Rome's imperial might. The initials SPQR stand for Senatus PopulusQue Romanus ("The Senate and People of Rome"). ©iStock.

Then, in A.D. 132, the Jew-hating Roman emperor Hadrian (who, two years earlier, had for a time made the practice of circumcision illegal) decided to rebuild Herod's temple, but announced that it would be a temple to the Roman god Jupiter (and, by association, to himself). The Jews, of course, rose up in rebellion. The rebels were led by a man named Simon ben Kosiba, whose early military successes caused the people to proclaim him the Messiah. As Messiah, he took the name of Bar Kokhba (Son of the Star). For a while he had the upper hand, and may have actually wiped out an entire Roman legion. But Rome soon prevailed and, in A.D. 135, Bar Kokhba and thousands of his followers were slaughtered at the Battle of Bethar. Hadrian and the senate had had enough. They decided to solve their "Jewish problem" once and for all. The Roman army ravaged the whole countryside, slaughtered thousands, sold more thousands into slavery, and dispersed the Jewish people into their two-millennial Diaspora that continued up until the foundation of the State of Israel in 1948.

The political unrest in this degree's story is caused by the Roman imperial emblem, a gigantic bronze eagle, which, as stated above, Herod had placed over the gate of his newly rebuilt temple in Jerusalem.

Most of our beliefs about the Pharisees come from stories in the four Gospels (out of about forty or more) that the emperor Constantine and the early Church Bishops decided to retain in their New Testament canon when they met at the Council of Nicea in A.D. 325. These stories usually portray the Pharisees confronting Jesus with hostile intent. Tradition has assigned authorship of these Gospels to four New Testament characters: Mathew, Mark, Luke and John. In fact, unknown parties wrote them at the end of the first century and the beginning of the second. All the men who actually wrote the Gospels were probably born after Jesus died and had never interacted either with him or his disciples.

Intellectually, the Gospel authors and their congregations in Damascus and Antioch were much more closely wedded to the Greek schools of philosophy than to the Judaism of Jesus and his disciples; they had more of Athens than of Jerusalem in their theology. A great deal of Church spirituality, for instance, derives from the Platonic schools' mystical philosophy of worshipping beauty for beauty's sake. In addition, the Church Fathers were heavily influenced by Aristotle's *Nicomachean Ethics* which Thomas Aquinas would later say contained everything necessary for living the good life.

So the political environment and philosophical underpinnings of the Gospel authors and the early Christian Church became somewhat different from that of Jesus and his Apostles. For instance, during his ministry Jesus had preached extensively about a mystical concept that he called "The Kingdom of Heaven." He invoked simile after simile to illustrate this concept to his listeners ("The Kingdom of Heaven is like a mustard seed; ...like a buried treasure; ... like a dragnet; ...like yeast, etc." [Mathew 13: 31-47]). This seems to have been an apocalyptic vision based on Jesus' prophetic analysis of certain sections of Old Testament wisdom.

Apparently, Jesus envisioned some sort of imminent cataclysmic event involving the appearance of an entity called The Son of Man, a violent Messianic figure from the Book of Ezekiel (whom he soon identified with himself) that would usher in the arrival of a utopian society. The old Jewish law of *halacha*, with its emphasis on Temple worship, would be replaced by a new law of universal love in which the heart of every person (who survived the butchery of the Son of Man) would be that person's own spiritual temple.

Jesus also came to regard himself as the long-expected Messiah, a sort of suffering superman of the line of David who would restore the Jewish nation to Solomonic glory and rid the land of the Roman occupation. He openly declares this when speaking to the much-married Samaritan woman at Jacob's Well on Mt. Gerizim:

> The woman said to him: "I know there is a Messiah coming...When he comes, he will tell us everything. Jesus replied, "I who speak to you am he."
>
> John 4:26

In fact, the Samaritans did not expect a conquering king descended from David; they were looking forward to a religious prophet similar to Moses.

It undoubtedly required meditation and other spiritual exercises for the average listener to be able to comprehend these doctrines. The neophyte would have to arrive at a sufficient stage of enlightenment to perceive Jesus' vision both of the Ground of Being and the advent of the all-conquering Son of Man that he was trying to communicate. The Gospel of Thomas probably comes closest to an exposition of this doctrine that might have been comprehensible to the average person. Both the Church and Constantine, however, found the doctrine of the Kingdom of Heaven distasteful and rejected Thomas' gospel from the canon. Both Catholic and Protestant denominations now ignore this, the fundamental teaching of Jesus, altogether.

All of the 40 or so Gospels, including the four currently accepted ones, were written at a time when Christian communities in Greek-influenced Mediterranean centers were downplaying their Judaic origins. They were trying to present a more ecumenical, welcoming attitude toward Gentiles. In particular the Gospel of John, which may have been written by a Greek Gentile, exhibits a decidedly anti-Semitic twist. This Gospel portrays Jesus as someone removed from his own countrymen and co-religionists. In several cases the Gospel's author sneeringly refers to them as "the Jews," as if Jesus and his disciples were something different. The reasons for this attitude may have been that the new cult of Christianity had come under attack by leaders of the Jewish communities scattered around the Mediterranean region.

Following the Roman destruction of the Temple in A.D. 70 and the dispersal of the Jewish population of Palestine in 135, the Pharisees of Jesus' time were becoming the rabbis of the Diaspora. They led the efforts to ostracize Christians, whom they looked upon as apostate Jews, from the Jewish enclaves.

Also, around A.D. 90 - 150, when most of the Gospels were being written, the Jews themselves were becoming unpopular in Rome. The Gospels' authors started to become anxious that Roman authorities not see the new Christian sect as being Jewish in origin. So, in their writings, they went out of their way to portray all rabbinical teachers other than Jesus in a negative light. Consequently, there are numerous Gospel incidents in which gangs of Pharisees "from Jerusalem" try to trap Jesus into making a seditious or blasphemous remark. Jesus, of course, always outwits the villains and they go away, foiled again.

The actual Pharisees of Jesus' time were almost certainly different from their portrayals in these Gospels. They were down-to-earth self-taught intellectuals who loved nothing more than a good argument over scripture or the law. If they ever did engage Jesus in debate it would have been because they respected him as a famous teacher, not because they wanted to see him come to harm. Besides, most of Jesus' recorded teachings were very much in agreement with Pharisaic philosophy anyway. It is very possible that, at some time in his life, Jesus had himself studied with Pharisees. Remember Hillel and his Golden Rule?[3]

The 17th Degree
of the Southern Jurisdiction:

KNIGHT OF THE EAST AND WEST

In the Southern Jurisdiction this degree has the same name but a different plot. It opens with the imprisonment and execution of John the Baptist after he rebukes Herod for his misconduct. Then a candidate who has crossed the desert and has been wandering on the shore of the Dead Sea is brought into a room called the Chamber of Council and is examined. The candidate is then ritually purified and made a Knight of the East and West. Much of the ritual is based on the Book of Revelation. The Book of Seven Seals remains closed because only Christ himself can open it. The plagues loosed by the breaking of the seals and the opening of the book are given Masonic interpretations. The phrase "East and West" refers to the combined wisdom one can garner by studying the Persian Zend-Avesta, the Hindu Vedas, the philosophies of Plato and Pythagoras, and the mystery religions of Phoenicia, Syria, Greece and Egypt as well as the Jewish scriptures.

The lessons are that :
1) God is one, immutable, infinitely just and good
2) light will finally overcome darkness
3) good will overcome evil and
4) truth will conquer error.[4]

18th Degree:

KNIGHT OF THE ROSE CROIX
OF H. R. D. M.
(From the old Law of Moses to the New Law of Jesus)

The Stage Drama

This is the ceremonial degree of the Chapter of Rose Croix, one in the Northern Masonic Jurisdiction of the Scottish Rite in which an exemplar is led through the ritual and takes an obligation at the altar. The ritual has a somewhat diffuse plot and does not reference any historical event but is a straightforward initiation ceremony. Therefore, I cannot describe the ritual in detail and will give only the general outline that has already appeared in print in other Scottish Rite books.

The setting for the Rose Croix degree consists of three "chambers": the Chamber of Darkness, the Chamber of the Mystic Rose and the Chamber of Light. Pike's candidate from the Southern Jurisdiction's 17th degree (see the previous degree, Southern Jurisdiction), who had wandered in the desert and along the shores of the Dead Sea, is introduced and examined. The candidate is taken from the first chamber (the Old Testament) through the second chamber (the "Mystic Rose'" – the Crucifixion of Christ) and ends up in the third (the Resurrection and beginning of the New Testament), where he is knighted as a Knight of the Rose Croix of Heredom. (The word "Heredom" means something like "holy house" or temple. It is also the name of an imaginary sacred mountain in Scotland.)

This degree symbolizes the transition in the Scottish Rite degree system from the Old to the New Testament. It tells of a new law of love coming from the Roman province of Judea, of a Kingdom that lives in the hearts of men and of a great Sacrifice made so that men could be free.

The lessons taught in this degree are that man must have a new temple in his heart where God is worshipped in spirit and in truth, and that he must have a new law of love which all men everywhere may understand and practice. This degree affirms the broad principles of universality and toleration.

Historical Background

This is the most beautiful, the most spiritual and, in some respects, the most problematic degree the Scottish Rite has to confer. As the pivotal degree of the entire Rite, turning attention from the Old to the New Testament, it deserves the most detailed examination of any degree in the repertory. Several observations are inescapable and have to be addressed.

Fig. 20 The Mystic Rose and the cross, representing Jesus' new law of love. This version is the coat of arms of Martin Luther and is the original icon, adopted by Johann Valentin Andrae (1586-1654), a Lutheran minister who may have authored the first three books of Rosicrucianism. See the 28th Degree, KNIGHT OF THE SUN. ©iStock.

First, the degree is unequivocally Christian in content and meaning. The ritual states with no uncertainty that the Old Testament religion (Judaism) is no longer acceptable (the implication is that it doesn't work anymore) because we now have a "new law". This new law is clearly presented as the teachings of Jesus of Nazareth; in other words, Christianity. The ritual also states that this new law is superior to the older Jewish law and deserving of supplanting it. Apparently this was so from the degree's first appearance, around 1783. Next, the Rose Croix ceremony is said to be the "spiritual heart" of the Scottish Rite. So the Scottish Rite, at some period in its history, saw itself as a Christian organization. Finally, we have to conclude that, at some point, non-Christian Masons were not fully welcome into the Scottish Rite. Or, at least, they were tacitly discouraged from advancing beyond the 17th degree. As we shall see, this may have been true in the past but is no longer the case, at least not in America.

The degree originated in pre-revolutionary 18th-century France. France then was a Roman Catholic country under an absolute monarchy. High-ranking churchmen, anxious to maintain favorable relations with Rome, advised the king. In this light, the ritual may be seen as an 18th-century political stratagem. However, some exclusionist features have surfaced and remained prominent at times during the 200 years that the degree has been under its American jurisdiction. This situation reached a peak in 1870 when a new ritual appeared. It contained such explicitly Christian dogmatic themes that it surly would have offended practicing non-Christians beyond endurance. The Ritual Committee deleted the offending passages and they have been gone from the Rite for the past 65 years.

In their book, *Uriel's Machine*, Christopher Knight and Robert Lomas, two English Freemasons writing in 2001, have this to say about the British version of the Rose Croix degree:

> "…the [degree of] Princes Rose Croix of Heredom… is now open only to Christian Freemasons [in the U.K.]. … in the 1996 edition of the ritual the opening notes show that the present rulers of the degree are extremely concerned to make sure that all the ceremonies are perceived as Christian and have changed the ritual to make sure this impression is maintained."[1]

They then go on to say that every candidate for the degree is now required to profess a belief in the "Holy and Undivided Trinity" before he can be invested.

It is to the everlasting credit of both Northern and Southern Scottish Rite jurisdictions in the United States that they have repudiated this path of small-minded bigotry and opened their higher degrees to all men. In this matter, the British could take a lesson from their former colonists. They gave America Freemasonry; we have shown them what Freemasonry is all about. Now we can truly say: "The Ancient Accepted Scottish Rite in the Northern Masonic Jurisdiction is an inclusive fellowship composed of Christians, whether Protestant or Catholic, Jews, Moslems, Parsees and other monotheists. A candidate for membership may take his obligation upon that Book which is to him the Volume of the Sacred Law."

One item that the degree mentions in passing is the worship of the god Moloch by the Hebrews. The worship of this loathsome deity is so repulsive that we should examine its history among the Hebrews more closely.

Moloch was originally the god of the Ammonites, a people traditionally said to be descended from Abraham's nephew Lot by incestuous relations with his younger daughter, after his wife had been turned in a pillar of sodium chloride as a punishment for looking back over her shoulder at the destruction of Sodom and Gomorrah.[2] Their territory was east of the Jordan River and north of the Dead Sea. An Ammonite woman was the mother of Solomon's stupid and undiplomatic son Rehoboam.[3] Solomon himself, perhaps to please Rehoboam's mother, introduced the worship of Moloch into Israel by erecting his idols on the Mount of Olives, outside of Jerusalem.[4] Whether or not the Hebrews practiced human sacrifice in Solomon's time is uncertain. But it was certainly practiced around Jerusalem at various times over the next three centuries.

The Valley of Gehenna (Hinnom, in Hebrew) is a long, shallow valley outside Jerusalem that ran along the entire south wall of the city. A section of the valley known as Tophet ("fire stove") came to be dedicated to the worship of Moloch. He was represented as a winged man with the horned head of a bull. His hands were spread and tilted upward to receive the little bodies of his victims and his mouth gaped open to swallow them. His bronze body was hollow and a hot fire burned in his belly. Parents who wanted the god to do them a favor rolled their little children into his mouth where they dropped down into the fire and were burned alive. Sometimes priests mercifully slit the children's throats before dropping them into the idol's mouth.

During the Yahwist reforms of King Josiah (620 B.C.) the king's forces obliterated all traces of this horrible practice and cleansed the valley of its evil heritage.[5] Later writers (perhaps the same ones who wrote the Book of Deuteronomy) claimed that it was King Manasseh, Josiah's anti-Yahwist predecessor, who had started the practice of infanticide in Gehenna and even said that he had sacrificed his own son to Moloch.[6]

At this remove in time it is hard to tell truth from propaganda. Josiah's writers were probably eager to vilify Manasseh's memory for political reasons. Although his statesmanship had secured peace and prosperity for Israel during his entire 55-year reign, he had persecuted the Yahwists and members of their prophetic party and probably had done much to further the worship of other gods, including foreign gods like Moloch and Chemosh. Whatever the case, the valley alongside of Jerusalem was a place of genuine horror and the names *Gehenna* and *Tophet* have become synonyms for Hell.

The 18th Degree
of the Southern Jurisdiction:

KNIGHT ROSE CROIX

The 18th degree in the Southern Jurisdiction is similar to the northern version. The candidate is led through three apartments. The first is the same as the one in the above ritual, a place of dimness and despair. Unlike the northern ritual, the second apartment represents Hell and the torments of the damned and the consequences of sin, as in the older rituals. The cross and the Mystic Rose (Plate 13) symbolize immortality won by suffering and sorrow. The third apartment is a place of brilliant light, symbolizing freedom from the principle of evil. Instruction on the interpretation of evil by various philosophies is given and the New Law of Love is explained. God is seen as more of a loving father than as a punishing tyrant. The degree teaches that we should have faith in God, mankind and ourselves. We should hope in victory over evil and practice charity by relieving the wants and tolerating the errors of others.[7]

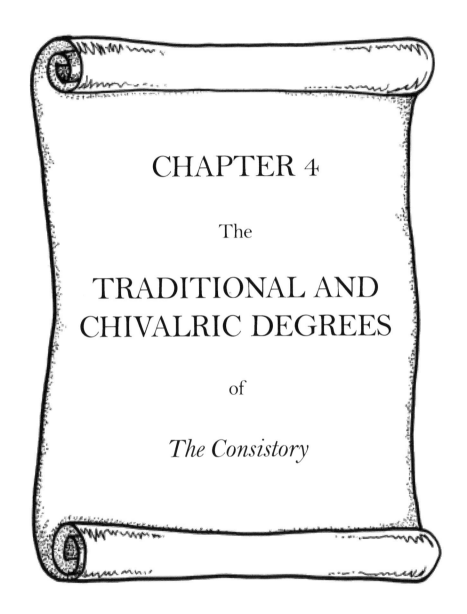

CHAPTER 4

The

TRADITIONAL AND CHIVALRIC DEGREES

of

The Consistory

19th Degree:

BROTHERS OF THE TRAIL
(The Oregon Trail degree)

The Stage Drama

This is the first "Americana" degree of the Scottish Rite in the Northern Masonic Jurisdiction (that is, the first degree based on an episode in American history). The time is 1849 and the place is a camp on the Oregon Trail by a rock formation called Register Cliff, not far from Fort Laramie in Wyoming. Two newly-met Masons, Aaron and Jake, have been travelling along the Oregon Trail to California. At Fort Laramie, Jake contracts cholera (the principal villain of the drama) and his brother Mason, Aaron, tries to nurse him back to health. The only character seen on stage during the play is Aaron; Jake remains an unseen presence in a tent. Jake dies and Aaron buries him and covers his grave with rocks. Throughout the play Aaron carries on a one-sided conversation with another unseen character named Henry (aka "Duke"), who seems to located somewhere out in the audience.

This degree expresses the Core Values of reverence to God and integrity. It's up to the viewer to decide how these values are important both in the drama and in his daily life. Another lesson might well be that we should seek more imaginative authors with better writing skills for our degrees (see my comments on the 31st degree in Appendix B, History and Development of the Degrees).

Historical Background

The 2,000-mile long wagon route known as the Oregon Trail began at Independence, Missouri and stretched, at its completion, to the Willamette Valley near Mt. Hood in Oregon. The trail crossed Kansas, Nebraska, Wyoming, Idaho and Oregon, where a branch led south to California. For this reason the route is sometimes called the Oregon-California Trail.

The trail started as a foot-path for fur trappers and mountain men around 1811, not long after Lewis and Clarke completed their famous survey of the lands gained from the Louisiana Purchase in 1803. Originally, before 1840, only men on foot or on horseback leading mule trains could use the trail. By around 1844 a passable wagon route had been cleared all the way to Oregon. Every passing year new roads, newly-cleared mountain passes, bridges and more stop-off points at the growing towns springing up along the way made the trip easier, faster and safer.

These improvements to the trail strengthened a new philosophy that had sprung up in America following the Louisiana Purchase. Politicians called the philosophy Manifest Destiny. Its premise was simple: It was undeniably apparent (*manifest*) that it was America's *destiny* to take possession of and settle all the land between the Atlantic and Pacific coasts. The fact that other people already lived there was not an obstacle because Manifest Destiny only applied to white Americans and the "other people" were neither white nor were they, at that time, considered to be Americans.

An 1872 painting titled *American Progress* (Plate 14) by John Gast shows the 50-foot tall goddess Columbia, wearing a toga to symbolize democratic Roman republicanism, striding across the western plains bringing settlers, soldiers, schoolbooks and modern 19th century transportation with her. If that's not enough, the energetic goddess is stringing out a telegraph line as she goes. Indians and wild animals cringe and run away to hide from the divine onslaught. The goddess, a fair-skinned blonde, has her eyes firmly fixed on the distant gold fields of California and doesn't even deign to look down at the red-skinned Indians and bison scurrying away from her feet as she leads hordes of white emigrants across their hunting grounds. The right side of the paining, representing the enlightened east coast, is brightly lit and she brings this eastern light along with her to illuminate the dark western plains ahead of her on the left.[1]

A typical wagon-train journey took about five or six months, depending on conditions. Travelers liked to begin the trek westward in early April for several reasons. The muddy trails would be drier and more passable. They could count on an abundance of fresh grass for the oxen and horses to graze upon throughout the spring and summer months. They stood a better chance of getting through the dangerous Rocky Mountain passes before the heavy snows began to fall in late October. There would also be better conditions for the men to hunt deer and buffalo to supplement the wagon train's usual take-along rations of bacon and hardtack bread.

Of the possibly 30,000 people who died traveling the Oregon trail, 90 per cent died of infectious diseases, principally cholera. Today, it is difficult for us to imagine the paralyzing panic that the very hint of cholera caused in these 19th-century pioneers. First appearing in the heavily polluted waters of Calcutta between 1800 and 1810, Asiatic cholera rapidly spread from Asia to Europe and then across the Atlantic to the Americas. Characterized by excessive diarrhea and vomiting, the disease has been responsible for eight major worldwide epidemics in which hundreds of thousands of people have died. It is caused by *Vibrio cholerae*, a rod-shaped bacterium that moves around using a long whip-like appendage called a *flagellum*. This creature lives in the intestines of humans and pigs. It can remain alive for days in fecal-contaminated water and in the bodies of filter-feeding shellfish (oysters, clams and mussels).

The Italian anatomist Filippo Pacini first isolated *V. cholerae* in Italy in 1855 during a cholera epidemic in Florence. But his paper was not widely distributed internationally and few other scientists read it. The medical community remained wedded to the theory that infectious diseases where caused by noxious vapors (*malaria* or "bad air") in the atmosphere. When a major cholera epidemic struck London in 1854, a local physician named John Snow noticed that families in certain sections of the city were heavily infected while families in other sections were almost untouched.[2] He investigated all significant differences he could uncover between the two groups and found only one: The infected families all drew their drinking water from the Broad Street water pumping station, located downstream from the pipes that emptied the city's untreated sewage into the Thames River. The healthy families received their water from another pumping station situated upstream from the sewage pipes. Snow's work convinced the public that sewage-contaminated water carried the disease.[3]

In 1861 the French scientist and pioneer microbiologist Louis Pasteur published his theory that tiny organisms (for which he may have popularized the word "germs" around 1871) caused disease. Then in 1885 the German pathologist Robert Koch read Pacini's paper, repeated his work and again identified *V. cholerae* as the contaminating agent in drinking water responsible for cholera. This time the scientific community listened.

In 1893 the great Russian composer Peter Tchaikovsky drank a glass of unboiled tap water during a cholera outbreak in Moscow. A careless waiter may have accidentally served the water to him during dinner at Leiner's, his favorite restaurant.[4] Or, as some think, unable to come to grips with his latent homosexuality he may have deliberately drank the contaminated water in his apartment to commit suicide.[5] He died two days later. Thanks to the work of Pacini, Snow, Pasteur and Koch, improved public health measures and sanitary engineering methods had eliminated the threat of cholera in most major cities in the western world by 1900.

American pioneers in the 1840s were not so fortunate. The travelers on the Oregon Trail knew only three things about cholera. It came out of nowhere, it could not be stopped and the only known way to avoid it was to run away. Far away. One such runner on the Oregon Trail was a Dr. MacBeth who fled west to escape a cholera epidemic on the east coast.

A pathetic photograph, titled "Dr. MacBeth in Costume He Wore Crossing the Plains to Flee Cholera," shows the terrified doctor posing with guns, a sword, hatchets, knives and billy clubs thrust into his belt, all in case of attack by hostile Indians.

Unfortunately the good doctor never got the chance to show his mettle in battle because, shortly after he arrived in California, he contracted cholera and died.

Although Dr. Mac-Beth never ran up against hostile Indians, other travelers on the Oregon Trail did. The plains Indians were at first friendly to the white settlers on the trail but that did not last. The westward-moving migrants on the Trail were

Fig. 21. The Harney Massacre of 1855 at Blue Water Creek. ©iStock.

driven to exhaustion by each day's journey and their patience with dark-skinned strangers who looked, dressed and spoke differently than they did quickly ran out. As a group, the wagon train trekkers had little formal education and no sensitivity training. They feared and distrusted the "savages" and only accepted their help out of desperation. The Indians, in turn, grew wary as more and more wagon trains, seemingly without end, passed through their territory. The white settlers were coming in enormous numbers, and they showed little regard for the rights of the red man. The Indians quickly realized that this westward migration was not just one summer's passing fancy; the white people were here to stay and the places they intended to stay were all on Indian land.

By 1850 relations between the races were rapidly deteriorating. Indians saw that the federal government was busily erecting fortified towns along the wagon route and manning the forts with soldiers. This could only mean that the government was planning to subject the tribes to armed coercion. The Army would drive the Indians from their traditional grass-covered hunting grounds onto reservations located on arid, desolate areas the white man had no use for. The Sioux, Cheyenne, Pawnee, Arapaho and Apache nations held intertribal councils but could see no answer to the situation.

In August of 1854 trouble erupted in Wyoming near Fort Laramie. About 4,000 Lakota Sioux were, by treaty, legally camped not far from the fort. Some Mormons had been traveling down the nearby Mormon Trail, a parallel route that crossed the Oregon Trail near Ft. Laramie. One of the Mormons' cows got loose and ran away. It wound up in the Sioux camp and a Lakota named High Forehead shot the cow. Hungry Indians quickly butchered and ate the animal. The cow's owner went to the fort and complained to the

Commanding Officer, a Lt. Fleming. Fleming, instead of following the terms of the treaty and waiting for the Fort's assigned Indian agent who would arrive in a few days, himself called in the Sioux chief, Conquering Bear. The Chief offered to let the Mormon take his pick of a horse from the Chief's personal herd of 60 animals but the white man insisted on a payment of $25 (about $720 in today's money), an impossible sum for the impoverished Indians to come up with.

When negotiations broke down, Fleming dispatched a recent West Point graduate, Second Lieutenant John Lawrence Grattan, with a detachment of 27 privates, two NCOs (Non-Commissioned Officers, a corporal and a sergeant) and a drunken French-American civilian. They took the civilian with them to act as an interpreter despite his known inability to speak much Lakota or any other Sioux dialect.

Fig. 22 Plains Indians having an inter-tribal council to discuss the problem of white settler incursions on their land. ©iStock.

When the party reached the camp, the "interpreter" staggered around aimlessly among the gathered Indians, waving an empty whiskey bottle in their faces. He insulted them in his childish Lakota vocabulary and jeered that the soldiers had come with only one purpose in mind: to kill them all.

Actually, he wasn't far from the truth. The troops' commanding officer, 2nd Lt. Grattan, despised Indians. He was eager to engage them in combat on one pretext or another just to have the opportunity of killing some of them. The two veteran NCOs nervously noted that the inexperienced officer, with no reinforcements, had led his detachment of 29 men deep into a camp of over a thousand armed warriors. Grattan also didn't notice that Indians were moving to surround his command and cut off his retreat. He loudly and insultingly demanded that the Sioux leaders deliver High Forehead, the cow killer, into U.S. custody. The leaders refused and Grattan became infuriated.

Chief Conquering Bear tried to ameliorate the situation by negotiating between the parties but Grattan spurned his efforts. By then Grattan had finally noticed that his tactical situation was deteriorating and that the Indians were taking up flanking positions around his command. As Grattan hastily retreated to mount his horse, Conquering Bear stood up to say something and a soldier shot him in the back, killing him. Another soldier fired randomly into the crowd. A Brule Sioux leader named Spotted Tail quickly took command and rallied the Indians. Following his lead, the Sioux returned fire and, within minutes, wiped out Grattan and his entire command, including the now terrified "interpreter."

The incident, which the press should have called "Grattan's Folly" was instead called "Grattan's Massacre."[6] Newspaper reporters back east used it to stir up revulsion against the "savages." As a result, traffic on the Oregon Trail began to fall off as people in the east worried about their safety on the westward trek. Land developers on the west coast complained to Washington that the Indians were holding up Manifest Destiny and something had to be done about it.

This led to a vendetta one year later in the form of a 600-man U.S. Army "Sioux Expedition" under the command of Brigadier General William Harney. The U.S. War Department dispatched the expedition in response to President Franklin Pierce's vow to avenge Grattan's death and secure safe passage for emigrants on the Trail.

The War Department choose Harney to lead the expedition because his superior officers knew that he had no scruples, would not hesitate to kill women and children and was heavily in debt. In other words, not a man likely to question orders. The government supplied his party with an arsenal of the latest weapons. These included Springfield rifles, deadly new six-shot .44 caliber Colt Dragoon revolvers and two wagon-mounted field howitzers. With the barrel elevated 5 degrees, the 1850 model Army howitzer could lob a 24-pound explosive shell up to 1,270 yards. It was accurate, quickly

Fig. 23. Covered wagons at Register Cliff, where travellers on the Oregon Trail frequently wrote their family names on the rock.
©iStock.

reloadable and rarely fouled or misfired. A trained artilleryman could estimate the range and trim the shell's fuses to explode on impact, scattering deadly shrapnel for dozens of yards in every direction.

The War Department's instructions to Harney were terse but broad; they told him to "go out and find some Indians and whip 'em." He complied, on September 3, 1855, by perpetrating what Indian Wars historians now call the Battle of Blue Water Creek although its alternate name – the Harney Massacre – is more appropriate.

Harney and his troops came across a band of Sioux families camped on the Platte River in present-day Garden County, Nebraska. Harney decided, based on some spotty information he had gathered, that these were the Indians responsible for the Grattan Massacre. After a night of preparation, he entered the village the next morning in a deceptively peaceful manner with 300 dismounted cavalry soldiers posing in the less-threatening role of infantrymen. He then treacherously engaged the village chief, Little Thunder, in sham peace talks, saying that he was only after the Indians who had fired on Grattan and his men. The chief admitted that some of the Grattan shooters were in camp but refused to identify them because he felt that, acting in self-defense, they had been justified. Meanwhile, Harney had dispatched 300 mounted soldiers the previous evening in an all-night flanking maneuver to surround the village. He ordered them to conceal themselves in the forest and await the signal to attack.

Then his careful plans fell apart. Several Sioux braves broke into Harney's pretended parley with the chief. They had stumbled across the hidden troopers in the forest. Harney took action. On his orders his "infantry" detachment opened fire on Little Thunder and his council with their newly issued state-of-the-art weapons: .58 caliber Springfield Model 1855 rifles. The grooved-bore Springfields had an effective range of 600 yards and their hollow-based Minié bullets retained sufficient muzzle velocity to splinter through four inches of pine boards 1000 yards away. If all that weren't enough, the soldiers' .44 caliber Colt Dragon revolvers could fracture a man's thigh bone at 25 yards. Most of the Indians had old smooth-bore muskets with a low muzzle velocity and a range of only 120 yards.

The infantry's concentrated rifle fire forced the entire village to turn and run into the waiting sabers of the concealed cavalry, who butchered them without mercy. Altogether they massacred 86 Brule and Oglala Sioux men, women and children. Seventy women and children were taken captive and the village was burned. Harney achieved his mission's goal: The Sioux signed a non-aggression treaty that guaranteed the safety of the Oregon Trail for decades to come.[7]

Shortly after the massacre, a lone young Oglala Lakota Sioux warrior named Curly Hair happened to be riding by and discovered the burned village. He described seeing many bodies of women and children, all of them mutilated and desecrated. He covered the bodies as best he could and then rescued a woman survivor whose husband and baby had been murdered and brought her back to his village. He became famous among the Sioux for this deed. Nine years later, in a battle during the Lakota-Crow War of 1858-1865, he again distinguished himself by leading a charge into a heavily defended Crow encampment and taking several scalps. In recognition of this and other deeds he was given the honorific name of "His Horse is Spirited" or, as he became known to the American public, "Crazy Horse." He entered American history when he led a war party against Custer at The Battle of the Little Big Horn in 1876.[8]

If cholera and hostile Indians weren't enough, yet another hazard on the trip west was starvation. Drifting snow could block the passes of the Sierra Nevada Mountains in a day or less. A delay of only a few weeks in setting out could trap a wagon party in the snow-filled passes with no hope of rescue until spring.

In May of 1846, a 20-wagon party of around 70 men, women and children led by George Donner and James Reed set out from Independence on the Oregon Trail. When they reached Fort Bridger in Wyoming, they fell in with a promoter named Lansford Hastings. Hastings had a financial interest in getting settlers to California as quickly as possible. He had his own inaccurate map that showed a detour he called "Hastings' Cutoff" which he claimed would shorten the journey by 300 miles. This would necessitate crossing the Wasatch Mountains, the Salt Desert and the Sierra Nevada Mountains before the winter snows fell. His map showed the desert stretch of the journey to be only 40 miles wide when, in fact, it was twice that distance with no drinkable water within a two-day journey.

Donner and Reed, their party already running behind most of the earlier wagon trains and knowing that it was now dangerously late in the season, decided to accept Hastings' advice. They were desperate to rejoin the Oregon Trail at Fort Hall and get to California before late autumn. They left Fort Bridger on July 31st and ran into trouble immediately. A supposed four-day stretch had taken a week to cross and when Reed rode ahead and finally caught up with Hastings who was with another group, Hastings refused to return and join them. Instead he gave Reed a crude, hastily drawn map showing another shortcut across the two mountain ranges.

The passage through the Wasatch Mountains proved difficult and took far more time than the party could afford. By the time they reached the Salt Desert on August 27 their desperation mounted as it became obvious that they would never make the passes through the Sierra Nevada range before the snows began. Also, they had been joined by another party of three wagons and 12 people. The spirit of camaraderie quickly evaporated and the party split as those with lighter, faster wagons pulled rapidly ahead and left those with heavier, slower wagons carrying Donner and Reed and their families behind.

The slower wagons abandoned some of their heavier luggage and continued on. They finally reached Fort Hall on September 30 and rejoined the Oregon Trail. They were by now the last wagon train of the season to leave the fort, an honor they had not sought. After leaving the fort the party was attacked by a band of Paiute Indians. Then they had internal dissentions including a fatal knife fight that caused Reed and his wagons to leave the party and travel ahead. They next had to cross 40 miles of desert during which time hostile Indians repeatedly attacked them.

By the time they reached the Sierra Nevada mountains the snow had begun to fall. A lone Paiute Indian shot and killed 19 of the party's oxen before the men in the party killed him. It was now the end of October and, with their path blocked by snowdrifts, the Donner Party turned back and sought shelter in some dilapidated abandoned cabins by a mountain lake. The men threw up some crude lean-tos and cabins and they settled in to try and survive the winter. There was no more food so they killed the few oxen that were left and ate them. Hunting and fishing sorties met with little success. Attempts by some of the men to break out of the 10-foot mountain snowdrifts and bring help all resulted in the expeditions returning to camp in defeat. Starvation threatened the entire camp.

A group of 15 of the strongest men and women left on December 16 in one last-ditch effort to reach the nearest fort and bring back a rescue party. This time they were finally able to get out of the snow-blocked pass. At some point on their journey they picked up two Indians who said they would act as guides. The group hadn't taken along much from the meager rations left to the survivors back at the lake and they soon ran out of food. One of the men was unable to go on and they had to leave him behind to die. The shortage of food was weakening them and threatening the success of their mission. If they died of exposure and starvation then the other families that they had left behind were doomed to the same fate.

Two more members of the party died and at that point an unpleasant solution to the food shortage presented itself. The men and women together made a unanimous agreement to cannibalize the body of the next one to die. This happened to be a man named Patrick Dolan and, in accord with their agreement, they cooked and ate his arms and legs along with parts of the other two men who had died. Another man died that night and they added him to the larder.

After many adventures the group finally reached Sutter's Fort and led a rescue party back through the snowy passes to the people left back at the lake. They found that over 13 people, including George Donner, had died of starvation and that survivors had cannibalized many of the bodies. Thus ended the worst disaster in the history of the Oregon Trail. Altogether 44 people in the Donner Party died and 47 survived.

Despite all the hardships of disease, starvation and Indian attack, a six-month journey by wagon was preferable to reaching California by a sea voyage around Cape Horn at the southern tip of South America. The sea route was more expensive, extremely dangerous, allowed for less luggage and, with sufficiently foul weather, could take longer than a trip along the Oregon Trail. Even more dangerous was the overland journey through the fever-infested jungles of Panama to reach the Pacific Ocean, a route few chose and fewer survived.

When the rail lines linking the Central and Union Pacific Railroads were joined on May 10, 1869, in Promontory Summit, Utah, the way to the west coast was thrown open to any citizen with $69 ($1,500 in today's money) to spend. That meant that the Oregon Trail's days were numbered. A trip by rail took only seven days and cost a fraction of the expense of outfitting a covered wagon. By 1880 the trail had fallen into disuse and was already fading back into the landscape. Today, if you drive along Interstate Highway 80 you will essentially be following the 21st-century remnants of the Oregon Trail.[9]

The 19th Degree
of the Southern Jurisdiction:

GRAND PONTIFF

This degree has the same name as its former counterpart in the NMJ (see the public play that follows) and a similar theme. The chief difference is that the Southern Jurisdiction follows Albert Pike's 1865 ritual in which the candidate is conducted to each of twelve pillars, representing the twelve tribes of Israel. At each pillar he is given a short lecture and witnesses symbolic outpourings of "the vials of wrath." The candidate does not enter the Land of Shades. At the end, the Spirit of Freemasonry triumphs over the Spirit of Evil and the candidate listens to one of Pike's lectures emphasizing his curious notion that "the dead govern, the living only obey." Somewhat odd considering that, in the Southern Jurisdiction version, the candidate doesn't actually get to see or hear any dead people. The lessons are that good shall triumph over evil, the human intellect cannot measure the designs of God and if lived properly, this life is a bridge to eternal life.[10]

INTERLUDE: A PUBLIC PLAY

GRAND PONTIFF
(The original 19th degree in its entirety)

The Stage Drama

This had been the 19th degree of the Northern Masonic Jurisdiction until the NMJ recently replaced it with the Brothers of the Trail degree. It was then declared to be a public play suitable for presentation to general audiences so I can present the entire drama.

In this play a neophyte is attempting to gain admission to a mystical brotherhood that oversees human destiny. He must first undergo his own Underworld Initiation and return with the gift of insight to give to the brotherhood and, by extension, to humanity in general. In doing this, he follows the traditional path of the hero's quest that Joseph Campbell traced in his book, *The Hero with a Thousand Faces*.

The play opens in the Chapter Hall of a mystical brotherhood called the Grand Pontiffs. The Pontiffs are apparently a group of immortal, super-priests of some unspecified eclectic quasi-Christian religion dedicated to the worship of a deity they call the Grand Architect of the Universe. They are organized in the manner of a Blue lodge under the leadership of a Master called the Grand Pontiff and meet in a guarded room on some secret mystical high place suggestive of Mt. Olympus. A newcomer, a candidate for initiation named Philetus, joins them.

Philetus, a philosopher, wishes to become a Pontiff. To see if he has the right stuff, the Grand Pontiff sends him on a Hero's quest. He is to enter the underworld (the Land of Shades) and seek advice from the spirits of famous teachers of the past. Traditionally, in most of the classical myths, the entrance to the Underworld is hard to find and the Hero has to undergo all sorts of tests to prove himself worthy of entrance. But not in this story; there happens to be a handy stairway nearby and down he goes. The lodge's Junior Deacon accompanies him as a psychopomp (a guide who conducts the souls of the dead into the underworld). The brotherhood charges Philetus with learning something about the problem of evil, why God permits bad things to happen to good people and whatever else he can dig up The first shade Philetus meets is Philo, a famous Jewish philosopher from Alexandria. Philo tells him to detach himself from the desires of the flesh. When Philetus asks how he is supposed to accomplish this, Philo unhelpfully disappears. Next, the Greek philosopher Epicurus comes on stage. Epicurus has a philosophy opposite that of Philo; he tells Philetus to eat, drink and be merry, to enjoy life to the hilt and stop worrying about all that self-denial nonsense. Then *he* disappears.

Next is the Egyptian ibis-headed god Thoth, here called Hermes (Thoth was frequently identified with the Greek god Hermes, the god the Romans knew as Mercury). After delivering an enigmatic three-sentence homily *he* disappears. Not much help there. Philetus is starting to feel like Dorothy in the film version of *The Wizard of Oz*, when she remarks to her dog: "My goodness,Toto, people come and go so *quickly* around here!" He's starting to wonder if this Pontiff business is really worth it when John the Christian Evangelist appears. John gives a sermon on love and charity and says that, in order to love God, a man must first learn to love his neighbor. Then he, too, is gone.

The Junior Deacon, who has been waiting off to one side, tries to find out if Philetus has learned anything. But Philetus has had enough of these conflicting enigmatic homilies; he's getting fed up with the whole idea of immortality and says so. Then a brightly-lighted cross appears. The cross flashes on and off three times. Philetus takes this to be a sign that there really is some kind of an afterlife (which, by this time, should have been obvious to him anyway since he's been talking to quite a few dead people).

In the classical myths, before he leaves the Underworld the Hero usually receives or steals a magical object of some kind to bring back to the land of the living as a gift to mankind and as proof that he's really been there. Philetus finds what appears to be a mirror in the shape of a globe that gives distorted reflections; he decides to take this back to the Pontiffs. He and the Junior Deacon climb back up the stairs.

Back in the Pontiffs' Chapter Hall everybody is congratulating Philetus on his successful journey when who should join them but Old Scratch himself (here called The Spirit of Evil), all dressed up in a hellish shade of red. This creature then boasts that it is he who really rules the world and, to prove his point, he delivers a diabolical rebuttal that mocks the Pontiffs' pious lifestyle. As he is on the point of winning the debate, he is challenged by the Spirit of Freemasonry, who suddenly appears as a knight in shining armor (we're not dealing in subtleties here). After a brief exchange of words, the knight kicks the Devil off the stage. He then gives the Pontiffs a short pep talk and disappears.

When the play was a degree it was said to have proclaimed the spiritual unity of all who believe in God and who cherish the hope of immortality, no matter what religious leader they follow or what creed they profess. It is concerned primarily with the perennial conflict between light and darkness, between good and evil, between God and Satan — and with the ultimate triumph of righteousness and peace in the hearts of men and in the councils of mankind.

The allegory dramatizes the lessons of the degree. In a very real sense, Philetus represents each one of us; his aspirations, his search for wisdom and understanding, his frustrations and trials are ours. If we are sincere in our search, and our minds and hearts are open to new insight and love, then the ultimate victory of Philetus also can be ours.

Historical Background

The plot of this play is taken from classical Mediterranean mythology in which the Hero (usually a demigod, the offspring produced when a god or goddess mates with a human being) must make an initiatory journey into the underworld and confront the ghosts of famous people in an attempt to extract information that is vital to his quest. Many classical heroes such as Gilgamesh, Aeneas, Odysseus and Hercules had to visit the Land of Shades in order to gain wisdom and insight before they succeeded in their task. Even Marlow, Joseph Conrad's hero in *Heart of Darkness,* had to retrace Aeneas' steps to confront the evil Kurtz who is hiding in the midst of a jungle empire of his own making. Marlow then gains unexpected insight into his own life from Kurtz's mistress, a black African woman who takes the part of a spirit guide.

The author of The Grand Pontiffs seems to have based this degree on the Theosophical concept of the Great White Brotherhood, an order made up of two classes of immortals who oversee the world and generally keep an eye on things. The first class is made up of what are called Ascended Masters. These are the great teachers and religious leaders of history: Lao-Tzu, Gautama Buddha, Moses, Jesus, Mohammad, Zarathustra, Socrates and so on. The second class consists of lesser-known thinkers and do-gooders who have chosen to remain on Earth as immortals and use their power and wisdom to help out wherever they are needed. These might include, for instance, Mother Teresa, Mohandas Gandhi, St. Francis of Assisi and the *bodhisattvas* of Buddhism.

The bodhisattvas are Buddhist monks and laypeople who have achieved *satori* (enlightenment) but have declined to enter the bliss of Nirvana and have chosen instead to remain incarnate in the cycle of rebirth and help the rest of us work out our salvation. People in Japan, China and Korea regard them in much the same light as Christians look upon saints. According to the *Kalachakra Tantra,* a Tibetan religious text written around A.D. 900, they live in an earthly paradise called Shambhala, thought to be located in a hidden valley somewhere in the Himalayan Mountains.

Fig. 24 Shambhala (or Shangri-La), the Earthly Buddhist paradise hidden away somewhere in the Himalayan mountains. ©iStock.

This doctrine formed James Hilton's concept of Shangri-La, a hidden utopia featured in his classic novel *Lost Horizon*. In Shambhala the bodhisattvas enjoy a kind of quasi-immortality, living utopian lives and looking after world affairs. Some day they will emerge from their mountain fastness in the form of a conquering Buddhist army to overcome the evil forces of the "Abrahamic" religions (Judaism, Christianity and Islam) and convert the world to Buddhism.

A more recent New Age version of the Hidden Gurus myth has the survivors of Atlantis and Lemuria (the Pacific version of Atlantis) living in the hollow interior of

Mount Shasta in northern California. There they keep tabs on things and watch over the destiny of the planet. Occasionally, to catch a breath of fresh California air, they take walks out on the mountainside. Every now and then people claim to have spotted them strolling about dressed in long white robes, presumably sipping cups of latte from Starbucks.

The choice of Philetus to be the newest addition to the Pontiffs is interesting. In a New Testament letter, Paul warns Timothy that Philetus and his friend Hymeneus were teaching heretical, destructive doctrines that were threatening the infant Church with serious injury.

> "This is the case with Hymeneus and Philetus, who have gone far wide
>
> of the truth in saying that the [bodily] resurrection [of the dead] has
>
> already taken place. They are upsetting some people's faith."

(2 Tim 2:17-19)

The Philetus that Paul was referring to taught that all talk of a future resurrection of the physical body was only figurative or metaphorical. He claimed that the only "resurrection" that was rationally possible was the one from ignorance to knowledge. He preached that there would never come a day when the Christian dead would actually hear Jesus of Nazareth call to them and raise them out of their graves, except in a metaphorical or spiritual sense. Philetus and Hymeneus exemplified the ferment of thought and the rich diversity of opinion that characterized the early Christian Church and that would eventually be snuffed out by power-hungry bishops at the Council of Nicea in A.D. 325. One would imagine that thinkers of this caliber would not be dissuaded from their beliefs by merely watching a symbol flash on and off.[1]

20ᵗʰ Degree:

MASTER AD VITAM
(The George Washington/Benedict Arnold degree)

"To the most brilliant soldier of the Continental army... winning for his countrymen the decisive battle of the American Revolution and for himself the rank of Major General."

Dedication on a monument to Benedict Arnold at Saratoga
that does not mention his name.

The Stage Drama

The time is November of 1784, one year after the Treaty of Paris, signed on September 3, 1783, ended the American Revolution and acknowledged American independence from England; the place is a blue lodge in Richmond, Virginia. George Washington (Plate 16) is acting as Worshipful Master of the lodge. The cast of characters consists mostly of famous historical men (Washington, Lafayette, etc.) and portrays an imaginary scenario of their post-war relationships as they might have been influenced by their shared Masonic brotherhood. There is talk of a British officer who was a Mason and who, during the war, had infiltrated American Masonic lodges to spy and pick up military information. Then Benedict Arnold makes an appearance. From this point on the principal activity involves a dialogue between Washington and Arnold, who has secretly returned to America from England and is seeking the forgiveness of his brother Masons for his treacherous behavior during the war. He does not succeed and Washington exiles him from America forever. Arnold is escorted back to his waiting ship and returns to England, a broken man.

This is the second of Northern Jurisdiction's "Americana" degrees. It is a drama of the American spirit, confronting the challenge of disloyalty and treason. Masonic principles and leadership are subjected to a crucial test. The degree demonstrates the Masonic condemnation of all who conspire against the security of their nation and the happiness of their fellow citizens.

Historical Background

On a beautiful spring morning in Philadelphia in 1780, the city's former Military Commandant, Major General Benedict Arnold, sat at his desk, shaking his head in despair and contemplating suicide. His office was in his home, the beautiful Masters-Penn mansion at 6th and Market Streets. This building was so splendid it would later become the presidential mansion for George Washington and then John Adams.

The reason for Arnold's despair was easy to understand: his world, his career and his life were crumbling around him. He had married a beautiful socialite twenty years younger than himself and the marriage had forced him into a lavish lifestyle that he could not afford. His meager salary from the Army had not been paid for two years, the new American currency was steadily plunging into devaluation from rampant inflation and the Continental Congress was in a shambles. He had wasted his wife's dowry in disastrous investments and had tried to redeem his fortune by graft and profiteering, practices which, when discovered by a hostile city council, had resulted in a court martial. His only friend in the military, George Washington, had publically rebuked him with humiliating language. On his present course, he was headed for debtor's prison and ruinous disgrace.

He could see only two ways out of his looming dilemma. One was suicide. The other was an equally terrible choice, one that made the patriotic Arnold sick in his soul but one that he had been contemplating for several months. In March of the previous year he had been forced to resign his post as Commandant. The court martial had isolated him from his few supporters in the Army and his almost total lack of social graces had turned away his even fewer friends in Philadelphia's snobbish social circles. He now had no one to turn to except his wife, Peggy Shippen Arnold, a pro-British Tory who, years before, had been courted by Captain John Andre, a British officer in the then-occupied city. She had a connection with the enemy, one that Arnold could use.

How had his life come to this? He loved his country. He was a brilliant strategist and fearless on the battlefield. He had sacrificed his health, his fortune and at times even his personal pride in his service to the Colonies. His friend Washington, the most respected officer in the Continental Army, had spent a good many of *his* campaigns running away from the British. It was well known that when British generals had pursued Washington across New Jersey as he fled from Manhattan, they had their buglers sound the fox-hunting call to show their contempt for him. They knew that Washington, who like every wealthy American, had been brought up as a British country gentleman was quite familiar with the tune. On the other hand, when the Brits heard that Arnold was coming, they frequently found a plausible excuse to execute an about-face and march the other way. Arnold felt that, by all rights, he should be an honored warrior, basking in the admiration of his countrymen and enjoying the rewards heaped on him by a grateful Congress. What had gone wrong?

Most historians now agree that the most resourceful, brilliant and competent commander of American forces during the Revolutionary War was Benedict Arnold. He was responsible for our victories at Fort Ticonderoga, the Battle of Valcour Island on Lake Champlain, and the battles of Danbury and Ridgefield in Connecticut. His most important victory was the Battle of Saratoga, the turning point of the war. Why did such a courageous, gifted man turn traitor? Let's revue Arnold's military career and see if we can find out what drove this battlefield genius to his own destruction.

Benedict Arnold was born on January 14, 1741 in Norwich, Connecticut. His alcoholic father left the family in reduced circumstances and Arnold was apprenticed to his two cousins as an apothecary (druggist). Like Washington, he had fought as a red-coated British colonial auxiliary in the French and Indian War (1754 – 1763). In one of the engagements his battalion was forced to surrender a fort to the French, who had promised safe passage to the fort's inhabitants. But as soon as the British laid down their arms, the Indian allies of the French massacred and scalped the women and children while the French soldiers looked on, doing nothing to stop the savagery. This instilled in Arnold a lifelong loathing and distrust of the French.

After the war, he soon had his own apothecary shop and then his own ship, which he sailed to the West Indies. He became deft at smuggling, an honorable and commonplace practice among sea-going American colonists. They had nothing but contempt for England's restrictive and crippling customs laws. During his travels he, like many sea captains of the time, may have been initiated into blue lodge Masonry on one of the British colonial islands in the West Indies. Or he may have been received into a military lodge while serving in the 15th Regiment of Foot under Lord Jeffrey Amherst during the French and Indian War. Hiram Lodge No. 1 of New Haven, Connecticut has him on the books as a member in 1765, and he may have been initiated there.

Back at home in New England, Arnold acquired a commission as Captain of the Governor's Second Company of Guards. When the Revolution broke out and news of the Battles of Lexington and Concord reached him, Arnold, without orders, marched off to the action with his men. He had acquired a taste for combat in his youthful campaigns during the French and Indian War. He paused long enough to request and receive a letter of authority from the Massachusetts Committee of Safety to capture Fort Ticonderoga. The fort was considered a prime target because it protected the southern tip of Lake Champlain against a feared British naval incursion from Canada. The British, with no need for the fort in peacetime, had allowed the defenses to fall into ruin. Rumor also had it that only 12 or 15 old British pensioners (retired soldiers) manned the fort. The capture of Fort Ticonderoga would be a plum assignment, indeed.

Others thought so, too. When Arnold arrived at Ticonderoga with his Massachusetts permit, he found that the rival colony of Connecticut had hired Ethan Allen and his mercenary Green Mountain Boys to take the fort. These characters were not regular soldiers by any stretch of the imagination. They were an undisciplined armed gang, closer to Robin Hood's Merry Men than to a troop of militia. They laughed at Arnold with his fancy officer's uniform and his letter from the Committee of Safety. Arnold, who was supposed to have been the CO (Commanding Officer) of the operation, was forced to share command with the gigantic 6' 6" Allen, a gruff, hard-drinking frontier character.

On May 10, 1775, the fort was easily taken, mostly because the old soldiers inside hadn't known that there was a war going on. Allen claimed in his memoirs that he had shouted "I take this fort in the name of the great Jehovah and the Continental Congress!" In fact, he kicked open the door to the quarters of the fort's commanding officer and yelled "Come out of there, you damned old rat!" The Green Mountain Boys celebrated their victory by breaking into the British rum stores and getting stinking drunk. This did not improve their social graces and they mocked the prickly Arnold mercilessly.

Fig. 25 "Come out of there, you damned old rat!"
Ethan Allen at the capture of Ft. Ticonderoga, May 10, 1775. ©iStock.

If that weren't bad enough, a Massachusetts officer with whom Arnold had previously quarreled reported back to the Committee of Safety, maliciously minimizing Arnold's role in the fort's capture. Then, when Arnold returned to Massachusetts, the

Committee of Safety refused to reimburse him for his out-of-pocket expenses. (Sometimes the CO of a financially-strapped colonial militia unit would pay for his men's uniforms, ammunition and supplies, with the understanding that the government would settle accounts with him later). Arnold had to get a lawyer and take the case to the Continental Congress before the Committee of Safety paid the whole amount.[1]

Ticonderoga was only the beginning of what was surely the most difficult, acrimonious and vituperative military career ever endured by a brilliant and courageous officer in the history of this nation. Each of the American colonies considered itself a small separate political unit unto itself. Rivalry among them for supremacy in the emerging nation was sharp. This had placed Arnold, the least diplomatic of men, in a vicious political confrontation between Connecticut and Massachusetts and – true to his nature – he had not behaved very well. He soon made for himself a small army of well-connected enemies in Congress that would plague him for the rest of the war.

Next came Washington's ill-conceived scheme to invade Canada. He thought that if we arrived in Quebec with a show of force then surely the French-Canadians would rise up and join us in overthrowing their British overlords. They would then petition Congress to welcome them as the 14th colony. Remember President Kennedy and the Bay of Pigs, when the war pundits in his administration were sure the Cuban citizenry would join our invasion force and rise up against Castro? Kennedy refused to give the invading rebels air support, the Cuban people remained loyal to Castro and the whole affair became a fiasco of historic proportions. The invasion of Canada was Washington's Bay of Pigs.

The French *Quebecois* still remembered the French and Indian War and wanted no part of us. They lived under an unusually mild British rule. The Colonial Office in Whitehall (Britain's Foreign Office headquarters near London) had allowed them to keep their French language and their Roman Catholic religion and had left them alone to live impoverished but semi-autonomous agrarian lives in peace. They saw no need to ally themselves to a bellicose group of bigoted English-speaking Americans who would look down on their language, their ethnicity and their Church.

Washington promoted his friend Arnold to Colonel and placed him under Brig. General Richard Montgomery to be second-in-command of the invasion. But before he even got near the border, Arnold was betrayed by an Indian scout who handed over his invasion plans to the British. Having lost any element of surprise, the invasion failed miserably. Montgomery was killed in combat and enemies in Congress wrongly blamed Arnold, who had fought bravely, for the defeat. During a major engagement on December 31, 1775, Arnold took the larger half of a split .75-caliber musket ball in his left leg. He refused let his orderlies carry him from the battlefield. He limped through the streets of Quebec with his men, his boot filling with blood.[2]

Afterwards, while evacuating Montreal, Arnold "liberated" some desperately needed supplies – food, boots and blankets – from captured British stores. This was a perfectly acceptable practice at that time and should have garnered no censure. But his enemies in Congress brought him up on charges of plundering (enemy stores!) and demanded his arrest. His friend Washington and General Horatio Gates (a British officer who had retired from the British Royal American Army and, when the Revolution broke out, joined the American side) managed to exonerate him. Both knew that a man of Arnold's abilities would be far more valuable commanding an Army unit in the field than languishing in a jail cell.

In the fall of 1776 the British began their anticipated naval incursion from Canada down into Lake Champlain. They planned to retake Fort Ticonderoga and establish a beachhead on the southern tip of Champlain that they could use as a staging area for amphibious troop landings. This would constitute a dagger thrust deep into the heart of the colonies, isolating New York from New England. This would effectively split the colonies in half and isolate New England's military contributions from the war effort. Washington once again called on Arnold, promoted him to Brigadier General, and sent him up to Lake Champlain, under the command of General Gates, to handle the matter.

The British Commanding Officer in Canada, Major General Sir Guy Carleton, knew that his country had the best navy in the world. He assumed that any colonial officer that Washington could dispatch to counter their offensive would be a hayseed and a landlubber with no knowledge of naval tactics. He was wrong. Arnold had been a sea captain and a world traveler; here he was able to put his maritime experience to good use. Gates, who admitted he had no experience with "Marine Affairs," was happy to put the sea-going Arnold completely in charge of the lake's naval operations, giving him command of the American fleet.

In 1775 Carleton, foreseeing the coming trouble on Lake Champlain, had ordered prefabricated ships sent from England.[3] By the time of the battle he had received ten. They were assembled by skilled Canadian shipwrights working for the British. One large ship of the line put together for Carleton was HMS *Inflexible*, an 180-ton warship. The 25 vessels of the British fleet outgunned the Americans' 15 vessels by six guns, all of them firing heavier ordinance than the smaller American guns.

The Americans were at a tactical disadvantage. Skilled shipwrights were hard to come by and they demanded exorbitant wages. Although Arnold worked for three months, his men were only able to find or assemble sixteen small ships. Arnold's flotilla consisted of a few small oared galleys that carried only eight guns and several "gundalows," flat-bottomed New England cargo boats 60 to 70 feet long, that had each been fitted out with three small-bore field cannons. Carlton, on the other hand, had a fleet of three ocean-going ships of the line, twenty gunboats and an enormous raft armed with cannon and carrying

Royal Marines trained for boarding operations. These ships were commanded by experienced naval officers, five of whom would later become admirals.

On October 11, 1776, Arnold lured the British ships into a narrow passage between the shore and Valcour Island where they had no sea-room to maneuver. The wind started to blow from the north and the huge British ships of the line, now sailing into the wind in a narrow passage, became unmanageable. Arnold's small oared galleys were not dependent on the wind and his men rowed them right up to the three largest British ships, safely under the enemy cannons' long-range arc of fire. The Americans gave the larger ships such a close-range pounding that the British could not use their ships to any tactical purpose. By sundown the battle was a draw with neither side having the advantage.

But Arnold knew that his tiny squadron of makeshift boats could not stand another day's assault from the British gunboats. There was also that raft full of marines, lost somewhere in the gathering darkness, to consider. When night fell, Arnold ordered his flotilla to retreat southward in the darkness toward Crown Point, an American fort near Ticonderoga.[1] The next day Carleton's fleet pursued them and, in a two-day chase, managed to capture and burn ten of the sixteen American boats. The British, frustrated and now far from their supply lines, finally had to withdraw back to Canada. By the time they could regroup for another assault, winter had set in and Lake Champlain was frozen over. By the following spring the Americans had garrisoned the region with so many troops that the opportunity for an unopposed amphibious landing by the Royal Marines had passed. Another naval invasion was unfeasible.

The Battle of Lake Champlain, while not a complete victory, had been the greatest success any American commanding officer could boast of up until then. A bunch of farmers in rowboats had humiliated the mighty British navy, the best in the world! The British General Staff now realized that the rebels had a military genius, a threat on both land and sea, in their ranks. Putting down this rebellion was not going to be a stroll in Hyde Park.

And what was Arnold's reward? Congress censured him for the loss of ten boats! They also refused to grant him seniority of rank (that is, they would not recognize his time in grade) and promoted several younger officers over his head to flag rank. These newly promoted men would now be able to give him orders. In their arrogance, Congress had not even consulted Washington on the promotions and Washington was unhappy about that. As Commander-in-Chief, he was not accustomed to being snubbed by civilians. He wrote a letter to Congress praising Arnold and recommending that they restore his seniority. The letter was ignored, another snub. Washington was infuriated but held his temper, an art Arnold never learned.

Arnold, fuming, marched his men down to Philadelphia to confront his enemies personally. On the way he routed a superior force of British Marines who had made an amphibious landing on the beach and who were starting to burn the town of Danbury, Connecticut. With help from Generals David Wooster and Gold Silliman who were stationed in New Haven, Arnold and his army chased the marines and soldiers back to their boats and continued on their way.[5]

Congress nervously eyed the approach of this short-tempered military prodigy, much as the Roman senate had eyed Julius Caesar's march on Rome in 49 B.C. and the French would regard Napoleon's advance on Paris, after he escaped from Elba, in the spring of 1815. Like them, Arnold was accompanied by a victorious, battle-hardened army loyal to him. And, like them, Arnold was noted for his short temper, incredible battlefield skills and his abrupt, unexpected actions. Congress executed a prudent about-face. They commended Arnold on the victory at Danbury and promoted him to Major General. However, they still would not restore his seniority. Neither would they repay him any of his recent expenses. Arnold replied as only Arnold could: in July of 1777, he resigned his commission.

And then, on the same day, he asked Congress to put his resignation on hold. Washington had, that afternoon, requested him to take command of a large force of men and proceed north at once. There was trouble brewing north of Albany, near a town called Saratoga. That meant some good fighting was in store and the always combat-ready Arnold, who enjoyed the battlefield more than the

Fig. 26 Major Gen. Benedict Arnold. Engraving by H.B. Hall after John Trumbull, published 1879. ©iStock.

boardroom, could not pass up the opportunity.

The British once again were attempting to capture the Hudson River Valley and split New York away from New England, paralyzing the American cause. This time, thanks to Arnold's brilliant maneuvers at the Battle of Lake Champlain, they had no convenient staging area at Ticonderoga. They would have to start their assault from the far-away Canadian border. A British major general, John Burgoyne, a vain actor, dandy and playwright, planned to push down through the wilderness route along Lake Champlain to Albany where he would join forces with General William Howe, who Burgoyne assumed would be coming up from New York City, Howe's last reported position.

Thinking the campaign would be an easy path to military glory, the well-connected Burgoyne, nicknamed "Gentleman Johnny" by his soldiers, had gone behind the back of his superior officer in Canada, Sir Guy Carleton. Burgoyne had sailed to London a few months earlier to lobby Parliament for Carleton's position of Commander-in-Chief of Canada. For success in this venture, he was heavily dependent on the support of his friend and patron, Lord George Germain.

Germain had started his political career as George Sackville and had worked his way up in the army to become Colonel of the 20th Foot (the Lancashire Fusiliers). During the Battle of Minden (August 1, 1759) in the Seven Years war, the French threatened to overrun Sackville's position. Terrified, he deserted his regiment and fled from the battlefield. The War Office charged him with cowardice in the face of the enemy and cashiered him from the service. Exploiting his friendship with George III, he returned to London and managed to move up in government to Secretary of War and eventually acquire the title of Lord Germain.

With Germain's help, Burgoyne succeeded. He sold Parliament on his plan to split New England away from the other colonies. He would march down from Canada through the wilderness toward Albany, retaking Ticonderoga along the way. In England, his friend Lord Germain, now head of the War Office, would issue written orders to Howe, thought to be operating around Manhattan Island, ordering him to march north up the Hudson Valley to join with Burgoyne's troops at Albany. The thought that Howe might ignore these orders never occurred to anyone. Once at Albany, Germain ordered Howe to relinquish his command and put himself under Burgoyne's authority. No one cared that the more experienced Carleton, back in Canada, had been by-passed in favor of the better-connected Burgoyne.

John Burgoyne had entered military service at the age of 15 and had used his prominent family's influence to climb up in rank to major general. Although a competent officer who had seen a great deal of action, he was completely unfamiliar with the American wilderness and was relying heavily on Howe's military experience in North America that he intended to exploit when they joined forces.

But Howe, tiring of besieging New York City, had other plans. On his own, with no orders from the War Office, he decided to travel south and take the rebel capital, Philadelphia, during the summer months. Unbeknown to Burgoyne or anyone at Whitehall, Howe boarded his men onto naval troop transports and sailed down the New Jersey coast. Some reports indicate that, for some reason, he may have spent the entire month of August at sea, finally sailing up the Delaware Bay and attacking Philadelphia in September. He took the largely pro-British capital with little fighting and settled down for the fall.

Howe was a tough, courageous soldier who had distinguished himself during the French and Indian War. During the British assault on Quebec on the 13th of September, 1759, a *Quebecois* sniper killed his commanding officer, Gen. James Wolfe. Howe took command, led the British assault on the Heights of Abraham and captured Quebec City. When the Revolution broke out, the Crown appointed him Acting Commander-in-Chief of all British forces in the Colonies.

Fig. 27 "Gentleman Johnny" Burgoyne. ©iStock

But age and battlefield hardship had mellowed Howe's tastes and blunted both his energy and his decision-making abilities. He had become fond of good food and gala social events. Once in Philadelphia, he fell in love with the clean, charming capital city so far removed from the filthy streets of crime-ridden London. Philadelphia was full of upper-class American Tories and British sympathizers who had no qualms about fraternizing with British officers; parties and balls abounded. Benjamin Franklin, in France at the time, quipped that it was not so much that Howe had captured Philadelphia but rather that Philadelphia had captured Howe.

Howe knew very well what Burgoyne was up to, and he had no intention of surrendering his command to a man he considered a pretentious fop. The pleasure-loving general was in no hurry to begin a long march north through the New York wilderness in the late fall with a harsh winter coming on, just to support the ambitions of a man he despised. He was also in no hurry to face companies of dead-shot American riflemen who, rumor had it, could hit a man's head at 300 yards. For personal reasons he found the company of his mistress, the wife of one of his junior officers, to be more agreeable and he stayed put in the City of Brotherly Love.

Meanwhile Burgoyne was struggling through the wilderness with a company of 3,700 British regulars, 3,000 Hessians, 250 Canadians and American loyalists and 400 Indians. A cumbersome train of baggage wagons, cooks and personal servants accompanied them. There were also a large number of women, the wives and "companions" of his men. He had loaded most of his field artillery on barges and was floating them down nearby Lake Champlain.

Burgoyne's forces had to waste time and energy diverting their march to retake the increasingly irrelevant fort at Ticonderoga with the half-hearted intent of turning it into a staging area. The mere approach of Burgoyne's army so unnerved the fort's few defenders that they promptly deserted their post and disappeared into the forest. After many hardships on the wilderness journey, Burgoyne finally met the Americans near Saratoga on September 19, 1777. He seemed to regard the American colonials as an inferior breed of "natives," one step above the Indians, whom the racist British considered to be one step above the forest animals. He fully expected them to run away in a panic when they caught sight of his troops' stunning red uniforms and heard the unnerving skirl of the regimental bagpipes. He had a few lessons coming.

His first lesson was the loss of an "impregnable" fort manned by two thousand British and Hessian troops. Arnold, serving under the command of General Horatio Gates, was the only officer who volunteered to attack the fort. He had to do this with less than a thousand men, all that the cautious Gates would allow. He succeeded by convincing the fort's defenders that he was leading a force of several thousand soldiers and Indians. He knew that the British and Germans were terrified of the savage Indians, who routinely tortured their captives to death. Sure enough, when they heard the American soldiers' imitations of Indian war whoops, the fort's defenders panicked and advanced smartly to the rear, disappearing into the pine woods. Arnold entered an empty fort.

Both the British and the American armies depended for their field artillery on the humble three-pounder battalion cannon. These guns were light and easily moved long distances by muscular draught horses. Their ammunition was an iron ball the size of a softball that, issuing from a yard-long barrel packed with a pound and a half of powder, would float through the air with deceptively apparent slowness for about a half a mile before striking the enemy. There it could burst through the bodies of four men lined up one behind the other and still have enough kinetic energy left to bounce on the ground and take off the arm or leg or head of one more man. If the ball struck stony ground in front of the troops it could impart enough energy to the loose stones and pebbles to scatter them with the force of a pistol-shot at close range, killing or wounding an entire front rank. The American cannon and cannonballs were made of bog iron dug up in the Pine Barrens of New Jersey. The British favored melted-down church bells.

The Battle of Saratoga was actually two separate battles, fought 18 days apart. The first was the Battle of Freeman's Farm on September 19, 1777, in which Arnold, alone, personally led the Americans to victory. This was too big a feat to ignore and Gates was now becoming wary of Arnold's bravery and leadership skills, two attributes that the cautious Gates lacked. Afraid that Arnold would outshine him, Gates falsified his written reports and refused to acknowledge Arnold as the officer responsible for the victory. He also began surreptitiously to reassign Arnold's troops to other officers. When Arnold found out, he exploded and quarreled with Gates in front of Gates' staff. Gates, who had been looking for just such an opportunity, relieved Arnold of his command and confined him to quarters.

Arnold, furious, paced and fumed in his tent until the second major engagement, the Battle of Bemis Heights, broke out on October 7. Unable to remain still while other men were fighting and dying for the American cause, Arnold sent for his horse. He galloped off to the front lines, waving his sword. Gates had concentrated his forces on the British right and left flanks, hoping that the British line would coalesce on either flank and give way in the center. Under Gates' conservative plan of attack, the center held and the Americans were being mowed down by timed, disciplined volleys of musket fire from Burgoyne's regulars.

Then Arnold appeared out of nowhere. He quickly sized up the situation and saw that the Americans' advance under the hesitant Gates was slow, allowing the Redcoats too much time to reload their muskets. A trained British soldier could reload and fire his Brown Bess musket once every 16 seconds. Arnold correctly surmised that if the Americans charged at a run they could reach the British line between volleys and settle the matter with bayonets.

Also, the British-born Gates wasn't making proper use of the long-range Pennsylvania rifles carried by Colonel Daniel Morgan's Rifle Company, relying on his regular soldiers' conventional-issue muskets instead. The smooth-bore army-issue Brown Bess musket lost so much muzzle velocity that its .75 caliber lead ball had an effective killing range of only about 70 yards. An individual soldier could not aim his musket with any accuracy. Only by lining up a regiment of several hundred trained men who could raise and fire their muskets simultaneously on command could a commander hope to do any damage to the enemy.

This was the original purpose of close-order drill (Right face! Left face!). Today officers use the drill only for ceremonial purposes or as an exercise to teach recruits obedience to commands. In Arnold's day it was a very practical and necessary maneuver that was used on the battlefield to wheel a forward-marching column of men into an effective firing line in a matter of seconds. In the same vein, the modern-day manual of arms (Present arms! Shoulder arms!) descends from the commands used to ensure the uniform delivery of musket fire and the subsequent reloading of weapons in unison by 200 men at a time.

In the hands of a practiced shooter a Pennsylvania rifle with a grooved bore and a .45 caliber ball wrapped in a greased patch could kill at 400 yards. Arnold, ignoring the fact that he had no command but knowing that American rifle fire was especially demoralizing to British troops, ordered Morgan to direct his riflemen to lay down a long-range volley. Morgan, who had served with Arnold before and who respected him, complied and Morgan's Rifles opened fire, safely out of range of the British muskets. Their volleys were devastating and the British, realizing they were now under rifle fire, began to break ranks and run.

Riding out in front, Arnold led the Americans in a charge that broke the thinning British line. As the Brits were retreating, Arnold's horse was shot out from under him and fell on his wounded leg, further injuring it. Arnold's tactics forced Burgoyne to retreat and wait for Howe to arrive with reinforcements.

He's still waiting. Howe, comfortably ensconced in Philadelphia, could not have cared less whether Burgoyne was winning or losing his battles in the wilderness and saw no reason to leave the charming city for an unwelcome campaign in the cold, wet forests of northern New York. He only intended to move if he received direct orders from London to do so. The orders would have to come from Burgoyne's patron, George Lord Germain, the Secretary of War.

The story goes that, back in England, Lord Germain was eager to go off on a weekend holiday in Kent. On the way, he had his carriage stop by the War Office at Whitehall so he could sign the requisite orders. There were two sets of orders, one for Burgoyne to conduct his march south from Canada and one for Howe to move north and meet him at Albany. Germain signed Burgoyne's orders but the orders for Howe had been sloppily written and Germain refused to sign them until a better copy was made. This would take about three quarters of an hour, and he didn't want to keep his carriage waiting.

Germain's office staff, a careless, slovenly bunch of civil servants, assured him that they would get the rewritten copy of Howe's orders to Germain's holiday retreat by the next day, in plenty of time for him to sign them and put them on the next ship to America. As soon as Germain left, they quickly mailed Burgoyne's orders so that they reached a departing ship just in time. Then, without waiting for the fresh copy of Howe's orders, they all went home for the weekend. A staff member threw the orders for Howe, when they arrived, on Germain's desk, where they languished unnoticed for two or three days. Germain's Deputy Secretary, a man named D'Oyley, found the papers and, knowing Germain wouldn't be back for several days, signed them himself and got them onto the next ship departing for the colonies.

There are at least three versions of what happened next. One version is that the ship with Howe's orders met with unfavorable winds and was delayed so long that by the time the orders reached Philadelphia, Howe was no longer there, having been forced to evacuate the city. Another version is that Howe received the orders in time but, seeing D'Oyley's signature, thought (wrongly) that they were not binding and waited for orders signed by Germain to arrive. A sailing ship, even with favorable winds, could take eight to ten weeks or more to cross the Atlantic and Howe was quite willing to spend those weeks in Philadelphia. Yet another version holds that Howe received the orders, knew that Deputy D'Oyley's signature made them binding, but ignored them anyway.

The last version is most probably correct. Howe detested Burgoyne, thought that his campaign was doomed to failure and had already written a friend at the War Office, saying that he had no intention of helping Germain's toady. Whitehall had given Britain's generals, conducting a war in a far-away alien land, a great deal of latitude in making their own decisions, so Howe's independence was not as surreal as it may seem in today's world of rapid communication. Every officer in the British armed services despised Germain as a sycophant and a coward, and they frequently ignored his orders anyway. Meanwhile, up in northern New York, Burgoyne had no recourse but to surrender to the American forces, which he did on October 17, 1777 (Plate 15).

I cannot overemphasize the importance of our winning at Saratoga. Saratoga was the major turning point of the war, as important a battle in its own time as Midway would be to America in 1942. In 1777 the reason was France. Until our victory at Saratoga, we were barely holding our own against Britain. France feared to come to our aid as long as it looked like we might lose. The Battle of Saratoga exposed Britain's many Achille's heels – communication time, distance, logistics, incompetent officers and an inflexible slovenly bureaucracy. Also displayed was the brilliance, courage and fighting ability of the American troops.

After our victory at Saratoga France officially declared her alliance and flooded us with men, muskets and ammunition. French warships came over to make up most of our naval force and well-trained professional French soldiers quickly arrived to double our number of ground troops. We soon had large artillery parks of excellent French cannon. Without French aid our cause of independence, popular with only about one-third of America's colonial population, probably would have sputtered out. As the brilliant Stanford historian, Thomas A. Bailey, points out in his book, *The American Pageant*, for a colonial American to say that we won the Revolution with some help from France was like saying "Daddy and I killed the bear."

Most Americans remembered all too well the butchery that England had subjected the Scottish Highlanders to after the failed Jacobite rebellion of 1745. We would have had to sue for peace under the most humiliating terms to avoid a similar orgy of vindictive hangings and public torture. But with France on our side, we backed the British into the sea and forced them to ground their arms at Yorktown.

Saratoga was the key to our success in the War of Independence and the victory at Saratoga was unquestionably Arnold's. But Gates made sure that he, not Arnold, received the credit. Arnold's contribution was once again ignored. Congress finally granted him his seniority in rank but it came too late to do his military career any good and much too late to mollify Arnold's savaged feelings. A proud fighting man, he was now a cripple with little money and few friends.

Following his wound at Saratoga, Arnold was sent to a military hospital in Albany to recover. After several months of agony and primitive medical care, he left the hospital with his wounded leg two inches shorter than the other. He could no longer mount a horse unaided and walked only with the greatest difficulty using a cane. By then Howe had evacuated Philadelphia and Washington, perhaps as a consolation prize, appointed Arnold to be Military Commandant of the city.

Irony plays tricks on us all, and some of the tricks can be horrendous. Arnold had survived everything the battlefield could throw at him and had laughed in the face of death and crippling injury. But the peaceful occupation of a beautiful city dealt him a deadlier wound than any British musket ball could have.

It all came down to a clash of cultures. In contrast to his days in the rough-and-ready colonial army, he now found himself in command of an environment that placed great value on wealth, manners and social status. Arnold, who had none of these, had no idea where to turn. He was a widower and began to court an attractive and boisterous young woman named Peggy Shippen.

Peggy was the youngest daughter of a prominent Philadelphia judge. At 18, she was not particularly thrilled by the attentions of a 38-year old, hook-nosed, pot-bellied, rough-at-the-edges officer who limped around on a game leg. If truth be known, she really missed the company of handsome young Captain John Andre, a British officer who had been seeing her during Howe's occupation of the city. She came from a well-to-do Tory family that was sympathetic to the British and, like many wealthy young Philadelphia girls, she had enjoyed the British occupation with its parties and balls and dashing, cultivated young officers from Britain's upper classes.

Her father is thought to have been chagrined at Arnold's approaches. But I believe that, seeing that the American side was finally gaining the upper hand, it was probably he who persuaded his daughter to accept Arnold's proposal. He would have looked on this as insurance against any post-war repercussions ensuing from the family's blatant fraternization with the enemy. Peggy reluctantly agreed and became Mrs. Arnold. At the marriage ceremony, Arnold – too vain to use a cane at his own wedding – had to be assisted down the aisle supported by one of his officers. The marriage elevated Arnold to a high social status that he could not afford; he and Peggy lived far above their means. She and Arnold threw lavish balls for Army officers and civilians.

The cash-strapped Continental Congress had been dragging its feet on payments to the Army and Arnold soon found himself over a year behind in his meager salary. To make ends meet, he ordered his soldiers to close down certain shops. He then forced the owners to sell him their merchandise at a steep discount and later resold the same goods at a profit. For a fee, he gave illegal passes to Tory merchants to leave the city, knowing that they intended to sell food and other goods to the British at a huge profit. He entered into a scheme with a group of speculators to purloin half the profits from the capture of a British ship that belonged to someone else. He boasted that he intended to resign from the army and use his naval skills to command a fleet of privateer ships and accrue a fortune. Privateers were privately owned and armed pirate ships that operated under a license from Congress. They could legally overhaul and board any commercial ship sailing under an enemy flag, steal and sell its cargo.

On a bulletin board in the main hall of Philadelphia's Customs House, the captain of every ship that was going to put out from the city's busy port fastened a sheet of paper with the ship's name, cargo and destination written at the top. Whoever wanted to invest in the ship would put up an amount of money as an early kind of maritime insurance. The investor would write his name and the amount of his investment on the paper under the name of the ship (the origin of the insurance term *underwriter*). If the ship reached port successfully, the captain would sell its cargo and every investor who had underwritten the ship would receive a share of the profits from the sale proportionate to his investment.

Arnold and some fellow speculators invested in a large merchant ship, the *Charming Nancy*. They did not underwrite the ship publicly and kept their investment a secret. Although legal at that time, this was definitely a conflict of interest for the Military Commandant of the city, who controlled the access of every ship to Philadelphia's busy port, to engage in without public knowledge. The ship carried a great load of merchandise and Arnold's split from the sale would be significant.

Shortly after the *Charming Nancy* left port, however, the crew of a New Jersey privateer made her heave to and boarded her. The privateer's captain had spotted British warships off the Jersey coast and, fearful that her cargo would fall into British hands, forced the *Nancy* to turn back and dock in the New Jersey port of Egg Harbor until the danger passed.[6]

When the news reached Arnold, he panicked. He could not afford to lose his investment and, knowing the fragile nature of law enforcement among the half-patriotic, half-Tory citizenry living under the rigors of wartime conditions, was fearful that a mob would storm the ship and steal its cargo. Without any authority, he forcibly seized a dozen wagons belonging to the commonwealth of Pennsylvania and dispatched them under armed guard to Egg Harbor. His soldiers retrieved the *Charming Nancy*'s cargo and brought it back to Philadelphia, where Arnold and his partners sold it. Arnold then doctored his account books to conceal the transaction and the requisitioning of the wagons. This was the final straw for the city's authorities and they pounced on Arnold.[7]

The Tory president of Philadelphia's Executive Council, Joseph Reed, hated both Arnold and Washington with a passion. He had been biding his time and keeping note of Arnold's activities. The Council quickly brought Arnold up on charges of improper conduct and demanded that the Army court-martial him. Washington, who would have preferred to handle the matter privately, had no choice.

The court martial took place at Norris's Tavern in Morristown, New Jersey. Because of the hard winter and difficult travel conditions, it dragged on from December 23, 1779 until the end of January, 1780. Arnold, confident of an acquittal, acted as his own defense, limping up and down on a cane in full-dress uniform in front of the court-martial board members. He thought that, when the trial was over, the board would acclaim him a national hero, an acclamation that he felt he well deserved. He planned to make some money later on by publishing the transcript of the trial and the expected acquittal as a book.[8]

But there was no acquittal. The court marshal found Arnold guilty on two counts: Requisitioning government wagons for his personal use and allowing unauthorized ships to dock in Philadelphia's port. Even Washington, who had supported Arnold up to that point, had to rebuke him publicly. In the rebuke, he called Arnold's conduct "imprudent, improper and peculiarly reprehensible." That rebuke, although it was nothing more than a formal slap on the wrist, was the final straw. Arnold never forgave Washington for what he considered a betrayal of their friendship.

Arnold was at his wits end and could take no more. After the court-martial conviction he had no hope of a post-war military career and he was now hopelessly in debt. At that time the courts could send a man to prison for an unpaid debt of five pounds, and Arnold owed considerably more than five pounds. Arnold knew that the law could not touch him in time of war as long as he was a flag officer in the Continental Army. Even if his creditors ignored the wartime restriction they would have to use the municipal police force to arrest him and Arnold, a Major General who commanded a thousand bayonets wielded by combat veterans loyal to him, *was* the municipal police force. But he also knew that the war was coming to an end and that he would not be a flag-rank officer much longer.

Arnold saw no way out; sometime toward the end of 1779 or the beginning of 1780 he decided to sell out to the enemy and opened negotiations with the British. His Tory wife fully supported his treason and, at her suggestion, he used her former boyfriend, John Andre, as a go-between. Andre, now a Major (or, in some papers, a Colonel), was the chief intelligence officer for Sir Henry Clinton, the British commander in Canada.

The British warship *HMS Vulture*, an armed sloop, ferried Andre to and from Canada along the largely unguarded Hudson River. Dressed in civilian clothes, he had no trouble contacting Arnold. The colonies were full of people with British accents and Andre blended right in. The British particularly wanted West Point, a fort that controlled access to the critical New York City area to ships coming south from Canada. Located on an S-curve of the Hudson, any ships that passed West Point would have to slow down and progress awkwardly within easy range of the fort's huge cannons. This very narrow, treacherous part of the river under West Point was nicknamed "World's End" by both the British and the Americans in tribute to the difficulties it presented to shipping. The fort was perched on a high bluff and could rain cannon fire down on shipping in the river while the ships below would be unable to return fire upwards. Also, a heavy chain stretching between West Point and Constitution Island lay on the river bottom. Soldiers could quickly raise it at a moment's notice and it would become an impassable barrier to any vessel sailing down river. West Point, in American hands, effectively confined the British navy to the northern half of the river. Arnold agreed to see if he could somehow gain command of West Point and then turn it over in exchange for 10,000 pounds (over $1 million in today's money), land in Canada and a commission in the British army.

Andre's activities, however, were not going unnoticed. Washington had established his own personal secret service organization under the supervision of his confidant, Major Benjamin Tallmadge of Setauket, NY. Washington was getting word about reported seditious activities in New York and requested Tallmadge, a former schoolteacher and a classmate of Nathan Hale, to establish a spy ring there. Tallmadge placed his boyhood friend, Abraham Woodhull, in charge of the New York operation and had him enlist their old friends and neighbors in near-by Setauket as civilian operatives in the counterspy network. The New York operation was code-named the Culper Ring from the code names of the New York contact – "Culper Jr." – and his go-between with the Continental Army in Connecticut, "Culper Sr."

Woodhull's spies soon got word to Tallmadge and Washington that something big - *very* big - was afoot. It would involve the sell-out of a major American military stronghold

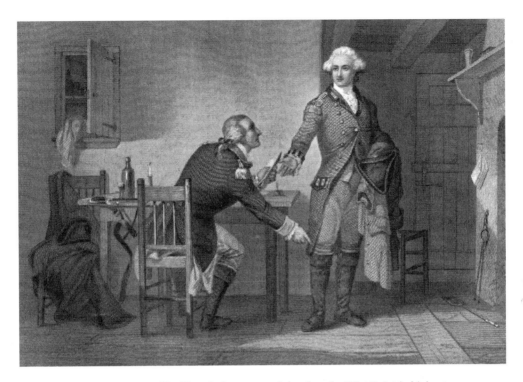

Fig.28 Arnold telling Andre to conceal the plans for West Point in his boots.
(© iStock)

to the British. Washington knew that only a high-ranking officer could bring about such a momentous transaction and pressed his spies to find out the traitor's identity and plans. Little did he suspect who the culprit would turn out to be.

Meanwhile, Washington was starting to feel that he had been too harsh with his old friend and offered Arnold command of the left wing of the colonial army, a great coup for any officer and one that would have delighted Arnold a few years earlier. But this was just the opportunity Arnold was waiting for. Using his crippled leg as an excuse he asked for command of West Point instead. Washington was happy to comply, thinking that now at least *that* particular stronghold would be in trustworthy hands. At last, events looked as though they were starting to come together for Arnold.

No sooner had Arnold taken command of West Point, however, when everything fell apart. When Andre tried to return to Canada after one of his visits with Arnold, he could not find the *Vulture*. A squad of American troops patrolling the Hudson had forced it into hiding. Dressed in civilian clothes, Andre was trying to make it to the Canadian border on foot when three highway robbers who doubled as frontier militiamen waylaid him.

Andre, a dandy who intended to marry well, was dressed foppishly in expensive clothes and his upper-class British accent marked him as fair game for the robbers. Who would punish them for despoiling a damned Tory? He had no money on him, but his beautiful shiny boots attracted the militiamen's attention and they ordered Andre to take them off. To their surprise, they found papers that looked like military documents stuffed into the boots. The men could not read very well but they figured Andre must be doing something underhanded so they tied him up and took him to the local sheriff, hoping for a reward.

The sheriff, a civilian, could not make sense of the maps and documents but he saw that some of them bore General Benedict Arnold's signature. And Arnold had scrawled his name on a margin of one of the pages. Relieved, the sheriff dispatched a rider to carry some of the papers to Arnold at West Point; this was Army business and the general would know what to do. After the rider had left, the sheriff sent another messenger to carry the rest of the documents to Washington's headquarters in Connecticut. He spent the rest of the afternoon daydreaming of the reward he would get from Washington and Arnold for returning the stolen documents and turning over the thief, who now languished in the town jail. He imagined Arnold would be especially happy and would probably have him and his wife over for dinner at the Point.

Arnold, however, was not especially happy when he saw the papers that the rider delivered. He immediately loaded two pistols and bolted from his office. He could not take his wife and child with him so, before leaving, he convinced Peggy that she could persuade the authorities of her innocence in the matter by feigning hysteria. Down at the river's edge he ordered two of his men to seize a boat and row him north up the river. When the men balked and pointed out that he was venturing into enemy territory, Arnold leveled his pistols at their heads and informed them that they could either obey or have their heads blown off on the spot. Good soldiers, they decided to obey.

The papers intended for Washington were intercepted by the master spy-catcher Tallmadge who immediately saw what was going on. He gathered a squad of men and made a beeline for West Point to arrest Arnold but they arrived too late. The traitor was gone. Washington himself had arrived at the Point that very morning on a routine inspection visit. He was miffed that his old friend Arnold was not on hand to greet him. Then Tallmadge's group galloped up and gave Washington the bad news. The consummate gentleman Washington, who knew nothing of Peggy's compliance in Arnold's treachery, was completely taken in by her phony hysterics and allowed her to return to Philadelphia with her child.

Arnold, thanks to his enthusiastic rowers, was able to find the Vulture that then took him safely up to Canada. Washington, stunned and grieving at his trusted friend's treachery, offered to exchange Andre for Arnold but the British refused. Washington, in an uncharacteristic rage over Arnold's treachery, had young John Andre hanged as a spy and Arnold, now a British officer, donned a red uniform.

For a while, Arnold fought as well for the British as he had for his own country. In Virginia, he asked a captured American officer what the Americans would do to him if he were taken. Supposedly the officer replied: "We would cut off your right [wounded] leg and bury it with full military honors and then hang the rest of you." After the war, Arnold moved to London and was welcomed by King George but found a cold reception from the Tory government of Edmund Burke. Burke refused to put Arnold in charge of British soldiers on the grounds that, as a traitor, he was a dishonorable man. Arnold died in London in 1801, in considerable debt. His wife Peggy managed to repay all of the debt to the sum of 6000 pounds before her death in 1804.

Arnold, his wife Peggy and their daughter, Sophia Phipps, are buried in the crypt of a Georgian-era church, St. Mary's of Battersea, on the banks of the Thames. Their tombstone, donated in 2004 by an American well-wisher, is almost obscured by a large tropical fish tank; the brightly-painted crypt now doubles as the church's day-care center. [9]

Scholars have considered Arnold's treachery to be particularly reprehensible because he committed it not from long-held principles but for entirely selfish and egotistical reasons. While he was undeniably a victim of circumstance and of his own abrasive personality, I believe that, during the years that he was a loyal American officer, he deserved better treatment from Congress and from Washington's General Staff. Of course, our fledgling country – insecure and vulnerable – surely deserved better from this courageous, talented senior officer, one of the best in the service. In spite of the many unfortunate circumstances that bedeviled this brilliant, driven man, I don't think that history will ever exonerate Arnold, nor will his Masonic Fraternity.

Nevertheless, like it or not, we all owe Arnold a great debt. We owe him the victory at Saratoga.[10] That victory gained us the French intervention that turned the tide against the mightiest empire in the Western world. We almost certainly owe him our independence.

The 20ᵗʰ Degree
of the Southern Jurisdiction:

GRAND MASTER OF ALL SYMBOLIC LODGES

This degree is quite different in the Southern Jurisdiction. It is all about teaching leadership by means of mystical geometry, particularly the numbers nine (3 X 3) and 27 (3 X 9). First, the candidate is taught nine virtues that Pike thought were necessary for the proper governance of a blue lodge. These are illustrated by nine candles representing the "nine great lights in Masonry." The candidate is then lectured on no less than 27 more virtues represented by the image of a complex geometric figure containing squares, triangles and an octagon. Finally, he is given advice on virtuous government by nine famous lawgivers of history, including Hammurabi, Socrates and Confucius. The lessons of the degree are that truth, justice and tolerance are indispensable qualities for a Master of the Lodge and that example is the best teaching method known.[11]

21ˢᵗ Degree:

PATRIARCH NOACHITE
(A medieval kangaroo court and a trial by fire)

The Stage Drama

The time is the late 12ᵗʰ-century, around the year 1190. The place is a clearing in the forest near the Imperial Free City of Dortmund, Westphalia (a region in what is now west-central Germany). It is nighttime and a full moon illuminates the scene. A meeting of a self-appointed group of vigilantes calling themselves the *Vehmgericht* is in session. The story tells of a conflict between a nobleman and a young knight named Adolph the Saxon. Adolph claims that the nobleman has defrauded him out of his inheritance and, lacking evidence, demands a fiery trial by ordeal. God is on his side and Adolph is unharmed by the fire.

This degree teaches that Freemasonry is not a shield for evildoing and that justice is one of the chief supports of our Fraternity.

Historical Background

During the early Middle Ages, from AD 1100 to 1300, a vigilante secret society called the *Vehmgeright* operated in what is now west-central Germany. *Geright* is German for *court* or *tribunal*; the meaning of *vehm* is uncertain. It is pronounced *fehm* and may be a play on the Arabic word *fehm* (wisdom) picked up by German knights in the Middle East during the Crusades. The Vehmgericht consisted of traveling kangaroo courts made up of armed knights and nobles. They held court and either acquitted, tortured or executed the accused on the spot. If they found the accused guilty of a major crime (which could include heresy), they hanged him or her from the nearest tree immediately.[1]

The excuse usually given for these secret tribunals is that they were necessary to keep law and order due to the rapidly expanding German settlement of the formerly pagan frontier region. The Teutonic Knights were ravaging and looting the area during the time of the degree's story. They were also, with legal and Papal permission, hunting down and slaughtering the native pagan people to make way for the incoming German Christian settlers.

I find the name of this degree more intriguing than the kangaroo court melodrama it recounts. The original Patriarch Noachite degree was very likely a "floating" degree circulating among Masonic bodies in France. The word *Noachite* is a relic of an extinct 17th-century Masonic myth. The myth holds that speculative Masonry descends (spiritually, perhaps) from Noah through his descendent Peleg.

The original Masonic exhumation myth (which predates the Hiramic legend), maintained that the three sons of Noah – Shem, Ham and Japheth – went to their father's grave and dug up his body. They were hoping to find some unspecified lost secret that he had taken with him to the grave. They tried to pull the body up by grasping a finger, but the decayed finger came off. When they tried to pull on his hand, the hand came off. The same happened with his forearm. In desperation, they finally wrestled him up out of the grave using a complicated five-point embrace. To complete the grisly story, the embrace forced the air of his last breath out of his lungs and the brothers thought that this gasp formed a magic word that gave them the secret they were after.[2]

From 1719 to 1722, a French clergyman named Jean Theophilus Desaguliers was Grand Master of the Grand Lodge of England. He did not like the Noah legend and decided to give it a remake. In place of Noah he substituted an obscure Biblical character named *Huram Abi* or, as we now call him, Hiram Abiff. This man, with a Hebrew mother and a Phoenician father, was a skilled bronze worker from Tyre whom Hiram, King of Tyre, had sent to Jerusalem to cast and finish most of the bronze decorations for Solomon's temple.[3]

Desaguliers and Anderson[4] wrote a story that promoted Hiram from a mere artisan to becoming the chief architect and master builder of the temple and a virtual peer of Solomon and Hiram, King of Tyre. He then made up a drama that detailed Hiram's death, burial and subsequent exhumation à la Noah. After this version became ascendant in Masonry, earlier Masons began calling themselves Noachites to distinguish themselves from the later Masons who had adopted Desaguliers' Hiramic story.

Here's another point. Some Biblical genealogists think that Peleg, who was born 101 years after the flood, was the director of works at the Tower of Babel. Others say that work on the tower began when Peleg was only five years old. Many scholars think that Nimrod, a great-grandson of Noah, was the tower's work director and chief architect. Nimrod supposedly founded the first world empire, centered on the Tower of Babel and its surrounding city, which became known as Babylon (Genesis 10:8-12; 11:1-9). There is also

Fig. 29 The Tower of Babel. The first recorded work of masons? ©iStock.

the possibility that Nimrod was originally a minor Babylonian god who appeared in the Mesopotamian "Epic of Gilgamesh."

Why is this important? Because whoever was the construction boss at the Tower of Babel is the first recorded master builder in the Bible. Now, the Babel myth probably originated during the Babylonian Captivity with the Hebrews' first awed view of a magnificent Babylonian ziggurat. A ziggurat, as mentioned earlier, is a stepped, mountainous temple-tower, especially striking when lit up and glowing at night. Now the men of Sumer (called Shinar in Genesis) supposedly built the Tower of Babel, like the later Babylonian ziggurats, of fired brick rather than dressed stone.[5] The principle, the architectural planning and execution of such a monumental building project, however, would have been the same as a stone structure and Medieval illustrations in psalters and church windows always show the tower as a stone structure with stonemasons at work on it, like their contemporary cathedrals. I have always wondered why Freemasonry makes such a fuss over an obscure character named Tubal Cain, the first known artificer in bronze and iron, when Nimrod or Peleg, the first operative masons mentioned in the Bible, workers in brick or stone, would seem to be more logical choices.

The reason may lie in choices that Grand Lodge ritualists made during the 18th century. Older documents from the 1600s trace Freemasonry's pedigree from either Enoch (see my comments on the 13th degree), Noah, Peleg or Nimrod rather than from Solomon. These older theories taught that we received our rituals (along with the skills of stone masonry, geometry, agriculture, government and other secrets of civilization) from the "ancients." We were supposed to have obtained the information in the form of data inscribed on two stone pillars fashioned by antediluvian patriarchs who knew that the flood was coming and did not want the knowledge lost. Later, three of Solomon's workmen dug up the pillars which then became the source of Solomon's vaunted wisdom.

Our present-day ritual, however, maintains that Solomon was already wise and did not need to study engraved pillars. He is now said to have started the whole Masonry-as-a-secret-brotherhood idea as a means to maintain order among the workmen on his temple. According to this system we Masons descend in spirit from Solomon's Phoenician workmen (whom modern ritual always portrays as Yahwist Hebrews rather than the goddess-worshipping Canaanites they were) who built his temple. At some point after 1750 the Solomonic-Hiramic doctrine won out over the Noachite and Enochian versions, possibly because the Grand Masters of the Grand Lodge of England gave it their support.

Also, after 1717, when it looked like it was safe to do so, Church of England clergymen began joining the Masonic lodges in droves. They pressured the ritualists to favor conventional, familiar material taken from the King James Bible, with which the clergymen felt more comfortable. They disparaged any irregular, alternative documents that they feared had been derived from alchemical, magical or (horrors!) Roman Catholic sources. Also, there is so much more material written about Solomon in the Bible whereas Enoch, Peleg, Nimrod and the Tower of Babel only get a couple of sentences each, at most.

Today, instead of being Enochs or Noahs or Nimrods, we're all Hirams. The Solomonic reformists reduced all references to the two stone pillars and their preserved scientific knowledge to a couple of sentences in the Middle Chamber lecture. Even there the ritualists conflated them with the two bronze pillars of Asherah that were supposed to have stood on the porch of Solomon's Phoenician temple. I think it is a pity that the only remnants of those imaginative, romantic notions from the Age of Enlightenment are a few scraps of ritual that pop up, now mostly unrecognized, in blue lodge, Scottish or York Rite degree work. The pioneering, self-taught intellectual giants who made up the first speculative lodges of the 1600s deserve better.

The 21st Degree
of the Southern Jurisdiction:

NOACHITE, OR PRUSSIAN KNIGHT

This degree in the Southern Jurisdiction is very nearly identical to its northern counterpart. Like the NMJ's 21st degree the SJ's also includes a reference to the original Noachite exhumation legend of the degree's ritual. The story line is the same as in the Northern Jurisdiction. It teaches that the downfall of evil is certain and that a free and independent judiciary (although hopefully with more government oversight than the Vehmgericht seem to have had!) is necessary to human progress. Pike thought that the ritual also taught the need for responsible, fair and just journalism as well, although this connection is difficult to discern in a story that takes place before the invention of the printing press.[6]

22nd Degree:

PRINCE OF LIBANUS
(The Lumberjack Degree)

The Stage Drama

The present-day version of this ritual opens in a lumberjack camp somewhere in the forests of the Pacific Northwest. The men sing (much of the ritual is sung in the manner of an operetta) about their working tools, the pleasures and dignity of hard work and their camaraderie. In the degree's original version they worked in the forests of Lebanon and all belonged to an elite guild called the Princes of Lebanus, although none of this is mentioned in the new, rewritten version. The story details the initiation and education of a candidate (*again* said to be a Noachite Mason, interestingly) in the ways of the guild.

In this degree the dignity of labor is demonstrated. It is not a curse, but a privilege for a man to be allowed to earn his sustenance by work. Idleness, not labor, is disgraceful. For instance, a self-confessed idler is found among the lumberjacks in the camp and is punished for slacking.

Historical Background

"Libanus" is the Latin name for Lebanon. The name of this degree comes from an 18th-century Masonic legend. According to the legend, men of Sidon (a coastal Phoenician city near Tyre) cut the cedars of Lebanon for Noah's ark, although according to Genesis 6:14, the ark was made of something called "gopherwood". The legend also says that their descendants supplied cedar wood for the Ark of the Covenant (supposedly made of acacia wood). Anyway, such an alliance would not have been likely, given the strained relations between the aggressive, invading Hebrew tribes and the native Phoenicians at the early time period when the artisans Bezalel and Oholiab[1] are said to have fashioned the Ark of the Covenent. Later Phoenicians, living in the fortified city of Tyre, felled the cedars of

Lebanon for Solomon's temple and, centuries later, are supposed to have supplied wood for Zerubbabel's Post-Exilic temple.

This degree's ritual is the only one in the Scottish Rite that is sung, rather than spoken. Because of the difficulty in finding and assembling six or more Scottish Rite Masons who are trained singers, valleys had seldom presented it. That was unfortunate, because the presentation is dignified and impressive and the lessons are plain and easily understood. Stage directors varied the setting from a workshop scenario with costumed workmen to having the singers simply stand at podiums on the stage dressed in tuxedos. However, there were Masons who had been in the Scottish Rite for decades who had never seen it presented.

Now the degree has been rewritten and the workmen are American lumberjacks working in the Pacific Northwest. The songs are new words sung to familiar tunes ("I've Been Working on the Railroad," "We Gather Together," "Morning Has Broken," etc.) and the audience is encouraged to join in. About halfway through the degree we are given a break where beer and pretzels are served! It's a delightful experience and one that is rapidly proving popular in the Northern Masonic Jurisdiction.

Fig. 30 Cover of a brochure announcing a presentation of the 22nd degree, September, 2014 in Chicago by the Massachusetts Consistory. Courtesy of the Massachusetts Consistory, Valley of Boston, MA.

The 22nd Degree
of the Southern Jurisdiction:

KNIGHT OF THE ROYAL AXE,
OR PRINCE OF LEBANUS

A very similar story (probably Pike's original version) but here the candidate is a Prussian Knight, which Pike evidently preferred to a Noachite (Pike seems to have liked things Germanic). The ritual goes on as in the Northern version, except that another scene, an ornate lodge-like Council Room draped in red, is included along with the humble carpenters' workshop. The lessons are that we are to respect labor for its own sake, that we are to do the best work that we are capable of and that work is the mission of man.[2]

23rd Degree:

KNIGHT OF VALOR
(The Four Immortal Chaplains)

The Stage Drama

The degree's drama recounts a famous true story from World War II. At 1:00 AM on February 3, 1943, the German submarine *U-223* torpedoed the U.S. Army troopship *Dorchester*, carrying 900 men, off the coast of Greenland. The stricken ship, flooded with oil and ammonia fumes, began to sink rapidly. There were four Army chaplains on board: A Catholic priest, John Washington; a Jewish rabbi, Alexander Goode and two Protestant ministers, George Fox and Clarke Poling. All four chaplains immediately ran out on deck and began handing out life jackets, trying to calm the young, panicking soldiers. When the supply of life jackets ran out, the four chaplains, without hesitation, removed their own and gave them to the soldiers. They did not inquire into the religious beliefs of the recipients.

Approximately 18 minutes after the explosion, the ship went down. The four chaplains were last seen standing arm-in-arm on the deck of the ship, each praying for the men. Almost 700 servicemen died that night; it was the third largest American loss at sea during World War II. The Coast Guard Cutter *Tampa* escorted the other ships in the convoy safely to Greenland. The cutters *Comanche* and *Escanaba* disobeyed orders to begin searching for the German U-Boat and instead stayed in the area and managed to rescue 230 men from the frigid waters.

The degree's stage drama follows the background events outlined above with some fictionalized characters and dialogue thrown in.

This dramatic story demonstrates that those with faith in God and love for their fellow man will make great sacrifices, even giving up their lives, to help others.

Historical Background

Anyone who grew up in America during the 1950s knows the story of the Four Immortal Chaplains (Plate 17), as everyone called them at the time. Their pictures were everywhere – on posters, in comic books and on television public service messages. Everyone regarded them as real American heroes and my friends and I were especially proud that one of them was a Catholic priest. I cannot think of a better "Americana" ritual intended to illustrate Masonic virtues than their story of self-sacrifice; talk about practicing what you preach!

In the degree's story, a boyhood friend of Father Washington, the Catholic priest, meets him in a park in Newark, New Jersey, and refers to him as "a Prince of Peace." As a young Irish boy growing up in the Ewing Township farmland outside of Trenton, I can't recall that any of us ever used that epithet for a priest. I'm pretty sure that the title was reserved for Jesus Christ. Maybe they do things differently in Newark.

It was Father Washington who was chiefly responsible for the camaraderie among men of different faiths aboard ship. It began when Rabbi Goode wanted to conduct Friday evening Sabbath services in the mess hall. It seems that every evening, after the mess hall crew cleaned up after chow, the men would use the tables for poker games. They didn't want to give up their games and they gave the rabbi a hard time. Father Washington, a tough Jersey boy whom the men respected, spoke to them.[1]

He said something like: "Look, guys, if Rabbi Goode needs the mess hall to have a service once a week, he's gonna have it! You can do without a poker game one night out of seven. Anybody who doesn't like that can see me about it! The government sent us out here to fight the *Germans*, not each other. So knock off giving the Rabbi lip and let's get *gung ho* [a common military exhortation in WWII that my father, who was in the Navy during the war, told me had come from a Chinese expression meaning *pull together*]."

After that the crew stopped bickering among themselves and worked as a unit, the way the Navy intended them to work, and Rabbi Goode conducted Sabbath services for his men.

One point: I do find it strange that the men on the *Dorchester* all went back to bed after the watch sounded General Quarters. General Quarters is a serious state of affairs on board a ship in wartime, especially if a torpedo attack is imminent. The ship was under General Quarters for an hour or so before the attack. Every man on board should have had his life jacket on and been ready for combat maneuvers, including the exercise of Abandon Ship. Apparently this was not done, as the torpedo strike is said to have aroused the men from their sleep.

The 23rd Degree
of the Southern Jurisdiction:

CHIEF OF THE TABERNACLE

The Southern Jurisdiction has the same name as our former 23rd degree but a different story. In the SJ, the ritual recounts the story in Chapter 16 of the Book of Numbers. Moses had declared that only descendents of his brother Aaron can be true priests and offer sacrifices before the Tabernacle. Three Levites, Korah, Dathan and Abairam, rebel against Moses' restriction. As punishment for their rebellion, the three Levites and all their "possessions" (that is, their innocent wives and children) are swallowed up by a seismic fissure that opens up under their tents (Numbers 16: 31-33). During the ritual, a candidate is given the first (lowest) degree of the Mysteries of the Jewish priesthood. The degree teaches that simple faith is better than vain philosophy and that a society's concept of its deity is consistent with its development (a concept that I discussed earlier in this book; see The Search for God). Pike was pointing out that the Hebrews were in a process of transformation from perceiving Yahweh as a vengeful, merciless Indo-European war god to the beneficent and loving universal God of Masonry. A rather odd choice of fables to illustrate that particular point, I must say. I hope the rebels' innocent families appreciated this coming transformation as the fissure closed in on them. Too bad for them that the transformation didn't come a few days sooner.[2]

24th Degree:

BROTHER OF THE FOREST

(The American Indian Degree)

The Stage Drama

The time is some point during "the late 1700s," several years after the French and Indian War but before the end of the Revolution. An Indian has petitioned a blue lodge somewhere in New England for membership by initiation. The story's action moves between two scenes: the small blue lodge and a clearing somewhere in a forest. Since the setting is given as "Colonial," it must mean that the story takes place before the Treaty of Paris in 1783 when America ceased to be a colony of Great Britain.

The lodge brothers disagree over the propriety of allowing an American Indian, a Cherokee, to join their lodge. During the French and Indian War, Indians had captured and then released the (biological) brother of one of the members. The brother in the lodge now considers the Indians to be Red Devils.

In the forest clearing six Indians, all of different tribes, debate the pros and cons of the white man. Some of the Indians consider all Caucasians to be White Devils. Eventually the racial problems are resolved in a spirit of tolerance and brotherhood.

Universal brotherhood is the particular message of the Twenty-fourth Degree. This degree shows that the pursuit and acquisition of knowledge often can dispel the fears created by ignorance and prejudice and that a Scottish Rite Mason should not judge a man by his race or by anything except his own acts.

Historical Background

At the time of this story – the late 1770s – the three principal races living in the American colonies were European Caucasians, African Negroes and American Indians. This story illustrates the moral lesson that Freemasonry should not take a candidate's racial or ethnic background into account when considering him for membership.

The home range of a Cherokee Indian at the time of this story would have been the southern Appalachian Mountains, in a region comprising parts of North and South Carolina, Georgia, Alabama, southwest Virginia, and the Cumberland Basin of Tennessee. The Cherokees were heavily involved in the French and Indian War, fighting mostly on the British side after signing a treaty with them in 1754. But they always retained a fondness for the French, who had treated them more diplomatically than the haughty, racist British officers and soldiers.

Fig 31 A war party of Cherokee Indians stalking a French patrol during the French & Indian War. ©iStock.

Even so, the odds of finding a Cherokee brave in Colonial New England would have been somewhat slim. Even higher would have been the odds against finding six Indians, each from a different tribe and probably representing different nonconfederated nations sitting peacefully around the same campfire.

Anyway, if the lodge brothers in the New England town had wanted to make a show of universal brotherhood they didn't have to wait for the unlikely advent of a Cherokee Indian. There were plenty of black Africans near at hand, and not all of them were slaves. Many of them were free men, owned property and would serve in Colonial militias during the Revolution. Purely on the basis of race, however, they were excluded by the Grand

Lodge of Massachusetts (and, as America grew in the coming decades, all Grand Lodges in all states) and had to form their own "African" or "Prince Hall" lodges.

The original Prince Hall was a mulato said to have been born on the Caribbean island of Barbados on September 12, in either 1735 or 1748, of a white father and a freed black mother.[2] His father taught him leather working but Hall could see that there was no future for a black tradesman in the West Indies. He boarded an American trading vessel bound for Boston and worked his passage to America. He arrived in Boston in 1765 and may have earned his living as a schoolteacher for black children. Eventually he became a freeholder, meaning he owned property and could have served as a minor official in the county government. In 1774 he converted to the Methodist denomination and was ordained a preacher.

In March of 1775 he and fourteen other black men were initiated as Masons into the military lodge (Lodge No. 441, working under the Irish Constitution) of a British infantry regiment, the 28th Regiment of Foot. They paid a total of 25 guineas (around $266 each in today's money) for initiation into all three blue lodge degrees. When the Revolution forced the regiment to evacuate Boston in 1776, it granted Hall and his brothers a charter to meet as African Lodge #1 but did not authorize them to work any ritual or confer degrees.

Fig 32 Prince Hall. Artist and date unknown. Grand Lodge of British Columbia and Yukon.

The same year he was initiated Prince Hall petitioned to join the Continental Army but was refused. In June the petition was sent to Congress where it was ignored. Finally, Gen. Washington accepted it with the proviso that Hall serve with a Negro regiment in the Army at Cambridge, MA. Finally, in February of 1776, after proving himself to his officers, he was allowed to enlist in the Continental Army proper. He served Washington well and got him to approve the recruitment of free Negroes into the Army. He succeeded to the extent that five thousand volunteered for service.

In 1782, after his stint in the Army, Hall returned to Boston and married Miss Phoebe Baker, his second wife. His first wife, Sarah Richery, had died in 1769 at the age of 24. The municipal records of the City of Boston claimed that he married three more times after Phoebe.

Finally, in 1784, African Lodge #1 was able to secure a more liberal charter from the Grand Lodge of England and became African Lodge #459, a fully functional, fully sanctioned Masonic blue lodge. All Prince Hall African-American lodges are descended from this lodge, which has left a proud history of black Masonry in America. The African Grand Lodge was formed on June 24, 1791, and Prince Hall was elected Grand Master.

Hall died in December of 1807 after a month-long bout with pneumonia. He is buried on Copp's Hill, Boston's second oldest cemetery and the Prince Hall Masons of Massachusetts erected a memorial to him there. Besides Masonry, Hall is remembered for his advocacy of education for black children and for equality under the law for all black people. Today Prince Hall Masonry is represented by Districts in the United States, Canada, the United Kingdom, Europe and the Middle East.

Beginning in 1784, all "regular" (white) Masonic Lodges did not consider themselves to be in fraternal relations with the Prince Hall lodges. This condition of Masonic apartheid persisted until the latter part of the 20th century when American blue lodges finally erased the racial barriers.

The 24th Degree of the Southern Jurisdiction:

PRINCE OF THE TABERNACLE

The Southern Jurisdiction has retained Pike's 1857 ritual. A candidate is tested by the four elements and enters a dark chamber where he hears prayers of mourning and lamentation for various pagan deities (Osiris, Mithra, etc.). He is shown the body of the murdered Egyptian god Osiris and is told to bring him back to life. After two failed attempts, he is able to raise Osiris up out of his grave using a strong grip. The candidate is made a Prince of the Tabernacle and, in a long lecture, is taught that all good men, regardless of race, are welcome in Masonry (the same lesson of the NMJ's 24th Degree) and that all religions have something good to offer to men (the lesson of the NMJ's present 9th Degree). The degree teaches that the soul is immortal, that there is power in having faith in the promises of Deity and that there is One True God who is pure, absolute intellect and is the ground of all existence.[3]

25th Degree:

MASTER OF ACHIEVEMENT
(Benjamin Franklin Degree)

The Stage Drama

The time is January 17, 1788. The place is a Blue lodge somewhere in or around Philadelphia. Brother Benjamin Franklin is celebrating his 82nd birthday and the lodge has convened to accord him the many honors he has earned in his extraordinary life. In the degree's story, Franklin has managed, through trickery, to get a Defense and Militia Bill for the city of Philadelphia passed over Quaker opposition. He discusses the famous 13 virtues he had been attempting all his life to cultivate and the honors his Masonic brothers bestow upon him for his role in getting the Constitution ratified is mentioned.

This degree teaches that no man is perfect and that all men err. If, however, a man maintains a firm and unshakable reliance on God's grace, he can and will regain his direction, his humility, his faith and his goals. One of the symbols of a symbolic (blue) Masonic lodge is the beehive. The beehive is a symbol of industry and recommends the practice of that virtue to each candidate in search of Masonic Light. It teaches us that, in addition to being intelligent creatures, we must be industrious scholars, always adding to the common stock of knowledge and understanding. The 25th degree of Scottish Rite Freemasonry, NMJ, further develops the virtue of industriousness.

Historical Background

Benjamin Franklin (Plate 18) has become known to history as the First Civilized American. His pamphlet, *Poor Richard's Almanack*, was read and quoted by intellectuals and socialites throughout Europe and is said to have been the most widely read book in the Colonies next to the Bible. He had an incalculable amount of influence on the shaping of the American character, much of which is still in evidence today. He was a thinker of immense practicality and gave mankind such useful inventions as bifocal glasses, the lightening rod, the Franklin stove, a national Post Office and a working knowledge of electricity. Without the advantage of a formal education, Franklin was arguably the first world class scientist born and raised in the American colonies. He was also an ardent Freemason.[1]

The ritual of this degree is based on the format of a television show, popular in the 1970s and 80s, called "This is Your Life." In the show, the Master of Ceremonies brings a person in the audience up on stage. He then reintroduces him to various people who have influenced his life, most of whom he has not seen in years.

The incident in the first skit, in which Franklin tricks the Quakers, is a fictionalized version of an actual incident that Franklin recorded in his autobiography. According to Franklin's account, he and his friends were trying to establish a lottery to raise funds for an artillery battery for the defense of Philadelphia. The Quakers, who made up the voting majority in the Philadelphia Assembly, opposed both lotteries (gambling) and artillery batteries (warfare). Just before the Assembly was to convene for the vote, Franklin was having dinner with his friends in a tavern. Two Quaker leaders approached Franklin and discussed the attitudes of their co-religionists. Most of the voting Quakers of Philadelphia were secretly in favor of defensive warfare as long as they did not have to participate in it. So they made a gentleman's agreement in which most of the Quakers would not show up for the vote and Franklin's motion would carry the day. The bill alluded to in the degree may have been the Defense Bill that the Assembly passed on November 25, 1755. This bill allocated the amount of 60,000 pounds for the raising of a militia for defense against Indians.

In 1757 Franklin was sent to London as a kind of minister without portfolio for the Pennsylvania Assembly to see if he could use his charm and diplomatic skills on Parliament and get them to issue Pennsylvania a charter as a Royal Colony rather than a mere province. He quickly established his residence, a boarding house at 36 Craven Street, as an unofficial embassy where he held long consultations with British Prime Minister William Pitt. The subject of their talks, a full nineteen years before the Revolution, was the deteriorating condition of the relationships between the colonies and Whitehall, the headquarters of British government.

While in London Franklin's ever-active intellect was operating at its usual velocity. Every 18th-century gentleman knew that if he rubbed his finger around the inside of the moistened rim of a crystal wineglass the glass would vibrate and produce a lingering musical tone in the air. Seeing street musicians performing complete melodies this way with a table of crystal glasses filled to various depths, Franklin got an idea. He invented a pedal-operated contraption that rotated a series of different size crystal bowls, running their rims through a shallow water-filled trough. The musician used his foot to turn the rod that ran through the center of the bowls and used the fingers of both hands to play haunting melodies. Franklin called the instrument a glass harmonica and it became very popular in Europe and the American colonies. No less a composer than Mozart wrote pieces for it.

Franklin also developed the lightning rod in London and made several working models, one of which still protects the dome of St. Paul's cathedral.

Given Franklin's towering intellect, his extensive reading and the preeminent position he has in Masonry today, a brief discussion of his religious beliefs might be of interest. Franklin had been raised a Presbyterian but found neither comfort nor reason in any Christian dogma, Calvinistic or otherwise. Then, while quite young, he finally came across in his reading a religious philosophy to which he could give credence. In his autobiography he says:

> But I was scarce fifteen when… I began to doubt of the Revelation [Bible] itself. Some books against deism fell into my hands… they wrought an effect on me quite contrary to what was intended by them. For the arguments of the deists, which were quoted to be refuted, appeared to me much stronger than the refutations; in short I soon became a thorough deist.

Franklin soon saw, however, that pure deism, while intellectually satisfying, had no moral or behavioral tenets. It was therefore not very useful for improving one's life, an obsession of his. So he devised a modified version of deism to which he adhered for the rest of his life. Franklin's deism included pragmatic self-help exercises, moral principles and the pursuit of what he called "virtue."

He also decided that belief in what he called "One supreme most perfect being" was a useful tool for guiding the activities of life. His conception of God was that of a remote being, perfect and all-powerful but uninterested in human affairs. In spite of this, Franklin believed that personal prayer was an effective means of obtaining God's help when needed. So he composed a liturgy of his own deist prayers for all occasions.

Beyond this, Franklin did not subscribe to any sectarian dogma, revelation, scripture, or the arguments of any clergyman. He believed that his God was far above the influence of human praise or flattery. Franklin had no interest in spirituality, meditation, commandments handed down from on high or the life and teachings of Jesus of Nazareth. His most deeply held belief was that "the most acceptable service of God was doing good to man."

This would be a good juncture to point out that, besides Franklin, many of the other revolutionary leaders and Founding Fathers of our country – including Washington, Jefferson, Ethan Allen, John Adams, Thomas Paine, James Madison and James Monroe were all deists. The deity they worshipped was neither Yahweh of the Old Testament nor was it Jesus of Nazareth; it was an all-seeing, all-knowing, all-powerful astronomical entity in charge of everything whom they referred to as the Great Architect of the Universe (Washington), Governor of the Universe (Jefferson), Sovereign Dispenser of Life and

Health or The Supreme Disposer of All Events.[2] None of these men believed in the Scriptures, revelation, petitionary prayer or the divinity of Jesus Christ.

For instance, Arnold Friberg's famous painting, *The Prayer at Valley Forge*, that shows Washington kneeling in the snow, is a piece of sentimental kitsch. There are two reasons. First and most importantly, all his adult life Washington resolutely refused to kneel, even in the many different churches he occasionally visited (where he also refused to take Communion and frequently walked out in the middle of the services).[3] When asked by a group of ministers if he believed in Jesus Christ and the Bible, he would only smile and say nothing. His own minister, Ashbel Green, communicated to Jefferson that Washington was not a Christian but a Deist.[4] Jefferson, himself a Deist, laughed.

Secondly, Washington, although he was a brave soldier and a dedicated officer, was also said to be a fop who would never soil his expensive uniform by kneeling in snow. If he ever needed a favor from the entity he called the Great Architect of the Universe he asked for it standing up.

Franklin acknowledged that God probably manifested himself to each person according to that person's ability to comprehend his presence. Consequently, he acknowledged that ordinary organized religion suited the needs of most people. Franklin therefore supported a local Philadelphia church run by the Presbyterian minister Jedediah Andrews. He also admired the preaching style of a Mr. Whitefield, an itinerant preacher from Ireland. Franklin, an inveterate student of human behavior, was fascinated with Whitefield's ability to mesmerize his audience even as he screamed at them that they were all "half-beasts and half-devils!" They don't make preachers like that anymore.

The 25th Degree
of the Southern Jurisdiction:

KNIGHT OF THE BRAZEN SERPENT

The Southern version of the 25th degree has the same name as the Northern Jurisdiction's original 25th but a completely different story, Islamic in nature. In its modern revised version the story of Moses and the snakes has been eliminated. I can't do the degree's story justice in a paragraph but suffice it to say that the plot involves a candidate being initiated into the mysteries of the Sufi, an esoteric Islamic sect. He is taught that truth is elusive and, although present, is often not recognized. He is also taught that man is a reflection of the Divine and should not weary God with petitions.[5]

26th Degree:

FRIEND AND BROTHER ETERNAL
(The Battle of Gettysburg Degree)

The Stage Drama

The time is July 3, 1863. The place is Gettysburg, Pennsylvania. The degree tells the story of two Civil War generals, one – Winfield S. Hancock – a Yankee, and the other – Lewis A. Armistead – a Confederate. The two had been friends and Masonic brothers in the U.S. Army before the war. The play traces their friendship from service together in California, their dismay when Fort Sumter is fired upon and their adventures during the Battle of Gettysburg (July 1-3, 1863).

The play's script is well researched and accurately portrays the Confederate officers' misgivings about Lee's proposed assault, now known as Pickett's Charge, on the fortified Union "fishhook" line. The charge, which went wrong from the beginning, was the final straw in a series of misfortunes that had plagued the South for two days and ended in Lee's withdrawal from Pennsylvania.

Confederate Brig. General Lewis A. Armistead and Union Major General Winfield S. Hancock were both wounded at the Battle of Gettysburg while taking part in Pickett's Charge on July 3, 1863. The Armistead-Hancock Masonic Memorial stone in the National Cemetery at Gettysburg, the names of the two friends joined by a square and compass, is an eternal testament to the enduring power of good will and brotherly love.

The Twenty-sixth Degree teaches us that partisan strife, even when it descends to the level of armed conflict, does not dissolve our obligations as Masons. There is a second lesson to be learned. The virtues of brotherhood give rise to the practice of good citizenship.

Historical Background

It is sundown on July 1, 1863 in the Confederate camp near Gettysburg, a small town near the southern border of Pennsylvania. General Robert E. Lee, commander of the Army of Northern Virginia, paces back and forth in front of his tent. He faces a critical decision. He had that day successfully carried out what most of his colleagues thought was an impossibly quixotic mission: he had invaded a northern state and, on northern soil, won an unquestionable tactical victory. And he had won this victory over the North's much larger Army of the Potomac, ironically commanded by an old Army buddy of his, General George G. Meade.

Such a monumental victory ought to have satisfied Lee, but he wanted more. He was undecided. The problem was one of logistics: in his forced march north, he had outrun his supply lines and did not have sufficient ammunition or supplies for a prolonged defensive stand against Meade's army. On the other hand, his men were exhausted and a withdrawal would expose his flank to repeated attack by the Union Army's superior numbers and their unending stream of supplies coming down the Baltimore Pike. He decided to stay put and hammer the Union regiments to keep them from concentrating their numbers against him. Perhaps, if his luck held, his supply lines would catch up to him and he could mount a proper campaign.

This was Lee's second attempted invasion of the north. His first, begun eleven months earlier, had ended on September 17 when Union forces under the command of Major General George McClellan had surprised Lee's forces on their northward march through Sharpsburg, Maryland. This conflict, known as the Battle of Antietam Creek, resulted in the bloodiest single day in American military history. Due to McClellan's incompetence, the battle ended in a draw rather than a Union victory; nevertheless, Lee's staggering losses forced him to withdraw and march his men back to Virginia, frustrating his plans to penetrate the north.

Then, in May of 1863, Lee went to Richmond and presented Confederate President Jefferson Davis and his cabinet with yet another proposed invasion of the enemy's homeland. The citizens of Virginia, when they had heard of the 8,772 wounded and 1,546 dead at Antietam, had been outraged. They accused Lee of sacrificing their sons and husbands for his own vainglory. Davis' cabinet members, after being mercilessly pilloried by the Richmond press, were in no mood for another nightmare. But Lee argued for three days, using every bit of his authoritative personality. The cabinet finally gave in and approved his plans by a vote of 5 to 1.[1]

Now Lee knew that his back was against the wall. If he failed again, there would never be another chance for a northern incursion. If the South could not take the war into the North's own territory it would become nothing more than an immobile, isolated fortress, a helpless target under relentless siege by an unlimited power. This could only end in the South's surrender and the end of the Confederacy, which Lee found unendurable. Another southern withdrawal was not an option. But why should he worry? So far the Confederates looked as if they were going to win decisively on the next day and resume their march on to Harrisburg, the undefended Pennsylvania state capitol only 40 miles away.

That morning the battle had gotten off to a jarring start. As he was riding towards Gettysburg through the small Pennsylvania village of Cashtown, Lee had heard the distant rattle of musketry ahead that told him that fighting was starting prematurely, against his orders. Who, Lee wondered, had disobeyed his express commands to conceal the Southern presence until he, Lee, gave the word?

The disobedience was the work of Major General Henry Heth (pronounced "Heeth"), a division commander in the Third Corps serving under Gen. A. P. Hill. Heth was acting against Lee's strongly worded orders that no engagement with the Yankees was to begin until the widely scattered Army of Northern Virginia was sufficiently concentrated for battle. Ignoring orders, Heth had deliberately led his 7,000-man infantry division into Gettysburg hoping to smoke out a smaller Northern unit that would provide him with an easy victory.[2] He succeeded in locating the Yankees; Lt. Marcellus E. Jones of the 8th Illinois fired the first shot of the battle at a platoon of Heth's troops. But instead of snagging a victory, Heth's division was routed by Reynolds' Iron Brigade and Heth only succeeded in alerting the Union Army to the Confederate presence, something they had not expected so soon. Reynolds was killed a few hours later leading his brigade on a reconnaissance mission into the town. He was hit by the first artillery shell fired in the battle by Marye's battery of Pegram's battalion of the Army of Northern Virginia. This served to further alert the Yankees; until then they hadn't known that the Rebels had any artillery in the town.

Lee, infuriated, was set to chew Heth out to within an inch of his life when they met an hour later on the Cashtown Road atop Herr Ridge. But Heth and his staff officers were ready and quickly pointed out that the Confederate regiments were now perfectly set up to carry the day with a few well-led charges over easy ground.[3] Lee thought about it and viewed the battlefield with his binoculars. Sure enough, he could see that one of his generals, Jubal Early, had arrived and his division was poised to cut through the Union's XI Corps's overextended line while another general, Ambrose Hill, newly-appointed leader of the Army of Northern Virginia's III Corps, would attack the Yankee line from the other side. Hill was easily visible in his bright red "battle shirt" that he always wore in the field to show his contempt for Union marksmanship. Lee, mollified, ordered Heth to join with Penderson's division and attack immediately.[4] Things seemed to be looking good for a Confederate victory, after all.

But the first day's gains would prove to be elusive. On the next day, July 2, the battle started to turn sour for the South with events seeming to conspire against a southern victory. A series of strategic setbacks rattled Lee's nerves as he helplessly watched Union advances reverse his previous gains.

Exactly two months before, at the Battle of Chancellorsville, Lee had lost his most loyal and brilliant general to "friendly" fire. Confederate pickets mistakenly shot General Thomas "Stonewall" Jackson as he was returning at night from a reconnaissance patrol. He died eight days later. As Jackson lay dying, Lee, in all sincerity, wrote to him, "Could I have directed events, I would have chosen for the good of the country to have been disabled in your stead."[5]

Lee's gruff second-in-command, Gen. James Longstreet, was no Stonewall Jackson. He was a reluctant recalcitrant subordinate and was not shy about showing his feelings. He had arrived at Gettysburg on July 1 almost a day late and far ahead of his own troops, rendering him useless to implement Lee's plans. Lee who, under normal circumstances was close friends with Longstreet, tolerated Longstreet's insubordination on the battlefield and tried his best to devise an affectionate nickname for him, but all he could come up with was "My Old War Horse," a sobriquet perhaps open to interpretation.[6]

Longstreet sized up the battlefield situation, then forcefully and undiplomatically promoted his desire to lead an immediate movement around the Union's left flank. He thought it would force Meade into ordering what Longstreet saw as doomed attacks on heavily fortified Confederate positions. Lee, who considered the plan unworkable, refused to listen and Longstreet was mortified.

Worse was to come. Before dawn the next day, July 2, Lee is said to have ordered Longstreet to attack the Union's left flank at sunrise to support Ewell's assault on the right. Longstreet is accused of insubordinately delaying his attack by insisting on waiting for Law's brigade to arrive on the field before he would advance. This delayed his attack, which Lee is said to have planned to take place at sunrise, until noon.[7]

In fairness, we should know that the accusations of Longstreet's insubordination at this and other junctures of the battle were not made public until seven years later, after Lee's death in 1870. The charges were largely the work of two other Confederate generals, Jubal Early and William "Parson" Pendleton, both of whom were themselves accused of major blunders that contributed to the Southern loss of the battle. Some historians, particularly Glenn Tucker, have accused Early and Pendleton of inventing Lee's "sunrise attack" orders (for which no evidence exists) out of whole cloth while trying to make Longstreet a scapegoat to cover their own incompetence. What is true is that Lee and Longstreet disagreed hugely over both tactics and strategy at Gettysburg and that Longstreet's positions often made more sense than Lee's.[8]

Here we must acknowledge that Lee was not the battlefield genius that tradition has made of him. He never held war councils in which all of his officers could synchronize and coordinate their actions to maximize their efforts; many attacks and skirmishes did not occur on time and were needlessly duplicated with enormous loss of equipment and personnel. Also, Lee's "gentlemanly" upbringing influenced him to make his orders far too broad and vague, allowing his generals too much latitude to insert their own ideas and opinions into the operations to the extent that few of his officers wound up operating on the same page. Much of his early success in the war was due to the almost comically rampant incompetence of the Union generals he had the good fortune to oppose on the battlefield. These experiences generated his complete contempt for Union military leadership and led him into overconfident reckless actions like the frontal assaults for which he became famous instead of more cautious flank attacks.

Whatever the case, the "sunrise" attack failed and the Confederates lost both Little Round Top and Big Round Top, two hills that constituted valuable high ground. These were strategic positions that could have supported a large amount of Confederate artillery. Now they would hold Union cannon instead.

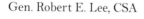

Gen. Robert E. Lee, CSA   Gen. James Longstreet, CSA
Fig. 33 ©iStock.

Ultimately, the Confederacy lost three valuable strategic items: Time, territory and men. This loss would be painfully evident on the following day and would cause future military historians (probably influenced by Early's and Pendleton's accusations) to place much of the blame for the battle's outcome on Longstreet's supposed insubordination, an attitude that has persisted up to the present day.

Next, Longstreet ordered Brigadier General William Barksdale to lead a spearheading charge to support a major Confederate assault on the Peach Orchard, a heavily defended

Union position. Instead of carefully advancing in a planned assault, Barksdale mounted his horse and, waving his sword around his head with his long grey hair flying in the wind, led his Mississippi Brigade in a glorious but reckless bayonet charge against the impregnable Union breastworks. The ill-conceived charge failed; Barksdale was killed and his ranks were torn to shreds by canister shot and rifle fire. The Confederate assault failed and the Peach Orchard, an important position, remained in the possession of the North.[9]

The 15th Alabama Infantry Regiment served alongside Gen. Law's Brigade in Hood's Division. Hood ordered the 15th Alabama under Col. William Oates to take the Union-held hill, Little Round Top, which Longstreet's delay had lost. This action, if successful, would expose the Union's left flank to artillery fire. The hill was defended by the 20th Maine Volunteers under the command of their fearless young Colonel, Joshua Lawrence Chamberlain. His brigade commander, Col. Strong Vincent, had ordered Chamberlain to "hold this ground at all costs!" Five times the 15th Alabama charged up the hill and five times the Union lines held firm and shot the Confederate companies to pieces.[10]

By 7:00 that evening 119 of the 358 Mainers had fallen. With one-third of his men down and ammunition running low, Chamberlain devised a new tactic to meet the anticipated sixth assault. He ordered his men, when they heard the Confederate buglers sound the charge, to leave their positions and themselves charge down the hill to meet the rebels half-way. The Mainers had to execute the charge almost entirely with bayonets because they had run out of ammunition. The unexpected onslaught caught the Alabamians by surprise and they fled, as Oates himself would later testify, "like a herd of wild cattle." Little Round Top, an important strategic point, remained in Union hands and the left flank of the Army of the Potomac, Lee's principal target for the day, remained secure.[11]

After the war, Chamberlain served four times as Governor of Maine and later as president of his *alma mater*, Bowdin College in Brunswick, Maine. He finally died in 1914 of the severe wounds he had received 50 years earlier at the 2nd Battle of Petersburg in 1864, the last Civil War veteran to die from battlefield injuries. Oates also survived the war and went on to become Governor of Alabama. He later served as a brigadier general in the United States Army and fought in the Spanish-American War.

Around sundown, General James Ewell Brown ("JEB") Stuart, Lee's cavalry commander who had been missing from action for a week, finally appeared in camp. He had taken his cavalry units away from Lee's main army days before and had disappeared, not reporting anything back to Lee in all that time. In those days, the cavalry, "the eyes and ears of the army," was one of only two long-range reconnaissance forces available to the infantry. Besides cavalry, Union troops used tethered hot-air balloons with baskets capable of carrying two men with long-range binoculars to over a thousand feet into the air, well out of Confederate rifle range. They could telegraph their observations of enemy troop movements to signal corpsmen on the ground. Lee sometimes used balloons but thought they hindered the army's mobility and preferred to rely on fast-moving cavalry.

With no information from Stuart's mobile units, Lee's army had had to grope its way into Gettysburg and through two days of intense combat "like a blindfolded giant."[12] Lee knew that, with Stuart's absence and no intelligence coming in, every troop movement he ordered would be a gamble. Riding through Cashtown on the way to the battlefield, he had complained to the officer riding beside him, "I cannot think what has become of Stuart; I ought to have heard from him long before now." Lee was dangerously in the dark and he remained that way for the first two days of the battle. When Stuart finally reported in, the usually congenial Lee greeted him with a glare and a frosty: "Well, General Stuart, I see you are here at last."[13]

Fig. 34 Gen. George Armstrong Custer at the Little Big Horn. ©iStock.

By the morning of the third day, July 3, the usually calm and collected Lee was getting desperate. To add to his military problems he was physically ill, weakened by days of field diarrhea and by a heart attack he had suffered four months before. He could sense that his defensive positions were crumbling and he knew that he needed a miracle to recover the victory that was slipping away from him. He needed to break the North's "fishhook" line that Union forces had established only a few hours earlier. They had overrun and held Culp's Hill, an action that many military historians would later recognize as the most significant event of the three-day battle.

Lee's first action on the third morning of the battle was to send the recently arrived and contrite Stuart to take his mounted forces around the heavily defended center of the fishhook line to attack the Union forces and supply lines from the rear. Lee's observers had spotted what they took to be a weak, poorly defended Union position on Cemetery Ridge. They could not see much in the way of field artillery defending the position. It looked to them as if a swift, massive infantry charge could break through the thin Yankee line and expose the Union rear. This would open the way for Lee to neutralize some Union hilltop artillery positions that were threatening his troop movements on the lower ground. This was the rationale for what became known as Picket's Charge, Lee's final roll of the dice.

Actually, "Pickett's Charge" is a misnomer on two counts. First, Longstreet was the officer in charge. George Pickett was one of three subordinate generals under Longstreet, Lee's senior corps commander who organized the action (as usual, against his better judgment) under Lee's orders. Also, the assault was technically not a charge because Pickett's men advanced in dressed ranks, shoulder to shoulder in lock step. A more accurate title would have been the "Pickett-Pettigrew Assault," since these were the only two brigades that actually reached the Union lines in any numbers. However, there is no denying that "Pickett's Charge" is a more colorful name and Pickett was a much more colorful character than either Longstreet or Pettigrew.

Pickett was every Southern lady's icon of a Confederate officer: courageous, handsome, dashing and aristocratic. He frequently rode up and down before his men waving his hat in his hand to show off his long brown hair that he wore down to his shoulders in oiled ringlets. In conscious imitation of Napoleon he wrote passionate love letters from the battlefield to the woman who would become his third wife, Sallie (LaSalle Corbell, a teenage Virginian beauty), who idolized him. At 38 years of age, he was the perfect officer to lead a doomed charge in support of a lost cause. Graduating last in his class at West Point, he had fought in the Mexican War (1846-1848), where he had distinguished himself by

Fig. 35 A contingent of Confederate cavalry led by Gen. JEB Stuart.
©iStock.

his impetuous daredevil bravery. He was a favorite of Longstreet, who admired him and advanced his military career.

Like many Southern men of the upper classes, Pickett regarded war in a romantic light as some kind of glorious adventure and expected his men to carry the day by sheer grit. He insisted that, to make a good appearance, they advance against the Union position marching in step and carrying their rifles at shoulder arms, as if on parade. They were forbidden to give the famous "Rebel yell" because Pickett thought it low-class and unseemly. Lew Armistead and James Kemper were two of Pickett's brigade commanders.

Lee decided that his generals needed a visible point of reference behind Union lines to center upon for the attack. He chose a group of tall trees known locally as Ziegler's Grove, sticking up from behind a stone wall on the north top of Cemetery Ridge and easily seen by the Confederates. (There was another, smaller copse of trees on Cemetery Ridge south of Ziegler's Grove, directly in front of Brig. General Alexander Webb's 106th Pennsylvania Infantry, that I believe may have also served as a landmark by the attackers. It can be seen as the "clump of trees on the right" in Edwin Forbes' painting of Pickett's Charge (Plate 19), made years after the war from sketches drawn on the battlefield.) What the Confederate observers could not see were the 7,000 Union troops concealed and waiting behind the stone wall.

The Confederate advance started late due either to some kind of miscommunication or, as was later charged, by further deliberate disobedience on the part of Gen. Longstreet. Longstreet – gruff, crude and sulking as usual – was temperamentally Lee's opposite. He had made it plain to his staff throughout the day that he strongly opposed Lee's strategy and thought Lee to be acting foolishly, which in some sense he was. Because of Longstreet's insubordinate delay of the previous day, Union artillery mounted on Little Round Top and Big Round Top could now prove fatal to the advance. Long-range Union artillery fire from deadly 10-pounder Parrott rifles – extremely accurate long-range cannons with rifled barrels – began to decimate Longstreet's forces even as they were forming up behind Seminary Ridge for the attack.

To make matters worse, a diversionary attack ordered by Lee on nearby, heavily defended Culp's Hill petered out before it could achieve its aim of distracting the Union forces on Cemetery Ridge.

A Confederate soldier who happened to be the rightful heir to Culp's Hill, Pvt. John Wesley Culp of the 2nd Virginia Infantry Division, died on the hill trying to take his family property back from the Yankees. A few years earlier Culp, a native of Gettysburg, had moved to Virginia and, when the Civil war broke out, enlisted in the 2nd Confederate Infantry Regiment under the command of Stonewall Jackson. When his companions recovered his body on Culp's Hill he was found to be carrying a love letter addressed to a young woman in Gettysburg, a Miss Mary Virginia "Ginnie" Wade. The letter had been given to him for safekeeping by a boyhood friend from Gettysburg, Johnston H. Skelly. Skelly was a Union soldier serving in the 87th Pennsylvania Regiment and Ginnie was his fiancée. Skelly died of his wounds from the Second Battle of Winchester where Culp had been captured and where Skelly, on his deathbed, gave him the letter. When Culp was later paroled he rejoined his regiment.[14]

Unfortunately, Miss Wade never got to read the last thoughts and endearments of her beloved. She was the only civilian killed in the battle. A stray bullet is said to have hit her while she was baking bread in her kitchen.

Meanwhile, JEB Stuart's attempt to circle his cavalry around behind Union lines was thwarted by the colorful figure of Brig. General George Armstrong Custer. At 23, Custer was the youngest flag-rank officer in the United States Army. He was a courageous, reckless leader who led his 7th Michigan Cavalry into combat by riding far out in front of the charge, waving his sword and shouting his battle-cry: "Come on, you Wolverines!" In those days, uniform regulations for flag-rank officers were lax and a general could wear whatever he wanted, as long as it looked military. (This laxity survived up until WW II when Gen. George Patton wore riding breeches and cavalry boots and carried a riding crop as if he were going to fight on horseback instead of in a tank.)

On that day Custer was wearing a uniform that he had himself designed and had ordered made especially to wear in battle. It was a tight-fitting European-style "Hussar's" suit of black velvet liberally ornamented with loops and curlicues of gold braid. He must have looked like a mounted toreador. Besides being the best cavalry officer in the Union Army Custer was also a grandstander, a gambler, a reformed drunkard and a showman. On the last day of his life, 13 years later, he would be wearing another outfit of his own design, a "Wild West" suit of tan fringed buckskin.

Custer believed heavily in his legendary luck and sometimes allowed this belief to influence his field tactics. His fellow officers often quipped: "I hope I'm not with Custer when his luck runs out!" Custer's favorite military tune was the Irish melody "Garry Owen" and, years later, his band was playing that tune as he and the 7th Cavalry rode into the Little Big Horn on the day his luck finally did run out.

But at Gettysburg on the 3rd of July, 1863, Custer's luck was operating in high gear. He had two horses shot out from under him and lost 219 men in 40 minutes of intense hand-to-hand fighting. Despite the ferocity of the engagement that upended colliding horses, crushing their own riders, Custer escaped without injury.[15]

Fig. 36 Statue of a Union soldier at Gettysburg holding a Spencer repeating rifle. ©iStock.

One reason for Custer's victory was that the soldiers of Brig. General David Greg's 5th Michigan Cavalry, equipped with brand-new Spencer repeating rifles, came to his aid. These lever-action rifles, their 7-round tubular magazines loaded with .56 caliber brass cartridges, could be fired at the rate of 14 rounds a minute and had an effective range of 700 yards. A mounted trooper in combat could easily reload one in the saddle.[16]

The Confederates, on the other hand, had to depend for in-the-saddle firepower on 1851 Colt Navy pistols.[17] These were .36 caliber percussion revolvers Colt had designed for the U.S. Navy to use in close-range shipboard action. While their dependability made them the most popular and widely used sidearm in the Civil War (Lee carried one; "Wild Bill" Hickok carried two) they were wildly inaccurate when fired one-handed from the back of a galloping horse, contained only six shots and were impossible to reload on horseback during combat. The only practical method of reloading in the saddle was to disassemble the pistol, remove the spent six-round cylinder and replace it with a fully loaded one from the trooper's pocket. The finely machined steel cylinders were expensive for the army to provide and heavy to carry so most troopers would only have one or two.

In the end, dash, courage and superior technology won the day. JEB Stuart and his "Invincibles" were forced to withdraw and the Union soldiers on Cemetery Ridge were left unmolested and able to give their full attention to Pickett's Charge.

At one o'clock in the afternoon, two Confederate cannon among the trees in the Peach Orchard fired a prearranged signal and the Southern artillery bombardment began. The artillery, perched on Seminary Ridge, was under the command of Colonel E. Porter Alexander,[18] a brilliant young officer in command of all the artillery in Longstreet's corps. He had up to 170 cannon at his command and he used them all in an hour-long bombardment that was the longest of the war, and even of the Western Hemisphere. It was certainly the loudest; contemporary newspapers reported that people in Harrisburg, 40 miles away, heard the noise of his guns. However, many of the Confederate fuses were defective and their shells did not explode. Also, Alexander's forward artillery observers overestimated the range by several hundred feet and most his shells landed harmlessly in the woods behind Union lines.

To Lee's surprise, the Confederate cannon were immediately answered by an even more intense bombardment from Union guns on Cemetery Hill and Cemetery Ridge. Where had all those Yankee guns come from? His observers hadn't seen them. Alexander's extensive artillery bombardment had almost no effect on the Union lines except to ready the defenders for the imminent attack.

General Meade, Commanding Officer of the Union forces at Gettysburg, had been expecting the Confederate assault all morning and his men were fully prepared to repulse it. Before the war, Meade and Lee had been close friends in the U. S. Army and Meade was the only Union general that Lee respected. Just three days prior to the battle he heard that Lincoln had chosen Meade to replace Gen. Joseph Hooker as Commanding Officer of the Army of the Potomac. The news upset the usually imperturbable Lee. He told his officer corps that morning that Meade "will commit no blunder on my front and, if I make one, he will make haste to take advantage of it."[19] He would soon see the truth of his own words.

After an hour of artillery dueling, the Confederate advance began with nine brigades totaling 12,500 men advancing in a mile-long line. From Seminary Ridge, they had to march across one mile of rolling open fields to reach the Union lines on Cemetery Ridge. The defending Union soldiers stared unbelievingly at the stately "charge" of Pickett's men. The Southerners were approaching at a walking pace in dressed ranks like cadets on review. The slow-moving Rebel units were under intense fire the entire time, both from flanking infantry units and from frontal artillery batteries. Some of the cannon fired canister shot. This was a cardboard tube stuffed with musket balls that turned the cannon into a giant shotgun. After one fusillade of canister from a line of cannon only a hundred yards away two entire Confederate battalions were said to have "disappeared." On that day Pickett lost between 60 and 80 percent of his men.

The advancing Confederates soon encountered an unexpected obstacle: the Emmitsburg Road. This was a sunken road flanked on each side by a long, split-rail fence. It ran from the northeast of the battlefield down to the Peach Orchard in the southwest, close to and directly in front of the Union position. From a distance, it had not looked as if it would present a problem; up close, it turned out to be a death trap for infantry advancing under fire. Heavy enfilades of Union rifle fire mowed the Confederates down as they took precious minutes to disassemble the split-rail fence. Those men who tried to save time by climbing over the fence were shot down like tin ducks in a shooting gallery. NCOs – sergeants and corporals – took over command from dead or wounded officers. Some men tried to take

Fig. 37 Bodies of dead Union sharpshooters on the crest of Little Round Top. ©iStock

cover from the unrelenting Union fire by lying flat and using the sunken road as a makeshift trench, but the Union soldiers were mostly firing down from elevated positions and the slight depression of the road gave little shelter. A trained Union soldier lying prone could reload and fire his rifle four times a minute and the Confederates found themselves trapped under an unrelenting shower of .58-caliber Minié bullets.[20]

Trimble's and Pettigrew's brigades, on the northern part of the Confederate line, finally crossed the road and advanced directly forward a short distance to the Union lines. But Pickett's and Anderson's men, making up the southern half of the line, had to first cross the deadly road and then advance a longer distance north under heavy fire. They also had to endure hand-to-hand combat from George J. Stannard's 2nd Vermont Infantry brigade, the unit that anchored the south end of the Union's fishhook line.

Lew Armistead's brigade got further into the Union position than any of the others. The Union forces concealed behind the stone wall on Cemetery Ridge poured volley after volley into his ranks. Armistead made it to the top of the ridge and straddled the stone wall, twirled his hat on the point of his sword and shouted "Give 'em the steel, boys!" But, despite their use of bayonets and clubbed muskets, his men were quickly repulsed by a Union counterattack. Armistead's units suffered more than 50% casualties.[21]

Armistead himself, just after crossing the wall, yelled at his men to seize some abandoned Union cannons and turn them on the enemy. Trying to push one of the big guns around, he was shot three times. As he went down, he gave a Masonic sign asking for assistance. A fellow Mason, Captain Henry H. Bingham, a Union officer who would later serve in Congress, came to Armistead's assistance and offered help. Bingham informed Armistead that his old friend, the Union general Hancock, had also been wounded. The news crushed the weakened Armistead. Although his wounds were at first thought to be minor, his condition deteriorated rapidly, probably from dehydration and heat shock. Armistead died two days later on July 5, 1863 in the Union Army's 11th Corps Field Hospital, near the George Spangler Farm.

Fig. 38 Gen. Louis Armstead, CSA, leading the attack on the fortified Union "fishook Line" at Gettysburg on July 3rd, 1863. He is about to try to turn the Union cannon in front of him and use it on the enemy. ©iStock.

Armistead's Yankee friend, Major General Winfield Hancock, had been fearlessly making a target of himself by riding back and forth on horseback to encourage his men when a Minié bullet struck him in the leg. The bullet, which I believe must have first splintered through a fence board, entered his right thigh along with some wood fragments and a large bent nail. Although he never fully recovered from the wound, Hancock survived the war and eventually ran for president, losing to another Civil War veteran, James Garfield. Hancock died on active duty at Governor's Island, New York on February 9, 1886.[22]

Pickett, who had been happy enough to lead his part of the charge when he thought victory was in the bag, never forgave Lee after the attack fell apart. Lee met him as Pickett came limping back from the failed charge and ordered, "General Pickett, reform your brigade!" Pickett glared at his commanding officer and spat out, "Sir, I have no brigade left!" and rudely walked away without asking the general's leave. He eventually became so bitter and insubordinate that Lee had to relieve him of his command at the Battle of Sayler's Creek, a few days before the South surrendered.

Six months after Gettysburg, Pickett committed an act that many in both the north and the south considered an atrocity and which nearly got him hanged after the war along with Henry Wirz, the commandant of the notorious Confederate Andersonville prison camp in Georgia.

In February of 1864 Pickett was campaigning in the Confederate state of North Carolina. His men captured a company of the U. S. Army fighting in the 2nd North Carolina Union Volunteer Infantry. All of the captured Union soldiers were native North Carolinians. Pickett considered them traitors to the Southern cause and probable deserters from the Confederate army. Of the 53 men captured, Pickett chose 22 and had them hanged in the public square of the town of Kinston as an example to others contemplating desertion. The men's wives, families and friends witnessed the executions. Desertion had been plaguing the Confederate army, sometimes amounting to 25% of the forces in a campaign and Lee himself had publically stated that only the threat and use of capital punishment could possibly stem the tide.[23]

People on both sides of the Mason-Dixon Line were infuriated by what they considered a senseless and brutal act perpetrated on helpless prisoners of war. Pickett narrowly escaped being tried as a war criminal during the war by the South and after the war by the North and suffering the same fate as the prisoners he executed. He never entirely lived down the stain on his character that the incident engendered.

For the rest of his life, spent selling insurance in Richmond, Pickett would say of Lee: "That old man destroyed over half my brigade for naught." He never acknowledged his own ineptitude in having his men march slowly in close formation over open ground while assaulting a heavily defended fortified position. In later years, when importuned at Richmond cocktail parties with endless inane questions as to what was responsible for the dismal failure of his infamous "charge," – his luck, his horoscope, his tactics – Pickett would grumblingly reply, "I always thought the Yankees had something to do with it."

Lee now had no further choices. The failure of Pickett's Charge had decided the battle's outcome beyond all doubt. Confederate casualties had been enormous and the Army of Northern Virginia, cut off from its overstretched supply lines, had almost no food or ammunition left. Meade, on the other hand, had access to almost unlimited supplies and reinforcements. Lee had to withdraw and he had to do it before the sun rose the next day.

Withdraw he did, and his army's retreat only succeeded because of Meade's indecisive pessimism and timidity. Meade found every excuse to stay put and sent only token units of cavalry to pursue the rebels. He even went to the extent of calling a council of war (against Lincoln's orders) and actually allowing his corps commanders to *vote* on whether or not to attack Lee as he retreated back into Virginia. Not surprisingly, given Lee's reputation, the attack was vetoed by a vote of 5 to 2. Lincoln's military chief, Henry Halleck, furiously wired Meade to order the attack at once but it was too late. Lee and the Army of Northern Virginia escaped.

The first movement of Gustav Holtz's symphonic suite, *The Planets*, is "Mars, the Bringer of War." The script of this degree's story calls for beautiful, sentimental music of the Civil War era to be played as the scenes change. I have always felt Holtz's grim orchestral dirge would be more appropriate. Like the recounting of Benedict Arnold's treachery (20th degree) and the story of the Four Immortal Chaplains (23rd degree) this degree recounts the tale of a genuine American tragedy. As in those stories, the genesis of the tragedy is war, perhaps the greatest tragedy of them all.

The 26th Degree
of the Southern Jurisdiction:

PRINCE OF MERCY

The Southern Jurisdiction retains the original Pike ritual. Although this is considered to be the first "Christian" degree in the South, it is more of a Trinitarian exercise in comparative religion in which we are taught that all religions – Hindus, Buddhists, Zoroastrians, Scandinavians, Jewish Cabbalists, etc. – imagine their respective deities to consist of three separate beings. Interestingly, in this degree we are first introduced to a character named Constans, who will be prominently featured, in quite a different role, in the final degree of the Northern Masonic Jurisdiction. In the Southern degree Constans' forehead is marked with a Tau cross and he is shown a statue of a virgin holding a silver arrow that represents divine justice. The degree, apparently a document promoting Trinitarianism, teaches that the notion of a three-part godhead (which Pike considered an indisputable truth) belongs to no single religion and that the truths of Masonry are contained within all the religions of the world.[24]

27th Degree:

KNIGHT OF JERUSALEM
(A Pope and an Emperor butt heads)

The Stage Drama

The time is the early 13th century, perhaps sometime in March of 1223. The place is a chapter hall of the Teutonic Knights at Ferentino, near Rome. The story describes the efforts of Pope Honorius III to recruit his one-time pupil, the Emperor Frederick II of Sicily, to organize and lead another Crusade against the Moslems. There is a lot of quarreling with accusations flying back and forth. An item featured prominently in the story is a legendary document called "The Three Imposters." Throughout the story, Frederick, who uses religion when it is convenient to his purposes and ignores it when it hinders his ambitions, treats the Holy Father, and anyone else who disagrees with him, with contempt and disrespect.

The degree teaches that Scottish Rite Freemasonry believes in the concept of a free church in a free state, each supreme in its own sphere, neither seeking to dominate the other but cooperating for the common good. This degree is brought to life by dramatic events from the period of the Crusades.

Historical Background

As soon as the College of Cardinals elected him pope in 1216, Honorius III began to preach a general crusade. He wanted to relieve the pummeled, bedraggled European knights who were trying unsuccessfully to beat back the Saracen hordes that were besieging Jerusalem. Honorius' effort, the Fifth Crusade, which at first looked like it was going to be a success, turned into a complete disaster. Working on their own and without his knowledge, a group of bishops had made the mistake of welcoming anyone into the ranks of the crusaders, without first ascertaining their fitness for combat. As a result, by 1218 "armies" of old men, women, cripples and thieves were arriving daily in distant seaports around the

Middle East. They were traveling, of course, at the expense of the Church and the taxpayers. This caused much embarrassment and weakened the public's support for crusades.

Finally, the stubborn, idiotic Spanish Cardinal Pelagius of Saint Lucia, leader of the Papal military contingent, had insisted on taking control of the expedition when they arrived in Egypt. He refused Sultan Malik al-Kamil's generous offer of all the Kingdom of Jerusalem west of the Jordan River and instead led the crusaders into unfortified encampments where the annual Nile flood trapped them and forced them to surrender.

Licking his wounds back in Rome, Honorius immediately began plans for the Sixth Crusade. He knew that the only man in Europe with the experience and prestige to head this mission was Frederick II, King of Sicily, whom the pope had briefly tutored as a small child. Honorius needed Frederick desperately. Frederick knew it and took every advantage he could. To further his territorial ambitions and demonstrate his military prowess, Frederick tried to humiliate and discredit Honorius, his aged former teacher, in every way possible. This degree's story details a small sample of Frederick's insolence and arrogance that Honorius had to put up with to achieve his goal.

The play's script portrays Frederick II as some sort of a hero, a precursor of our Founding Fathers, pursuing the ideal of separation of Church and State as expressed in the American Constitution. At the same time the story presents the Pope, Honorius III, as a clownish figure, foaming at the mouth with threats of excommunication every time something displeases him. Let's see what history has to say about them.

Fig. 39 Frederick II, Holy Roman Emperor.©iStock.

Whatever else Frederick may have been, he was no champion of Jeffersonian Democracy. The notion of separation of church and state as a philosophical idea meant no more to him than the idea of free elections would have. In the story, Frederick says "Temporal sovereignty is not the concern of the Church. It is the business of princes and rulers and peoples." In reality, Frederick would probably have left "peoples" out of his declaration. Neither he nor any other medieval monarch was ever very concerned about any "people" other than the powerful nobility. In 1223 the era of the Common Man was still a long way off.

Frederick had been raised and educated by Muslim scientists, mathematicians and philosophers. He respected the Islamic religion and spoke excellent Arabic. Preferring to negotiate with Muslim leaders rather than to engage them in armed conflict, Frederick had little enthusiasm for crusades. Although German by descent, he loved his Sicilian kingdom and hated to leave it.

From all accounts, Frederick was a shrewd but unprincipled warlord, living by the sword as long as others did most of the actual fighting. After his first wife died, he married the thirteen-year old Yolande of Jerusalem, a girl less than half his age. She interested him because, as the daughter of the King of Jerusalem, she would eventually become the queen of that city and marriage to her would make Frederick her king. Because Jerusalem was completely in Muslim hands at the time, Yolande and her father lived on the coast of Palestine in the Crusader-held fortress of Acre. No Christians had been allowed to enter the city for 50 years, so her royal title was tenuous, at best. She and her father were also penniless. Frederick saw them as two down-and-out people that he could push around with ease.

Immediately after the wedding he dispossessed Yolande's father, John of Brienne, of all his titles and possessions and appropriated them for himself. Even then he did not leave Sicily for a couple more years. He once started for Jerusalem in 1227 but after only a few days at sea he had to turn back because he had contracted a fever, either typhoid or cholera, which had swept through the Crusaders' camp in Apulia (a region on the Adriatic Sea in Southern Italy). Once safely home again, he recovered.

In the story, the Pope accuses Frederick and his nobles of living licentious lives with Saracen concubines (historically true). Frederick counters by bringing up the luxury and depravity of many high churchmen of the times (also true), and claims that he and his knights practice "the knightly virtue, chastity." The notion of Frederick practicing chastity, knightly or otherwise, is laughable, as he had a harem of concubines, guarded by eunuchs, which he took with him on campaigns. A few days after his marriage to Yolande he raped her cousin and, when Yolande complained, put the cousin in his harem.

History portrays Frederick as a man ahead of his time, a ruler who was a dedicated patron of the arts and sciences. There is no doubt that Frederick's early education by Muslim scientists, physicians and philosophers had put him, intellectually, decades ahead of most European thinkers, but he was still a child of his times. Frederick II was highly intelligent and free of most of his era's superstitions and prejudices, but he was no saint.

Cencio Savelli was no saint either, but that is no reason to portray him as the irascible, stereotypical Papal hobgoblin of anti-Catholic imagination. When the College of Cardinals elected him Pope in 1216 and he took the papal name of Honorius III, he was already in his late seventies and physically quite frail. And he came into office facing a great many problems.

Europe was under imminent threat of invasion by the Tatars (or Tartars, as Europeans came to call them), a nation of savage nomadic horsemen who belonged to the Mongol race. They came from the steppes of Central Asia where they were known as Kipchak Turks. Even the violent Genghis Khan, himself a Mongol, feared and distrusted them. In 1223, to get rid of them, he persuaded them to pack up their tents and migrate west into Europe, promising them rich lands to plunder. This led to the Mongol invasions of 1223 – 1241 that devastated Eastern Europe and even brought about the downfall of the vicious Shia Islamic murder cult known as the Assassins (from "hashashins", or "hashish eaters").

Honorius put the Mongol threat on the back burner, however. First and foremost, he wanted to reclaim the Holy Land which, by the time of his elevation to the Papacy, was mostly in Moslem hands. He intended to bring about the fervent desire of his predecessor, the great Pope Innocent III, to preach another Crusade. To bring this about, he knew that he would have to pacify the loutish, quarreling barons and petty nobles of Europe and reconcile them to work for the common cause with some semblance of unity. He accomplished this with unending diplomacy and cunning, winning over even such recalcitrant freebooters as Frederick II.

Honorius' other concern was to see all of Europe Christianized. At that time, areas around the Baltic coast were occupied by farmers and fishermen who still clung to the pagan nature religions of Old Europe. These people, known as Old Prussians, were of Latvian-Slavic ethnicity. They were semi-barbarian farmers and fishermen who minded their own business but could put up a fierce resistance to invaders. Honorius preached yet another crusade, this time against these peaceful European pagans. He even founded a military order of knights – the Sword Bearers – just for the purpose of teaching them a lesson. Like his previous crusades this one also failed; the Old Prussians obliterated the Sword Bearers. He would later try again with a better-armed and better-trained band of knights. Honorius died in 1227 without ever realizing his dreams of a Christian Holy Land or a totally Christian Europe.

The scroll referred to in this play as "The Three Imposters" ("De Tribus Impostoribus") was a literary curiosity that first appeared at Rackau, Germany, in 1598, although there are claims that one copy was seen in 1538 and another in 1573. There is no indication that it existed at the time of the story, around 1223. Some said it was a translation from an Arabic document of the Dark Ages (A.D. 500 – 1000), although no one has ever produced such a document. Church authorities have pointed to several men as the author, including such luminaries as Machiavelli, Rabelais, Erasmus and Milton.

The document is a dissertation on the falsity of the Abrahamic religions (Judaism, Christianity and Islam) and treats Moses, Jesus and Mohammad as three holy imposters. The document claimed that they had duped the people and made a good living at the expense of their gullible followers. Naturally, this theme did not please any group of religious authorities, be they Catholic, Protestant, Jewish or Islamic. Men died as a result of this universal ecclesiastical displeasure. One of them was Michael Servetus, burned at the stake in Geneva in 1553 during the religious persecutions conducted under John Calvin because Servetus did not believe either in the Trinity or in Jesus Christ as Redeemer. Also, Calvin suspected him of being the document's author. Two other reputed authors of the document were Etienne Dolit, a Parisian printer, and Lucilio Vanini, a noted Italian atheist. The Inquisition burned both of them at the stake.[1]

There is a remote possibility that the scroll that the ritual calls The Three Imposters may refer to another forged document, *The Donation of Constantine*. According to tradition, The Emperor Constantine was cured of leprosy and subsequently baptized on his deathbed by Pope Sylvester I (314-335). In gratitude he gave the Pope an imperial document giving the Church great temporal powers throughout Europe, particularly the authority to appoint and crown kings. In fact, the document didn't appear until 751 at the earliest, 400 years after Constantine's death, when the Greek Zacharias was Pope.

In his book, *Realm of the Ring Lords*, Laurence Gardner relates that when Stephen II became Pope in 752, he used the document to legitimize the crowning of Pepin the Short, father of the famous Charlemagne, as King of the Franks, thereby ending the Merovingian line of kings. The Merovingians had been hated by the Papacy because they claimed to be directly descended from the daughter (or, according to Gardner, one of the two sons) of Jesus Christ and Mary Magdalene and consequently thought they owed no allegiance to Rome.[2] However, John Norwich in his history of the Papacy, *Absolute Monarchs*, claims the Donation of Constantine is now thought not to have appeared until around 800, fifty years after Pepin's coronation.[3] The document was occasionally used for political purposes by the Church beginning about 1054, by Pope Hadrian I, although many scholars, including churchmen, thought it to be a forgery. In the Divine Comedy (circa 1320), Dante writes:

> Ah, Constantine! How much evil was born,
> not from your conversion, but from that Donation
> that the first wealthy Pope received from you!

The Italian priest and linguist, Lorenzo Valla, definitely proved the Donation to be spurious in 1440 and relegated it to the scrapheap of historical hoaxes.[4]

We should also take a closer look at the Teutonic Knights, in whose Chapter Hall the degree's story takes place. The play makes them out to be a band of noble Christian warriors. This is part of an idealistic myth that saintly monks and miracle-working preachers converted Europe from paganism to Christianity. This is almost certainly untrue. The pagan people of Europe would not have given up their beloved native religions voluntarily. For purposes of political gain, their rulers forced them to accept Christianity at the point of a sword, under threat of torture or death. The Teutonic Knights were one of the instruments of this process. They were no band of clean-living heroes. Like many military units of the Middle Ages, they were a crude, illiterate gang of sluggers, rapists and brigands.

After failing to Christianize the Middle East, the Teutonic Knights returned to Eastern Europe. There, a local ruler hired them to wage a viscous, brutal and one-sided war against the tribes of the Baltic coast, the last surviving European pagans. They were the above-mentioned Old Prussians, who had stubbornly clung to their native faith that centered on the worship of gods and goddesses of the rivers and forests. They had successfully resisted the coercions of Christian missionaries who had tried to force the new religion of Rome on them and, as we have seen, had even defeated Honorius' Sword Bearers.

A Polish Duke, Conrad of Massovia, probably to rid his own country of a band of undesirable troublemakers, persuaded the Teutonic Knights to invade the Old Prussian region. He directed them to massacre the inhabitants, promising them that they could keep whatever wealth they could plunder from the families they murdered. He also promised them exclusive sovereignty over a region he called Culm. The knights' leader was their Grand Master, Hermann von Salza. He operated under the authority of Pope Honorius III and Emperor Frederick II (who, in 1230, raised von Salza to the rank of Prince for his troubles). Von Salza appointed his fellow knight Hermann Balk to be the Provincial Grand master in charge of the invasion. Balk rounded up 28 masterless knights and raised an army of "crusaders" from the taverns, jails and farms of Germany.

After a 25-year struggle, the invaders finally managed to vanquish the Old Prussians. They "converted" the few survivors to Christianity under threat of death or torture. The pagan citizens of neighboring Lithuania fared no better. Mounted knights and supporting infantry invaded their lands, slaughtered as many people as they could, and intimidated the survivors into conversion. Bands of Teutonic Knights forced families of Lithuanian pagans to flee into the forest and then hunted them down for sport. Honorius and Frederick encouraged German colonists to move in and settle the depopulated lands. By 1390 the entire region, now known as Prussia, had been thoroughly Christianized and Germanized. The only surviving remnants of the Old Religion of Europe were the covens of wise women and healers that the Church called "witches" and, later, accused falsely of devil worship. A 200-year long persecution of torture and public burnings virtually exterminated them.

A modern Scottish Rite Mason searching for knightly role models to emulate can find far better examples than the Teutonic Knights. The Knights Templar, for instance, provide an excellent example of bravery and skill ameliorated by true Christian mercy and honor. The same can be said of the Knights of Malta. This order, first called The Military Hospitaller Order of Saint John of Jerusalem, still exists today in its original form. Headquartered in Rome, it is the oldest continuously existing order of chivalry in the world.

Fig. 40 Knights Templar. ©iStock.

The 27th Degree
of the Southern Jurisdiction:
KNIGHT COMMANDER OF THE TEMPLE

This degree of the Southern Jurisdiction has some things in common with the Northern Jurisdiction's 32nd degree. The hero, Constans, is a young Prince of Mercy about to be inducted into an exalted order of knighthood called the Chapter of Commanders. If accepted, he will become a Knight Commander of the Temple. He must first undergo an all-night vigil before the Chapter's altar. Monks instruct him not to abandon his vigil no matter what happens. During the night, when he is alone, he is tempted three times. First an officer enters and says that Constans' fiancé is outside in the town square, where a party is going on, and that she is being pursued by a rival suitor. If Constans does not join her immediately, she will break off the engagement and marry the rival. Constans does not budge. Next, Constans learns that an army is attacking his castle and if he does not appear to lead his troops his estates will be lost. Constans does not move. Finally, a monk comes in and tries to persuade Constans to join him in a life of penance and self denial. Constans refuses and the monk leaves, disgusted at the young man's apparent lack of spiritual fortitude. Then, Constans hears the sounds of battle at the city's gates. The enemy army is breaching the city walls and, because of his absence, is gaining the upper hand. He can take no more and rushes off to join the fighting.

Constans suddenly appears among the city troops and his skill and bravery turn the tide of battle. But nobody seems to recognize him. When the officers of the Chapter of Commanders return, they find Constans missing. Everyone agrees that Constans has abandoned his vigil to seek pleasure somewhere and is therefore unworthy of the honor they were going to confer upon him. When Constans comes back into the room everybody gives him a hard time for leaving his vigil and the Master of the Chapter declares that he is unfit for the honor of becoming a Knight Commander. Then a knight recognizes Constans as the unknown superhero who had saved the city. The master apologizes for his hasty condemnation and receives Constans into the chapter.[7]

28th Degree:

KNIGHT OF THE SUN
(An unlikely "hero" becomes a Rosicrucian)

The Stage Drama

The time is 1650, the dawn of the Age of Enlightenment, and the place is the headquarters of the Order of the Rosy Cross, known today as the Rosicrucians. The Council consists of historical men of the time and includes a future Pope, a Lutheran minister, a rabbi and a king. Their meeting was called to select a candidate for admission into their order. They examine four candidates for initiation. They find the first three unworthy and select the fourth, the famous Freemason Elias Ashmole, for admission.

This degree teaches that as nature hides her treasures under an external coat which must be hewn away before her wonders can be put to use by man, so Freemasonry helps us to strip the vices and superfluities of our lives so that we see and perform our duty to God and our fellow man.

Historical Background

In Germany, between 1612 and 1616, three anonymously-authored books appeared. The first was called *A Report of the Good Deeds* (or "Fame") *of the Brotherhood of the Rosy Cross*, the second *The Confessions of the Brotherhood of the Rosy Cross* and the third *The Chemical Marriage of Christian Rosenkreutz*. Supposedly, they were written by one Christian Rosenkreutz (1378-1484), a wandering German monk who had travelled to Egypt, Morocco and the Middle East in search of occult wisdom. (At the time the books appeared, scholars considered the study of magic and occult subjects to be a legitimate topic of intellectual research).

When he returned home to Germany, Rosenkreutz was said to have founded the House of the Holy Spirit, a religious fraternity consisting of him and seven other monks. They would travel the world separately in search of knowledge and then reunite once a year to share what they had learned with each other. Someone was said to have discovered Rosenkreutz's burial place in 1604. The discoverer supposedly found the monk's body perfectly preserved, along with many secret manuscripts detailing the order's teachings.

Johann Valentin Andrae (1586–1654), a Lutheran minister, may have written the three books. Andrae's goal was to found an order of mystical philosopher-scientists that would plumb the secrets of the universe. They would then reform 17th-century European culture by injecting their newfound knowledge and wisdom into everyday life. His ultimate ambition was to establish a utopian society resembling the Biblical vision of a New Jerusalem (Revelation 21: 9-27). He intended to teach his philosophical insights through the symbolism of Alchemy (another legitimate scientific discipline of the time).

As his order's logo, he adopted a revised version of Martin Luther's coat of arms, coming up with a white cross with an open red rose in the center (see Fig. 20). He called his new order the Brotherhood of the Rosy Cross, more commonly known today as the Rosicrucians. He never achieved the universal reformation of mankind that he desired, but the Order of the Rosy Cross became extremely popular among intellectuals of the European Enlightenment. The Rosicrucian Order, today surviving as an invitational research body in Freemasonry and in a few New Age organizations, died out among the general public around 1760 in France, its last stronghold.

Elias Ashmole, one of the earliest speculative Freemasons, was also a Rosicrucian as well as a practicing alchemist. The degree's story gives a fictitious account of Ashmole's reception into the Brotherhood of the Rosy Cross.

This excellent stage drama demonstrates everything that was right, outstanding and noble in early speculative Freemasonry. Important points included camaraderie among men of different religions and political beliefs, respect for the opinions of others, readiness to help a brother in need, desire to improve the lot of all men and social equality among fraternal brothers. Equally important were intellectual curiosity, the rejection of avarice and the refusal to take advantage of gullible men and women of lesser knowledge.

That the author did not base the degree's story on historical records is irrelevant; the core spirit is one of pure Masonic virtue and good will. I believe the historical setting and time is right. Although most historians date the Age of Enlightenment to the early 18th century, I believe that it really began with the efforts of intelligent men in the middle of the 1600s. These men were willing to devote their lives and their fortunes to the pursuit of scientific inquiry. Their opened minds enabled them to see beyond the religious bigotries and hatreds of their time. They spent their lives expanding humanity's knowledge base and searching for ways to turn the fruits of their self-education to the betterment of their fellow men. They toiled late into the night in their home laboratories, they ground the lenses for their own telescopes, they sailed the uncharted South Seas and scanned the night sky, attempting to discover God hiding somewhere in the recesses of the natural universe. They were the first candidates for speculative Masonry. It was their cultivation of empirical knowledge, honest good will and informed attitudes on social justice that laid the foundations of our fraternity and, 100 years later, of our country.

This rapprochement among men of different religious systems did not occur in a vacuum and was even more remarkable considering the historical circumstances of the period. At the time the story takes place, 1650, Europe was just recovering from the horrors of the Thirty Years' War. This began in 1618 as a conflict between Catholics and Protestants but soon metastasized into an all-consuming political conflagration throughout Europe. The Bourbon royal regime in France took up arms with their ancient rivals, the northern European Hapsburg dynasty. Before long, the entire Holy Roman Empire was in flames. Italy and the Czech lands were drawn in. The worst fighting took place in Germany and the Low Countries with the destruction of one-third of all the towns and villages and the extermination of somewhere between one-third and one-half of the total population.

Fig. 41 Combat during the Thirty Years War. ©iStock.

The Thirty Years War was a war of intense close-quarter combat on all sides. It was a war that saw the extensive use of firearms, primitive though they were. It spawned its own particular systems of battlefield strategy, centered on the use of pikes to repel cavalry.

Some infantry soldiers carried a clumsy proto-musket called a matchlock, firing a 17.5 mm (.75 caliber) ball. The musket's hammer was a hollow brass tube called a serpentine that carried a lighted fuse (the "slow-match").[2] When the musketeer pulled the trigger, the serpentine flipped backward toward the shooter and pushed the sputtering fuse into a touchhole, igniting the powder. Early matchlocks were so heavy that they could be fired only if the barrel were supported on a large wooden fork thrust into the ground; the musketeer had to be accompanied by an assistant who carried the fork. Matchlocks didn't work on a rainy day and took forever to reload. Every prudent musketeer carried a large sword at his side in case his position was overrun by enemy pikemen, a common occurrence.

A more dependable firearm used in the Thirty Years War was the wheellock.[3] When the trigger was pulled, the hammer snapped back toward the shooter and held a piece of iron pyrite against a spring-loaded spinning steel wheel with a roughened edge. The resultant shower of sparks into the touchhole ignited the powder in the barrel and fired a 14 mm (.65 caliber) ball. Wheellock firearms became especially popular with dragoons. Unlike cavalry troopers, who always fought on horseback, dragoons were soldiers who rode into battle on horseback and then dismounted and fought on foot. They were highly mobile infantrymen who could be moved from one part of the battlefield to the other at a moment's notice.

At this stage in the development of firearms these weapons were only a minor improvement over the firearms of the previous century, which had basically been small, hand-held canon barrels mounted in a wooden block. They had no sights and the musketeers just pointed them in the general direction of the target. Their usefulness came from the fact that the targets they were pointed at – tightly packed masses of musketeers surrounded by protective squares of pikemen – were large and couldn't move.[4] Also, their bullets were capable of piercing armor. Cavalry units would wait until the musketeers fired a volley. Then they would gallop up, stop just out of reach of the pikes, fire their pistols into the immobile mass of musketeers, wheel around and gallop away before the musketeers could reload.

Because of the extensive use of long wooden-handled pikes the war also saw the use of a giant two-handed sword with a six-foot long double-edged blade called a *zweihander* (German for "two-hander"). This was used by the largest and strongest soldiers to cut through rows of wooden pikes (and their handlers) to make way for mounted cavalry with their short-range pistols. A soldier who wielded a zweihander received double pay.[5] The use of the sword was discontinued after the war when pike formations were abandoned and it was discovered that the gigantic zweihander-using soldiers simply made better targets for the more accurate long-range firearms that were becoming commonplace.

Both sides employed foreign mercenary troops from Sweden and Norway that pillaged the countryside, burning and looting towns and showing no mercy to men, women or children. At that time the population of Europe was largely rural. To survive the winter they depended heavily on the annual fall harvest. Whole regions faced starvation when their livestock and crops were stolen or burned. The recorded atrocities committed by the mercenary soldiers of both Catholic and Protestant armies are so sickening as to defy description. The barren fields were strewn with rotting, unburied corpses, many of them obscenely mutilated. Many citizens that survived the ravages of invading armies succumbed to famine or disease. The Thirty Years' War ended with the signing of the Treaty of Münster, a portion of the Peace of Westphalia, in 1648.

One last item. The casting instructions for the character of Elias Ashmole describe him as:

"…the young man 'from next door' whom we would all like to have our daughter marry. He is young, open, and sincere. The 'hero'."

I am not so sure about that. I don't think that any father, after reading Ashmole's biography, would want him to come courting his daughter. The son of a saddler who had impoverished his family by running off to fight in foreign wars, Ashmole made his way in society by becoming a fortune hunter. He unsuccessfully courted several young rich widows. Finally, desperate for money and needing to improve his social station in life, he married Mary, Lady Mainwaring, a wealthy noblewoman twenty years his senior. She soon separated from him but he retained the money from one of her former husband's estates. Also, the social connections Ashmole had made when he was her husband served him well.

Ashmole befriended a famous botanist and collector named John Tradescant. Tradescant had acquired an enormous collection of plants, minerals and other exotic items that was known and admired throughout England. Ashmole, apparently after getting Tradescant drunk, persuaded the botanist to bequeath the entire collection to him. When Tradescant died three years later, his wife Hester fought the transference of the collection to Ashmole, citing her husband's drunken condition at the time he had signed the will. She lost the battle in court.

The court ordered that Hester hold the collection in trust for Ashmole until her death. Some years later Ashmole built a house next door to Tradescant's estate and, while Hester was still alive, began illegally moving items from Tradescant's house to his own. Hester took him to court again and began another legal battle over the matter. A few days later her servants found her drowned in a pool in her garden.

Ashmole's second wife was Elizabeth Dugdale, daughter of his friend, the antiquarian Sir William Dugdale. She was 15 years younger than Ashmole; the couple had no children.

Although modern Masonic scholars look upon Ashmole as one of the great early Freemasons, his zeal for the fraternity is questionable. According to his diary, he only attended two meetings in 35 years! The first was his initiation in October, 1646, of which he wrote:

> "I was made a Free Mason at Warrington in Lancashire, with Col. Henry Mainwaring [perhaps a relative of his first wife] of Karincham in Cheshire."

Fig. 42 A research laboratory during the time of Elias Ashmole. ©iStock.

The second was a meeting at Masons' Hall in London, March, 1682, 35 years later. He writes:

> "About 5 H: P.M. I received a Sumons to appeare at a Lodge to be held the next day, at Masons Hall London. Accordingly, I went ... I was the Senior Fellow among them (it being 35 yeares since I was admitted) ... We all dyned at the Halfe Moone Taverne in Cheapeside, at a Noble Dinner prepaired at the charge of the New-accepted Masons."

These diary entries are the earliest references to speculative Freemasonry in England that researchers have found. But that's all he wrote on the subject; in all his surviving writings he says nothing more about the Craft. To be fair, a fire in London's Middle Temple on January 26, 1679 destroyed most of Ashmole's papers and collected artifacts, so the record is far from complete.

There is no doubt, however, that Ashmole was an ardent Rosicrucian. That some people at the time looked upon Rosicrucianism as a weird cult can be seen in the following attempted defense of Ashmole by John Gadbury, a famous English astrologer of the period who was acquainted with him:

> "Anthony Wood hath falsly called him [Ashmole] a Rosicrucian, whereas no man was further from fost'ring such follies."

Ashmole, like most intellectuals of his time, probably regarded both Freemasonry and Rosicrucianism as scientific secret societies in which researchers could freely exchange intellectual views without interference from church or government authorities. And that's exactly what these fraternities were in the 17th century: scientific research societies. One Rosicrucian utopian ideal was that of a freely accessible repository of universal knowledge and wisdom. Some historians trace Ashmole's fervent desire to establish a large museum of science and natural history to this vision. Ashmole died at his home in May of 1692 and was buried in Lambeth. To some historians he was a heroic proto-scientist who exemplified all the best of the Enlightenment. To others he was an ambitious, ingratiating social climber with little in the way of ethical rectitude. The truth probably lies somewhere in between; either way, he was apparently not much of a Freemason.[6]

The 28th Degree
of the Southern Jurisdiction:

KNIGHT OF THE SUN, OR PRINCE ADEPT

The Southern Jurisdiction's version of the 27th degree differs both from the NMJ's degree as well as most of the SJ's previous rituals. Here, a candidate, presumably a 26th-degree Prince of Mercy, is introduced to a mystical figure called Father Adam who presides over a choir of seven angels called the *malakoth*, or "messengers." Each of these angels imparts bits of wisdom or knowledge regarding various mysteries. Each angel's name ends in *el* to signify its relation to El, the ancient Canaanite deity originally worshipped by the nomadic trans-Jordan pastoral tribes that became known as "Hebrews."

First, Father Adam presents a prologue to the class explaining the lessons that will follow. He explains the nature of symbols and the importance to mystical study of the pseudo-science of numerology. Then the angels present their respective "keys" of understanding: Cassiel (geometry), Sachiel (numerology), Zamael (geometry and numbers), Michael (the Pythagorean pyramid of dots called a Tetracty), Hanael (the *ichthys* fish symbol of the early Christians), Raphael (Hermetic symbolism and alchemy), and Gabriel (language and the evil nature of iron). Finally, a non-angelic entity called Brother Truth appears and lectures the class on symbolism in general, particularly the meaning of light in Masonry. Pike apparently considered this degree to be of utmost importance as his following lecture is the longest in *Morals and Dogma*, taking up almost one-fourth of the entire book.

The degree has several lessons: Nature reveals a power and wisdom that continually points to God; the visible is a manifestation of the invisible; in the universe two opposite forces provide balance – there is no death, only change, and the moral code of Masonry is more extensive than that of philosophy.[5]

29th Degree:

KNIGHT OF ST. ANDREW
(Incompetent amateurs decide the fate of Europe)

The Stage Drama

The place is the Cathedral of St. Andrew in Patras (ancient Patrae), in Western Greece. The time is evening following the Battle of Nicopolis on September 25, 1396 between the Christian forces of the Duke of Burgundy and the Turkish Sultan Bajazet el Ilderim (called Bayazid in the story). The Sultan has defeated the Christian French knights and has eight of them brought before him. The prisoners include such famous historical French noblemen as Enguerrand VII (or Sire de Coucy), de Nevers, De Vienne, De la Marche and Boucicaut (here called Boucicault). The Sultan demands an inordinately high ransom for them and threatens to behead them if the ransom is not paid.

The Duke De Nevers (a young man of 24 at the time of the battle) tells the Sultan that they could never raise his ransom demands. He offers his own head as the first to roll. His bravery impresses the Sultan who says that he now knows why people call de Nevers "John the Fearless" (a title the young man would not gain until years after the battle). Bajazet treats the knights leniently. At his request, the European knights induct him and his two sons into the Order of St. Andrew. In gratitude, he rescinds the knights' ransoms and allows them to depart.

This degree emphasizes the Masonic teachings of equality and toleration. Masonic equality is not an artificial leveling of wealth or outward conditions. It is the true equality that should exist between men of virtue and high ideals, regardless of such conditions. Masonic toleration is respect for the opinions of others. No one man, no one church, no one religion has a monopoly on truth. We should be true and faithful to our own opinions, and we should extend to the opinions of others the same respect we demand for our own.

Historical Background

By the end of the 13th century the once-mighty Seljuk Turks had finally succumbed to repeated raids by the Mongol cavalry units of Genghis Kahn. Around the year 1300 a new confederation of Muslim tribes seized the opportunity to break away from their weakened Seljuk rulers and strike out on their own path of conquest. They called themselves Ottoman Turks, after their chieftain, Osman, who had led them from their settlements on the shores of the Black Sea to conquer most of Anatolia (present-day Turkey). By 1325 they had towns and garrisons all along the Asiatic shore of the Bosporus, the strait separating Europe from Asia. Europeans heard distant rumors of the Muslim advance but paid little attention.

Fig 43 Sultan Bajazet battling a Christian army. ©*iStock.*

In 1353 the Ottoman leader Murad crossed the Bosporus into Europe and took Gallipoli. This made the Ottomans masters of the Dardanelles, the gateway from the Mediterranean to the Black Sea. Europeans, particularly in the maritime commercial seaports of Genoa and Venice, began to get nervous.[1] By 1365 Murad had conquered Adrianople, 120 miles into European territory. By 1389 Bajazet, Murad's successor, had his armies at the border of Hungary. He was declared Sultan at Kosovo and, to show everybody that he took his new title seriously, immediately had his brother strangled with a bowstring so there would be no rival claimant to the throne.[2] He then proceeded to subjugate Bulgaria, Macedonia, Attica (central Greece, including Athens), Bosnia and Croatia. His unstoppable blitzkrieg advances and rapid conquests earned Bajazet the nickname of *Ilderim* ("The

Thunderbolt").[3] Europeans in France and Germany finally woke up and realized they were facing an imminent threat: nothing less than a Muslim take-over of the Western World.

Fervor for a great crusade against the invaders soon overwhelmed France. The Duke of Burgundy, in 1394, decided to take the initiative and formed plans to mount a crusade against the "miscreants," a term of contempt the upper classes used against both Muslims and their own European peasants.[4] The Duke, who did not plan to go on the crusade himself, sent his 24-year old son, Jean de Nevers, in his stead. The ungainly Jean with his oversized head would, later in life, become known as *Jean sans Peur* (John the Fearless), not for bravery in battle but for the brazenness with which he conducted his evil life.[5] Two of Jean's kinsmen would accompany him. They were Raoul, Comte d'Eu et Guines (the Constable of France) and Jean Le Meingre, the Marshal of France who called himself "Boucicaut."

Like de Nevers, both of these two young men lacked any leadership experience in warfare so Burgundy called upon the services of the highly respected Enguerrand VII, Sire de Coucy, to head the expedition.[6] De Coucy, the most famous noblemen, diplomat and warrior in France, accepted. De Coucy selected Jacques, Comte De la Marche, as a counselor.

The expedition was one of extravagant, sumptuous display of class and privilege with little in the way of planning, strategy, reconnaissance or military intelligence. No one considered such details necessary when fighting the "miscreants." The Europeans assumed that God would favor the Christian forces and annihilate the Muslims with natural disasters, so-called "acts of God." Colorfully dressed minstrels and heralds preceded the army. Every knight had his own team of cooks with portable ovens to bake little pies when he was in the mood for them.

Burgundy supplied his son de Nevers with his own personal company of 200 servants, cooks and valets. He also gave him two dozen wagons full of shiny green satin for his tents and four enormous banners. The banners showed images of the Virgin Mary surrounded by fleurs-de-lis (the Virgin's image was popularly supposed to strike fear into the hearts of the Saracens). Twelve trumpeters dressed in heraldic silk costumes embroidered with gold and silver emblems were to precede de Nevers wherever he went. There were barrels of red wine and sack (a kind of sherry) and flocks of sheep, droves of long-legged northern European pigs and herds of cattle to provide fresh meat.[7]

There were no stone-hurling siege weapons, the artillery of the Middle Ages. The expedition did not take along one single catapult, ballista, trebuchet or mangonel (whose middle syllable has given us the word "gun"). Nor did they bother to bring along any skilled carpenters with the necessary tools to assemble such machines on the spot.[8]

As the expedition advanced through the countryside, De Coucy, a veteran of many campaigns, argued for dispatching reconnaissance parties to scout ahead for any signs of enemy presence. The band of young, inexperienced noblemen voted his suggestion down. They were reveling in their first taste of independent command and considered the middle-aged De Coucy to be both an overcautious old fuddy-duddy and their social inferior.

The knights camped in splendid tents and pavilions decorated with hanging pictures. They appeared every morning dressed in different outfits of gorgeous silks in every imaginable color. Jugglers and jesters entertained them in the evening while they reveled in drunken orgies with the many prostitutes they had brought along. Later, when the crusaders entered what they considered "schismatic" (Eastern Orthodox) Christian lands, they allowed the common soldiers to entertain themselves by raping the local women and looting their villages.[9]

The crusaders traveled from France to Strasbourg, through Bavaria, and along the Danube to Budapest. There 44 shiploads of Knights Hospitaler who had arrived from their island fortresses on Rhodes joined them. At the insistence of the veteran Hospitalers and after quarreling among themselves, the young noblemen finally allowed De Coucy's good sense to prevail. They dispatched a reconnaissance party to the Hellespont to scout out Sultan Bajazet's intentions. The party found no trace of a Muslim presence and reported back that the cowardly heathen was hiding, afraid to face the might of Christian Europe.[10]

After easily taking several undermanned Turkish garrisons, the Christian forces finally arrived at the strategic fortified Muslim town of Nicopolis on the Adriatic Sea in western Greece.[11] With no catapults or other siege weapons, the crusaders could only camp around the city walls and play a waiting game with the inhabitants. This promised to be a long wait because the town's Turkish governor, Dogan Bey, was convinced that the Sultan was on his way to rescue the city and was prepared to hold out for months.[12] Marshal Boucicaut ordered the construction of siege ladders, which he thought were more useful than catapults anyway. The more experienced De Coucy, eyeing Nicopolis' high walls perched on towering limestone cliffs, was not so sure but, to keep the peace, did not object. At least building ladders would keep the men busy.

Then, unexpectedly, a reconnaissance party brought news that the Great Turk was on his way, rapidly closing the distance with large units of cavalry and infantry. De Coucy, unhappy with the arrogant over-confidence of his untested young comrades-in-arms, said, "Let us find out what sort of men our enemies are."[13] He personally led a party of 1000 men, 500 lancers and 500 mounted archers, to ambush an advance party of Turks as they issued from a narrow pass. His strategy worked and his men slaughtered the entire Turkish party with no trouble. His party returned to camp in triumph.

That night at dinner, as the crusaders were drunk with wine celebrating their victory, word came into camp that the rapidly moving Bajazet, master of the blitzkrieg attack, was only six hours away. He would greet them at dawn with all his forces. The panic-stricken knights stumbled around, all discipline and organization gone. Some called for their armor. Then, to get themselves warmed up for the coming battle, the drunken French knights massacred all of their 1000 prisoners, Turks and Eastern Orthodox Christians, that they had captured from the small garrisons they had taken along the way.[14]

Before the sun rose next morning, the heavily armored French knights mounted their warhorses. These creatures were not the small, clip-clopping palfreys that Chaucer's pilgrims rode as they told bawdy stories on their way to Canterbury. They were savage chargers called *Destriers*, bred by Benedictine monks to spring into a crazed frenzy at the sound of military kettle drums and trumpets. They would charge fearlessly into the enemy lines, running down with churning hooves anyone who got in their way. Farriers had equipped their rear hooves with steel blades; at a signal from its rider a horse would jump into the air, kick back viciously with its hind legs and shred any enemy soldier coming up from behind. Then the horse had to land squarely on all fours, facing forward. This maneuver has survived into modern times as the *capriole*, said to be the most difficult exercise for a horseman to master in formal dressage.

Contrary to Hollywood, the knights were perfectly capable of mounting their horses without being hoisted up into their saddles with the aid of wooden cranes. If a knight's horse was killed in battle he could simply grab the reigns of the first riderless horse (there were usually plenty on a Medieval battlefield) he came across and swing himself up into the saddle – armor, weapons and all.

The French also had large, fierce war-dogs called *aulants*, similar to modern German shepards, that would run into enemy lines to attack and terrorize infantrymen. In case the dogs' teeth weren't enough of a threat, the animals would have pots of flaming pitch strapped to their sides. This was especially fearsome to Moslem soldiers who frequently wore flammable resin-impregnated canvas armor.

The French knights lined up for the customary cavalry charge that began most European battles.[15] Each man carried an eighteen-foot long wooden lance, three times the height of a man, tipped with an armor-piercing steel point, certain death for any infantryman caught in the knight's path. In addition, each knight carried a 5-pound sword, a steel battle-ax, a mace and a long, double-edged Pistoian dagger capable of penetrating chain mail. Some also carried a hammer with a long sharp spike that, when swung by a strong man, could penetrate a steel helmet and the head within the helmet. Each knight was wearing either a coat of mail or a set of plate armor over a padded linen shirt. Thus armed and outfitted, he was thought to be invincible.

Fig 44 Knights in combat. (14th century) ©iStock

The previous night the stupid, vainglorious Constable d'Eu had seized command of the army from De Coucy.[16] De Coucy could not countermand him because the Constable was of royal blood and he, De Coucy, was not. D'Eu himself led the charge that morning, waving the royal banner, and the mounted knights followed at a break-neck gallop. Each knight screaming his family's battle cry, each man's leg armor clinking against the leg armor of the rider on either side of him, lances couched at the level of an enemy's head, they made a thundering tsunami of steel, an unstoppable wave of death. A contingent of mounted crossbowmen formed a supporting unit bringing up the rear. The knights were charging at what they thought was Bajazet's main force. In their youthful bravado they had left their reinforcing infantry units behind to catch up on foot as best they could. All this day's glory would be theirs. The infantry, made up of lower-class pikemen and yeoman archers, could mop up after them.

What they met, however, was not the main Turkish army. The knights instead encountered a small group of ragged, poorly armed and untrained peasant conscripts that the Turks had forced to precede their main infantry squads as a buffer unit. The mounted knights easily scattered the frightened peasants. Thinking they had encountered and defeated Bajazet's entire army, they happily began to slaughter the fleeing farmers without mercy.

Then the main Turkish infantry appeared. These soldiers were trained professionals who shot armor-piercing arrows from compound bows and skillfully wielded long pikes capable of unhorsing armored riders. They quickly set up a perimeter of sharpened outward-pointing stakes planted in the ground to foil any more cavalry charges. The stunned French knights and crossbowmen, with their just-arriving echelons of allies and infantry reinforcements, waded without hesitation into the field of stakes. Then the Turkish cavalry, that Bajazet had held back, appeared and mounted a counter-charge. Most of the knights' European allies fled the scene.

The French knights and the Hospitalers did not flee. They stood their ground and fought in the face of worsening odds. Whatever one thinks about the knights of medieval Europe, no one can say they were cowards. They may not have lived exemplary lives but they knew how to die with honor.

At that point a European vassal of Bajazet arrived on the scene with 1,500 mounted cavalry and attacked the French and Hospitaler knights, many of whom had lost their horses to the stakes and enemy arrows and now were fighting on foot.[17] The dismounted knights struggled to maneuver and fight in the churned-up mud, hampered by 30 pounds of cumbersome steel plate armor. By afternoon, the battle was over and the Turks were victorious. Three thousand corpses littered the battlefield with heads, arms and legs scattered around piecemeal. The dismemberment was due to the choice of weapons: The Turks used razor-sharp scimitars while the French favored two-handed swords and 15-pound battle-axes.

Following his victory, the Sultan did not behave nearly as graciously as the degree's story depicts. For one thing, he had no interest in joining an imaginary mystical order of European knighthood. For another, he had lost twice as many men as had the better-armored French. As the final straw, he found out about the French massacre of the garrison prisoners the night before. He had the leading French nobles and Hospitaler Grandmaster rounded up for ransom and forced them to stand beside his pavilion and witness his vengeance.

And Bajazet's vengeance was terrible. He had some two thousand captured French foot soldiers massacred for his amusement.[18] He had some disemboweled while his soldiers cut the throats of others. Most he simply ordered beheaded. When Bajazet grew bored with the screams and the stench of blood, he ordered the slaughter stopped and had the survivors marched off to be sold into slavery. Instead of inviting De Coucy, De Nevers and the other nobles to an ecumenical tea party, the Sultan forced them to go on a 350-mile Bataan-style death march from Nicopolis to Gallipoli on the Dardanelles Strait, where they stayed for two months. Then, fearing a rescue attempt from the sea, he had them moved 40 miles inland to the fortified city of Bursa, the Ottoman capital, in present-day Turkey. There he imprisoned them until their relatives in France could pay their ransoms. Admiral

Jean de Vienne, listed in the story as one of the prisoners, had actually been killed in the battle. His body was found with the royal banner still clutched in his hand.[19]

The Battle of Nicopolis, lost because of French vanity and arrogance, changed the course of European history for the next 600 years. Fifty years later Constantinople fell to the Turks and today is the Muslim city of Istanbul. An enormous region of Orthodox Christianity was forcibly converted to Islam and remains so today. De Coucy, the eldest of the French prisoners, died in captivity at Bursa.[20] Jean de Nevers lived to succeed his father as Duke of Burgundy. In 1407 he had his cousin,

Fig. 45 The Battle of Nicopolis (1396). ©iStock.

Louis d'Orleans, hacked to death by assassins in a Paris gutter. His brazen public defense of this act combined with his extravagant and licentious life-style earned him the nickname of "John the Fearless." He quieted public dissention by giving the people a tax break. Arriving on the bridge at Montereau in 1419 for a parlay with his rival, the Dauphin of France, De Nevers was himself hacked to death by followers of the Dauphin.[21] In 1415 the English under Henry V captured Boucicaut at the disastrous Battle of Agincourt. He died six years later.[22]

The 29th Degree
of the Southern Jurisdiction:

SCOTTISH KNIGHT OF SAINT ANDREW

In the Southern Jurisdiction this degree follows the original Pike ritual. In his reception into the Order of Scottish Knights of St. Andrew in the ruins of an old Scottish castle, guardians challenge a candidate for the degree and then accept him into the Order. They give him a brief history of the degree, repeating the legend of Robert the Bruce of Scotland, and tell him stories about the valor of the Crusaders. The duty of a Knight is "to practice active charity and practical philanthropy, and to inculcate the principles of toleration and free government." They admonish the candidate to believe in God and to lay aside all pride, to be humble, and to practice patience and self-denial as the virtues of a true Knight. They exhort him to practice loyalty and knightly duty and tell him the symbolic lights of Charity, Clemency, Generosity, Virtue, Truth and Honor will guide him.[23]

30th Degree:

GRAND INSPECTOR
(Wake me up when it's over)

The Stage Drama

This degree's story, supposedly an accurate rendition of a 14th century English courtroom trial, centers around an imaginary secret order of knighthood called the Knights Kadosh. Kadosh is a Hebrew word meaning "holy" or "set apart." A newly-inducted Knight Kadosh is the defendant and stands accused of betraying the order's secret passwords and signs to a wandering monk. His accuser is the order's treasurer.

The trial takes place in England sometime during the reign of Edward II (1307 – 1327). The location is Chester, a city on the River Dee near the Welsh-English border. There are charges and countercharges, false witnesses and missing documents. It reads like a boring, tedious play in which it's difficult to keep track of the characters. The villainous plaintiff appears to be winning the case until the defendant, the play's hero, is saved by the timely arrival of one Higg, son of Snell, a scrivener (a secretary who makes copies of legal documents). Higg has the torn half of a critical document. The heroic defendant is saved by a brave Templar who arrives just in time with the other half of the document. The judges advance William, the innocent defendant, to the degree of Inspector General.

The degree teaches us to be attentive, impartial and equitable in judging others. I think it also reinforces one of the lessons I believe is exemplified by the 19th and the 31st degrees.

Historical Background

This degree's play is tedious. There is too much needless dialogue, taking of oaths, technical exchanges in pseudo-medieval legal jargon, back-and-forth bickering between the lawyers and endless cross-examinations that seem to go on forever. The characters' long-winded names and titles confuse their identities and obscure what little action the play provides. Throughout the play I kept losing track of what was happening to whom and why. And the entire premise of the play is silly. A knight is tried in a court of civil law because he gave away his fraternity's passwords? And why, when he is declared innocent, do the judges confer a Masonic degree on him? Very strange.

Fig. 46 A Medieval courtroom trial. ©iStock.

Anyway, it was good to see an old acquaintance – Higg, son of Snell – in court again. In Sir Walter Scott's novel, *Ivanhoe*, Higg, son of Snell, is a Saxon peasant. He is a witness for the defense at the Templars' trial of Rebecca, the Jewish woman whom the Templars' Grand Master has accused of witchcraft. Higg tries to explain that the lotion that Rebecca had given him to ease the pain in his legs is not diabolical, but his testimony does not move the grumpy old Templar Grand Master. In desperation, Rebecca entrusts Higg with a scroll, written in Hebrew, which Higg delivers to her father, Isaac of York. Spoiler alert: As a result, Ivanhoe rides to the rescue and saves Rebecca. In a similar vein, the Higg in this ritual also produces a document (or half of one, anyway), also written in Hebrew, which also saves the day. Ironically, in this story, a Templar supplies the other half of the redeeming document.

Is this the same Higg? Were there two men named Higg who had a father named Snell? Now, in Scott's novel Rebecca's trial took place when Richard the Lionhearted had returned to England to crush his brother John's attempted *coup d'état*. That would have been in 1194. Richard *Coeur de Lion* hated England; he thought the climate was terrible and the common people uncouth. He spoke only Norman French and never learned the Anglo-Saxon language of his subjects. Richard spent only several months in his native land during the ten years he was king. The earliest that the trial in this degree's story could have taken place would have been 1307, the first year of Edward II's reign. If the original Higg, son of Snell, was 30 years old at Rebecca's trial, he would have had to have been at least 140 years old when Sir William was brought into court. Rebecca's ointment must been rejuvenating, to say the least. Anyway, I am glad that, in the intervening years, Higg managed to advance from peasant to scrivener (which pays a lot better). Old Man Snell would have been proud of him.

The 30th Degree
of the Southern Jurisdiction:

KNIGHT KADOSH, OR KNIGHT OF THE WHITE AND BLACK EAGLE

The third body in the Southern Jurisdiction is called the Council of Kadosh; it is responsible for 12 degrees, from the 19th to the 30th. The 30th degree is the culmination of the Council. It depicts the reception and initiation of a Knight Kadosh into the Council. The candidate is conducted through four apartments. In the first he sees a tomb with three skulls, one with a crown, one with a Pope's tiara and one wrapped in laurel leaves. These represent, respectively, King Phillip the Fair, Pope Clement V and the last Grand Master of the Knights Templar, Jacques De Molay. In another apartment he sees a two-sided ladder with seven rungs on either side. On one side the rungs are labeled with the Seven Liberal Arts and Sciences: Grammar, Rhetoric, Logic, Arithmetic, Geometry, Music and Astronomy. The rungs on the other side are labeled with Hebrew letters and represent various mystical elements from the Kabala. The lessons of this impressive and solemn degree are that we must arm ourselves with faith in God, love toward your fellow man and knowledge.[1]

31st Degree:

MY BROTHER'S KEEPER
(Paul Revere Degree)

The Stage Drama

The time is March, 1770 and the place is Boston. This degree's drama is said to be a retelling of Jesus' parable of the Good Samaritan, set in Boston during the years preceding the outbreak of the American Revolution. The Boston Massacre has just taken place and a newly-initiated member of Marblehead Lodge, John Pulling, has been given the task of conveying Henry Pelham's drawing of the event to engraver Paul Revere. Revere would then engrave a colored print that could be reproduced and distributed all over the Colonies and England (Plate 20).

Pulling sets out in the evening with his drawings. He is accosted by two ruffians who, thinking he is carrying something of great value, club him into unconsciousness when he refuses to surrender his parcel. Finding only worthless drawings, the ruffians flee the scene. Three men, a clergyman and two citizens, all members of the nearby Masonic Lodge that is meeting that evening, see the semiconscious, groaning Pulling and all three find some flimsy excuse to pass on by without rendering help. A fourth man, Thomas Dawes, sees Pulling and gives him aid, carrying him to the nearby tavern where the Lodge meeting is in session. The surly innkeeper, the lodge Tyler, at first refuses to interrupt the meeting until Joseph Warren enters and explains the meaning of Brotherhood to him. Five years later Warren would meet his death in the Battle of Bunker Hill.

The degree, said to be based on both the Old Testament story of Cain and Abel (not evident in the script) and Jesus' parable of the Good Samaritan, illustrates the Core Values of Service and Integrity. Its lesson is that we must fulfill our obligation to help and assist a brother in distress. Hopefully, it will also teach us that we have the same obligation to help *anyone*, Mason or not, in distress.

Fig. 47 The death of Joseph Warren on Bunker Hill. By John Trumull (1786).

In the Boston Museum of Fine Arts. ©iStock

Historical Background

On the chilly evening of March 5th in 1770, young Edward Garrick trudged home through the snowy streets of Boston with two companions. He was a wigmaker's apprentice and his master had complained to him that morning that a British officer, a Captain-Lieutenant Goldfinch, still hadn't paid his bill. As he approached the Massachutsets State House on Devonshire Street, Garrick spied Goldfinch talking to a lone British sentry posted on the street in front of the State House's steps. As he passed Goldfinch, Garrick called out to him that he should be more prompt in paying his debts. Goldfinch, who had settled his account with the wigmaker earlier that afternoon, ignored Garrick's insulting tone and walked away.

The sentry, Private Hugh White of the 29th Regiment of Foot, stepped up to Garrick and demanded that the boy apologize to the officer. Garrick began exchanging insults with White until the private lost his temper and struck Garrick on the side of his head with the butt of his musket. Garrick cried out from the pain of the blow and Bartholomew

Broaders, one of Garrick's friends standing nearby, began to loudly berate White for his brutality against an unarmed civilian.

It was evening and the streets were filling with men leaving their work places to head home for dinner. Broaders' shouting started to attract a crowd of sympathetic citizens, none of whom had any love for the red-coated foreign soldier. A teen-aged bookseller named Henry Knox, who would later fight in the Revolution as one of Washington's generals, warned Private White that "If you fire your musket, you'll die for it!"

Understandably, given that he was on duty alone and three thousand miles away from civilization in a rough-and-ready colonial environment, Private White became nervous and retreated to a safer position at the top of the State House's steps. He hailed a runner from the street and dispatched him to request back-up from Captain Thomas Preston,[1] the officer of the watch at nearby regimental headquarters.

A runaway mixed-race slave named Crispus Attucks had assembled a mob of around fifty Bostonians from the nearby taverns and led them to the State House. Attucks hated the British because it was they who maintained the African slave trade to procure workers for their sugar cane plantations in the West Indies.

The British colonial Home Office had developed a lucrative "triangle of trade" that profited both the English government and American ship captains.[2] New England had large distilleries that distilled molasses into rum. New England sea captains would take the cheap rum to West Africa and trade it to the coastal tribes of Kaanu, Sine, Mane and Akan for prisoners of inter-tribal wars that these tribes had taken (or had purchased from Arab traders). The New Englanders would then chain the prisoners and transport them in slave ships to the British West Indies and trade them for money (a slave bought in West Africa for five pounds sterling would fetch thirty pounds in Jamaica or Barbados) and molasses. Then the molasses would go to New England where it was bought (at a heavily marked-up price) and distilled into rum that would begin the journey all over again. The captains (and their ship's underwriters) made a huge profit at every point of the triangle and, since the life expectancy of a slave on a sugar plantation was only about six years, the planters were always in the market for fresh merchandise.

The mob was growing larger and more boisterous when Captain Preston appeared with a detail of one corporal and six privates from the 29th Regiment to reinforce Private White. As they pushed through the crowd, Knox drew up next to Preston and again warned "For God's sake, keep control of your men! If they fire their muskets, you'll all die for it!" Preston brushed him off with a curt "I'm aware of that" and pressed on to the top of the steps where a now badly frightened Private White stood shaking in his Army-issue "ammunition" boots. Preston ordered his men to load their muskets and to form a semicircular firing team.[3]

By now the crowd had grown to over three hundred angry men and the situation was becoming critical. The citizens ascended the State House steps and crowded around the soldiers, daring them to fire and throwing snowballs and horse dung at them from the street. Preston was asked by a club-wielding innkeeper if his men's muskets were loaded. He replied that they most assuredly were but that the men were trained veterans and would not fire unless he gave the order to do so. He added dryly that he was not likely to give that particular order since he himself was standing in front of the firing team!

Then some hard object, perhaps frozen horse dung, was thrown from the street and struck one of the men, Private Hugh Montgomery, on the head and knocked him down. He pulled himself back up, picked up his musket in a rage and, without orders, fired it into the crowd. The infuriated innkeeper swung his club first at Montgomery and then at Preston, hitting each of them in the arm.

Fig 48 The Boston Massacre. . ©iStock.

Everything became suddenly still as the people looked up at the soldiers in shocked disbelief. Then the other seven enlisted soldiers, acting without orders, brought their muskets to their shoulders and fired a random, unaimed volley into the crowd. If this seems like an unbelievably barbaric act for trained, uniformed soldiers to have perpetrated, we should remember that they came from an England that was undergoing a lawless and loosely governed phase of its history. At about the same time period as the one in which the degree takes place, London was a beehive of criminal and riotous mischief, in which chaotic civil disobedience was rife and even armed soldiers were vulnerable to an enraged mob. Firing on citizen rioters was routine, as described by Charles Dickens in the opening of his novel, *A Tale of Two Cities*:

> "...musketeers went into St. Giles's, to search for contraband goods, and the mob fired on the musketeers, and the musketeers fired on the mob, and nobody thought any of these occurrences much out of the common way."

Although no more than seven shots could have been fired, eleven men were said to have been struck. This brought a later charge that four armed workers in the Customs House had also fired into the crowd from the second-story windows. Three citizens, including Crispus Attucks, were struck at point blank range by .75 caliber lead balls and died instantly. Samuel Maverick, a seventeen year-old apprentice ivory carver, died the next morning after being hit by a musket ball that had ricocheted from a building at the back of the crowd. Patrick Carr, an Irishman from the old country, died of his wound two weeks later and an apprentice named Christopher Monk survived in a crippled condition for ten years before finally succumbing, it would be alleged, to the wounds he had received that evening.

The crowd finally had had enough and dispersed, still boisterous, to safer positions in neighboring streets. Acting Governor Thomas Hutchinson arrived on the scene and somehow managed to restore some degree of order. Meanwhile, Captain Preston had called out all available officers and men of the 29th Regiment and lined them up across the street in front of the State House. There would no more rioting that night.

But these were not the lawless streets of London; this was the law-abiding colony of Massachusetts. Everyone involved, soldier and citizen alike, was a British subject and, as such, was both constrained and protected by the stringent regulations of English law. Soldiers could not fire into a crowd of helpless citizens any time they felt threatened by snowball-throwing tavern revelers. Preston and the back-up detail of enlisted men under his command that evening were arrested. So were four men who had been working on the second floor of the Customs house. The army removed both the 14th and the 29th Regiments of foot from the city and quartered them in nearby Castle William on Castle Island in the bay off South Boston.

Captain Preston, the eight enlisted men who had been with him and the four civilians taken from the Customs House were indicted and brought to trial on charges of murder. Ironically, their defense attorney was none other than John Adams, the future second President of the United States. He had agreed to represent the soldiers because he was an ardent believer in the English system of justice and in a fair trial by jury for everyone. The prosecuting attorneys were Solicitor General Samuel Quincy and attorney Robert Paine. Adams succeeded in securing a complete acquittal for six of the soldiers. The remaining two soldiers, Private Montgomery and Private Matthew Kilroy, were convicted of manslaughter and sentenced to be branded on the thumb with a hot iron in open court (a "slap on the wrist" in that day and age).

Captain Preston was tried in a separate court later that year and his lawyer, again John Adams, convinced the jury that he had not ordered his men to fire. The jury acquitted him. After his trial he resigned his commission and retired to Ireland. He and Adams would meet once again in London in the late 1780s when Adams was serving as Minister to Britain.

The four civilians from the Customs House were the last to be tried. The case against them was weak to begin with and finally, after the servant of one of them made claims against his master that were easily refuted, all four were acquitted. The lying servant was whipped at the pillory and banished from the colony.[4]

Members of some paramilitary group, perhaps the Sons of Liberty, commissioned silversmith and engraver Paul Revere with engraving a colored print (Plate 20) of the incident that had been quickly dubbed The Boston Massacre. The original drawing for Revere's engraving was made by a local young artist named Henry Pelham. In an article in the Boston Gazette Pelham would later accuse Revere of using his drawing without giving him either credit or a fee. Also, Revere incorrectly portrayed Captain Preston in the act of ordering his men to fire (which he did not do) and showed a musket firing from a second-story window in the Customs House, which Revere labeled "Butcher's Hall."[5] In Revere's original engraving all the faces of the wounded citizens are white but in 1858, just before the Civil War, an African American abolitionist named William Cooper Nell convinced engravers to make one of the faces black to represent Crispus Attucks.

The 31st Degree
of the Southern Jurisdiction:

INSPECTOR INQUISITOR

The Southern version of this degree, INSPECTOR INQUISITOR, is totally different. The scene takes place in the Hall of the Last Judgment as portrayed the Ancient Egyptian Book of the Dead. The characters are the gods and goddesses of Ancient Egypt; they are judging the soul of a recently deceased Egyptian architect named Cheres. Osiris, Isis, Nephthys and Ptah grill the dead man mercilessly. They weigh his merits and review his life. He finally makes it into Heaven when Osiris, who had once been a man and understands human frailty, declares him to be worthy of a good afterlife. Although quite different in its ritual, the Southern Jurisdiction's 31st degree teaches a similar lesson: Judge yourself in the same light as you judge others; consider both actions and motives.[6]

32ⁿᵈ DEGREE:

SUBLIME PRINCE OF THE ROYAL SECRET
(The knights of the Middle Ages)

The Stage Drama

The time is an unspecified period during the Middle Ages, perhaps the 13ᵗʰ or 14ᵗʰ century. The place is a cathedral in the midst of an unnamed fortified city somewhere in Europe that is apparently at war with a neighboring city. A young aspirant to knighthood, Constans, prepares to undergo an all-night formal Vigil of Arms. Three times during the night tempters – a drunken reveler, a wizard and the Prince of Darkness himself – sneak in to lure him away from his vigil. Each time he repulses the tempters and remains true to his vigil. But, just before dawn, enemies attack the city. Constans hears the battle and realizes that the fight is going against the defenders. He must make a decision: to remain faithful to his vigil or abandon his post and join the men fighting for the city. He decides to fight, with unfortunate consequences for himself. He is awarded the Sublime Prince of the Royal Secret degree posthumously.

As with some of the preceding degrees, this is a type of play called an *allegory*. In an allegory, the characters represent abstract concepts such as courage, honesty or gluttony. Allegorical plays were very popular in the Middle Ages because, in the short space of one act, they could illustrate to an illiterate and uneducated audience the Church's approved ways to lead a virtuous and moral life.

This allegory teaches us that we should not rush to judgment in condemning the acts of another person when we do not know all the facts and that he who would judge others must first judge himself. It also teaches that possession of the Royal Secret will enable the candidate to withstand temptations and spiritual tribulations and to correctly see his way to the performance of his real duties in life.

As the culmination of 32ⁿᵈ-degree Scottish Rite Masonry, this degree celebrates the triumph of individual integrity and our obligation to serve humanity. This is the ceremonial degree of the Consistory and it has been recast to deepen its dignity and solemnity while enhancing the experience of the candidates, for most of whom this will be their ultimate degree in the Scottish Rite.

Historical Background

In view of the fascination that knights and knighthood holds for Scottish Rite Masons we will take a closer look at knights and at Medieval life in general. We will find much that is familiar mingled with some unexpectedly alien and bizarre features.

The story of knighthood begins in the ancient Roman Republic, around 510 B.C. A Roman knight was called an *eques*, from the Latin word for "horse." An eques was a noble of the second class, between a senator and a common citizen, whom the Senators expected to volunteer for military service when needed. They required him to supply his own horse, arms and armor and to maintain a certain standard of behavior in public (the Romans did not care what anyone did in private). As befitted his highborn rank, the eques received preferential treatment while serving in the field. For instance, the Roman army paid a common foot soldier a small daily wage with which he could buy his own salt. This was his *salarium* ("salt money" from *sal*, the Latin for salt) and is where our word "salary" originated. An eques received three times the salarium of a foot soldier. In civilian life, the sumptuary (clothing and jewelry) laws allowed him to wear a thin purple stripe around the edges of his toga. He could also sit on juries. In return, everyone expected him to be courageous, kind and generous and to hold the good of the Republic above his own personal welfare and safety.

For instance, in his book *The White Goddess*, Robert Graves tells the story of the legendary young eques named Mettus Curtius. One day in 326 B.C., a bottomless chasm opened suddenly in the Roman Forum. Everyone recognized this as a sign from the gods: a demand that Rome must sacrifice its most precious possession immediately or they would destroy the Republic. Someone had to do this in a matter of minutes; there was no time to talk it over. Curtius, reasoning that the Republic's most precious possession would be a brave warrior, mounted his horse and, waving his sword, jumped fully armed into the chasm that closed upon him at once. The spot was later covered by a marshy pond the Senate named Lake Curtius.[1]

After Rome fell in the 5th century A.D. the equestrian class with its noble virtues disappeared from European society. During the Dark Ages (roughly A.D. 450 – 1000), there was no societal demand on soldiers to be anything but fighting men. Only histories written centuries later, when knighthood was in full flower, refer to "knights" during this period. Take, for example, the romantic tales of King Arthur written from the 12th all the way up to the 20th centuries.

Fig. 49. Pages practicing jousting against a revolving dummy. If the page does not hit the dummy just right it will swivel around and whack him with the club it holds. ©iStock

When the legendary Celtic warlord now known as Arthur ("The Bear") defeated the invading Saxons at the Battle of Badon Hill (around A.D. 500) he did not have any Knights of the Round Table with him because there were no knights. There was also no Round Table and no knightly courtesies or courtly table manners on display at Camelot. A Welsh monk, Geoffrey of Monmouth, wrote the legend of King Arthur in his book, *Historia Regnum Britanniae* (The History of the Kings of Britian), around 1138 when he was a teacher at Oxford. Geoffrey depicted the 5th-century Arthur as if the king were one of his own contemporaries, a 12th-century medieval Christian king complete with knights in armor, coats of arms, tournaments and codes of chivalry. When the real Arthur, a Latin-speaking Romanized Celt, sat at his dining table, his companions were not the pious, virginal, Grail-seeking Christians of medieval and Victorian legend.[2] They were hard-drinking, fiery-tempered, blue-painted pagan clansmen who fought naked and collected the heads of their enemies as souvenirs. These delightful party animals were as likely to maim or kill one another during the victory feast as they were to kill an enemy on the battlefield.[3]

A century or two before the Norman invasion of England in 1066 a new social class was rearing its head in feudal Europe. The class consisted of noble mounted warriors called *knights.* The modern English word "knight" comes from the Anglo-Saxon word *cniht* that means "young servant." The *Anglo-Saxon Chronicle* is a Dark Age history of England written during the late 800s, when Alfred the Great was king of Saxon England. In the Chronicle a *cniht* was an armed servant who fought either on foot or on horseback when the king required his master to provide military service. By the time of Chaucer's Canterbury Tales (circa 1390) the same word in Middle English had come to mean "youthful hero." In most other European languages, the word for knight means "a man who rides on horseback." Examples are *chevalier* (French), *caballero* (Spanish) and *Ritter* (German).

As Barbara Tuchman points out in *The Proud Tower*, her best-selling history of pre-World War I England, "The man on horseback was the symbol of dominance, and in no other class anywhere in the world was the horse so intrinsic a part as of the English aristocracy."

After 1066 a man who wanted to become a knight had to supply his own horse, arms and armor. This limited the profession of knighthood to the wealthier classes and a social distinction soon arose that separated the common foot soldier with his leather tunic and pike from the mounted, elaborately armored warrior. During the early period of knighthood, a lord could knight any young man who had fought bravely on the battlefield. He would do this on the spot with little or no ceremony. The young warrior would kneel on the ground bareheaded, holding three blades of grass (symbolizing the Blessed Trinity) between his fingers. The lord would simply say "You are henceforth a knight," and that was that. As dubbing ceremonies became more elaborate and expensive, a king or baron would sometimes knight groups of impoverished squires in this manner on the battlefield knowing that they would never be able to afford a formal ceremony.

By the year 1200, the road to knighthood had become long, rigorous and infused with religious ceremony by the Church. Only a young man of noble birth could hope to become a knight. Society had standardized and planned every step along the way and had instituted rules that would make sure that no commoner could afford to undertake the journey.

Among the European upper classes during the Middle Ages, the actual parents spent little time with their children. Female servants would raise and educate a boy of noble birth at home until he was seven years old.[1] Then his father sent him to live a neighboring castle where other servants trained him to be a page to the castle's lord. This training went on until he was 14. During this time he would wait on table at mealtimes, help his lord to dress and bathe, comb his lord's hair and see that his clothes were cleaned and ready to wear. In return, servants and the younger knights would train him and his fellow page-boys to ride on horseback, hunt birds with a hawk and play chess and backgammon. He might also learn to sing, dance and play a zither-like musical instrument called a *psalterie*, which could be played by ear without requiring the ability to read music.

He would sometimes have to master the rudiments of reading and writing Latin or French romantic poetry.

At the age of 14 the young page became a squire. The term *esquire* means "shield-bearer."[5] The young squire rode in front of his knight, leading the knight's horse and carrying the knight's shield with its coat-of-arms prominently displayed. At this point in his education combat training became serious and the squire practiced with lance, sword, battle-ax and mace. The training at this stage was also dangerous, because the squire had to participate in jousts and tournaments. Although everyone considered these affairs to be sporting events, they could be as hazardous as actual combat.

Fig. 50 Knights jousting in a tournament. ©iStock.

For instance, in 1186 Richard the Lionheart's brother, Geoffrey, died in a joust at the court of Phillip in Paris. His horse threw him to the ground, trampling and dragging him to death.[6] In the early tournaments, there were no rules of engagement and the opposing knights could go at each other in deadly earnest. In one tournament, no less than 60 knights were killed in the general melee. In another tournament, a father killed his own son.

Even a king was not safe. On July 1, 1559, Henry II of France entered into a friendly joust with the Comte Gabriel de Montgomery, a skilled jouster six years younger than the king and the Captain of the King's Scottish Guards. All went well until the final round. Montgomery, aiming at the king's head, did not lower his lance in time and the wooden point shattered on Henry's helmet, sending a long sharp fragment through the king's right eye and into his brain. With no anesthesia available, doctors had to tie Henry to his bed where he screamed and convulsed for ten days until he died. As he lay dying he repeatedly called for his mistress, Diane de Poitiers, but his wife, Queen Catherine de Medici, would not allow the woman to come to his bedside.[7]

By the rules of medieval warfare, a squire could only aid and defend his knight on the battlefield; he could not engage the enemy in direct combat. Sometimes when a king arrived at the scene of a battle he found that the enemy hopelessly outnumbered him. He would then immediately knight as many squires as possible so they could engage in combat and even the odds. The medieval historian Froissart tells us that, on August 14 in 1385, King John I of Portugal knighted no less than 140 squires before the battle of Aljubarota. Why? Because he had seen that the opposing army of John of Castile with its Aragonese, Italian and French allies was twice the size of his own army. The tactic worked; he won.

The squire would also learn about financial and business matters from the castle's *seneschal* (administrator) and would be responsible for attending to the lord's purse when they were on a journey.

By the 14th century a squire had to be 21 years old to be considered for knighthood. In earlier centuries this rule did not always apply. In 1173 the Crown Prince Henry led a rebellion against his father, King Henry II of England. But only a knight could lead an army and young Henry was still a squire. So he had William Marshal, the head of his royal household, knight him in the field at the age of 18. Instead of the customary *colée* (an open-handed smack to the side of the head) the politically astute Marshal gave the new knight a kiss on the cheek. Forty years later the long-lived Marshal knighted nine-year old Henry III on the evening before his coronation. A tender age to become a knight, one would think, let alone a king! No doubt Marshal again replaced the *colée* with a kiss. Not one to be outdone, to celebrate his victory at the Battle of St. Albans in 1461 during the Wars of the Roses, the Lancastrian king, Henry VI, knighted his *seven*-year old son Edward, Prince of Wales.

Finally, the day would come when the young squire would be ready for the ceremony of initiation into full knighthood. To be eligible he had to have appeared in battle at least once, fighting at the side of the knight he served. The night before this first qualifying battle, he would undergo a standard vigil, an informal ceremony in which he stayed up late into the night, praying to the Blessed Virgin Mary or his patron saint that he would survive the coming fight. During the battle he would be closely observed for any signs of timidity or cowardice. Two highly valued traits looked for in a knight *aspirant* (one who aspired to become a knight) were recklessness and bravado. Veteran knights considered compassion on enemy foot soldiers and over-reliance on pre-battle planning to be unmanly.

On the evening before the dubbing ceremony that would make him a knight, the squire would have to undergo a formal Vigil of Arms. This was a much more complex ritual than a standard vigil and consisted of several parts. First, the aspirant fasted for 24 hours to purge his body and soul of sin and to make him compassionate toward the poor and hungry. Then, as an antidote to upper-class vanity, barbers would cut and shave his hair off in the manner of a monk entering a religious order.

Next he would take a symbolic, purifying bath in rose-strewn water. (Urban and upper-class people – and even some peasants – during the Middle Ages bathed much more frequently than we now imagine. Bathing did not become unpopular until the Renaissance. The Middle Ages was not, as one wit put it, "A thousand years without a bath.") After the bath he would lie down in bed like a young bride to signify his new virginal state of body, mind and soul. When he got up, attendants would clothe him in a long white tunic to show his purity. Over the tunic, he would don a bright red garment that signified he was ready to shed his blood in the service of his feudal lord. Finally, over everything else, he put on a black cloak to remind him that death comes to all men, be they knight, noble or commoner and that he should never fear to meet death in a just cause.

After placing the squire's armor and weapons on the altar, everyone left the church. The squire, humbled and purified, was alone before the altar. Standing or kneeling (he was not allowed to sit), he had to remain awake and keep watch through the night for at least 10 hours (Plate 21). Sometimes the bishop would post a priest or monk to spy on him and make sure that he did not fall asleep. At dawn, his sponsors, along with a crowd of people, entered the church. The highest-ranking priest or bishop said Mass before an assembly of knights and nobles. He then prayed over and blessed the squire's weapons and individual pieces of armor as monks fitted the squire with each one. When he was completely armed and armored his sponsors formally presented him to his feudal lord where he knelt and swore fealty as his lord's liege man.

The dubbing ceremony was not the light touch with a sword on the shoulder that we see in the movies. Either the castle's lord or the knight's father would hit the squire on the side of the head with a vicious open-handed whack, the above-mentioned *colée*. In English, this became known as the "accolade" (lit., "a blow to the neck"). Though the squire anticipated the swat and steeled himself to receive it, the force of the blow knocked more than one aspirant off his feet. The man who had delivered the blow would then exhort the young man to be a knight, good and true, and would give him a pair of golden spurs. He had "earned his spurs," as we now say. Finally, he received a shield decorated with his family's heraldic coat of arms.[8]

The European knight had much in common with his Far Eastern counterpart, the *samurai* of Japan. Both lived in a feudal society governed by hereditary nobility and both earned their living by military service. Like the word knight, the word samurai derives from the word *saburau*, ("servant"), and a samurai ranked between a *Daimyo* (the equivalent of a European baron) and a common citizen. Like the knight's code of chivalry, the samurai lived by his code of *bushidô,* a way of life dedicated to loyalty, fearlessness and practice of the martial arts, particularly *kendô,* the Way of the Sword.

Both knight and samurai spent their lives traveling the land in search of a wealthy lord in need of their fighting skills. Failing that, they would have to humble themselves and accept menial work. Unlike European knights, most samurai were cultured and literate. In times of peace they could turn their efforts to civil service, poetry and the arts. European knights who found themselves in a similar situation were frequently illiterate and sometimes turned to looting and brigandage against the peasantry of their own country. Another major difference was that a samurai would frequently fight on foot as an infantry soldier whereas a knight, encumbered by up to forty pounds of steel armor, could fight effectively only on horseback (and on a stallion; a knight was never to be seen riding a mare).[9]

By modern American standards, neither knight nor samurai lived in a free society. Civil and ecclesiastical law regulated every detail of everyone's life. In Japan only a Samurai could carry both a long and a short sword and wear a hairdo in which the front part of his hairline was shaved away and the back of his hair was done up in a topknot. Commoners could shave their heads but had to leave a patch of hair above the forehead to show that they were not samurai. A Japanese commoner could not wear silk; he could carry a short *wakizashi* sword but not the samurai's long *katana* sword. And only a samurai was allowed the privilege of regaining his lost honor by committing *seppuku,* a ceremony in which he knelt, smiling politely, and disemboweled himself with a short sword before a crowd of onlookers.

Similarly, in Medieval Europe, people could not dress as they pleased. The *sumptuary laws* decreed the kind of fabric, color, decoration, and trim of every article of clothing people of every occupation, religion, ethnic group and social class could legally wear in public. How rigidly society enforced those laws was a matter of time and place. Over time, most sumptuary laws proved to be unenforceable and had to be abandoned. The laws' original purpose was to distinguish between the hierarchal ranks of clergymen when they went about dressed in the ordinary street clothes of laypeople (as they frequently did in those times). By 1250, the laws had infiltrated into every corner of society.[10]

The wearing of ermine was restricted to physicians, magistrates and the nobility; even the richest merchant, who could well afford ermine, had to trim his garments in squirrel or fox. Ordinary peasants wore rough wool, usually dyed brown or black, the cheapest pigments. Well-off peasants sported tunics of bright red and blue.

Merchants' wives were forbidden the use of multicolored gowns, velvet, or gold embroidery on their outfits. Urban men wore short tunics, flared at the hips, over very tight-fitting leotards. Merchants had to wear leotards of all one color but the nobility and their servants were allowed to wear parti-colored tights in which one leg was a different color than the other. Upper-class men, both commoners and nobility, wore long, pointed shoes called *poulaines* that had toes extending out as much as 20 inches. In many cases the points of the long floppy toes had to be tied to the wearer's shins to allow him to walk. Even armored knights sometimes wore steel poulaines into battle. The fashion became so pervasive that eventually the Church condemned long-toed shoes as marks of vanity foisted on society by the devil. Everyone, men and women, wore daggers but only males of the nobility could wear swords. With men's clothing too tight to admit pockets, they had to carry everything - keys, purses, daggers, holy relics - hanging from a broad leather belt.

All non-Christians had to wear identifying cloth badges sewn to the left breast of their coats or tunics. Jews had to wear a yellow six-pointed star (or the Tablets of the Ten Commandments) while Muslims wore a green crescent. Cathars ("Purified Ones," a heretical sect in southern France) wore the yellow Cathar cross and repentant heretics wore a devil's head. Besides their badges, Jews also had to wear a pointed, knobbed hat resembling the pawn on a chessboard. Muslims wore a yellow turban and, in some jurisdictions, heretics wore a conical paper cap (the origin of the modern "dunce's cap").[11]

Although many knights could not read or write, they were not as ignorant as they are sometimes portrayed nowadays. Most knights knew that the world was round and that the moon was the closest planet to the earth. A well-educated knight knew that the stars were very far away, that epilepsy and insanity were natural illnesses caused by spasms of the brain and that fireflies were the souls of unbaptized babies doomed to drift on the night wind until the Second Coming of Christ.

If his eyes troubled him as he grew older a knight could buy himself a pair of eyeglasses (invented at Oxford between 1250 and 1300). When he had a bone broken in combat or in a joust, he could have it expertly set by a specialist. The specialist was usually the village blacksmith, the strongest man available, because stretching an arm or leg to allow the broken bone to snap back into place required a great deal of strength. If all these problems gave the knight a headache he would go to the local barber, who doubled as a physician. The barber would grind him a mixture of peony root and oil of roses, which did little good. If, instead, the knight sought help from a local witch ("wise woman") she would have him chew on a mouthful of willow bark that would promptly take the pain away. (Willow bark contains large quantities of salicylic acid, the active ingredient of aspirin.)

A knight, like any other citizen of the Middle Ages, knew many witches. These women were adherents of the ancient pre-Christian nature religions of the European countryside. The peasant population respected these women; they lived and practiced their arts freely in rural villages throughout Europe. Then, around 1400, agents of the Holy Inquisition arrested them along with Jews and non-conformist Christians ("heretics"). The Inquisitors tortured all of their victims to extract confessions of guilt and burned them alive by the tens of thousands. The monks who wrote down the witches' "confessions" (and who did not like to admit that the Old Religion was still popular with the people) claimed that the women had admitted to worshiping the devil, a capital offense in Medieval Europe.

In fact, British witches did not believe that the Devil existed; they worshipped a nature deity they called Red Champion. This may have referred to a bright red hallucinogenic mushroom (*Amanita muscaria*) that the witches ate to make them think they could fly to their religious services on a broomstick. The mushroom, commonly known as fly agaric, was well known to the Church. Plaincourault Abbey in Indre, France, has a fresco showing Adam and Eve standing on either side of a gigantic *Amanita muscaria* mushroom. In this case, the fungus took the place of the more conventional Biblical Tree of Knowledge of Good and Evil. (Plate 22)

Fig. 51 Goings-on in a Late Medieval tavern. The sleeping woman on the left is probably drunk. If no one intercedes, the two children on the right will soon be in the same condition. Note the use of pewter and ceramic plates at this later time, even in a lower-class tavern. Detail from "The Fat Kitchen" by Jan Steen. Liechtenstein Museum, The Princely Collections, Vienna. {PD-US}

Life in the Middle Ages was collective; no one, even the king, knew much privacy. People ate, worshipped, worked and slept in groups. The lord of a castle and his lady might have their own bedroom, but his knights, servants and dogs all slept together in the great hall. In smaller homes the entire family, servants and overnight guests all slept together in one room. Frequently they even slept in the same bed as Chaucer tells us in the naughty Miller's Tale. On the road, travelers overnighting at an inn ate and slept in a common room and travelled together in armed bands for mutual protection.[12] Sanitation everywhere was rudimentary. Builders always located toilets at the edge of the castle where they could drain into the moat; men and women used them, sometimes at the same time.[13] Travelers said that they always knew when they were approaching a castle that was not yet in sight just by smelling the moat.[14]

The knight's day began at sunrise with morning prayers and a Mass said in the castle's chapel. In Medieval times, all upper class people kept track of the time of day by following the liturgical hours of prayer established by the Church. There was the hour of Lauds (dawn), Prime (early morning), Terce (mid-morning), Sext (midday, about noon), None (mid-afternoon), Vespers (evening, about sundown "at the lighting of the lamps"), Compline (night), Nocturns or Vigils (late night), and Matins (early morning hours, before

Fig. 52. A Medieval castle. ©iStock.

sunrise).[15] Each of the hours had its own set of prayers appropriate to it. The Church called this system of timekeeping The Divine Office and the various liturgical hours were announced by the ringing of local church bells.[16] People in the Middle Ages took their praying seriously.

There was no meal equivalent to our breakfast; after Mass people began their day with a sip of red wine and a bite of bread.[17] Everyone spent the morning hours on routine chores that varied dramatically depending upon the social class of the person doing the chore. Chores ranged from going over the estate's business affairs (the lord of the castle, his seneschal and the chaplains as recording secretaries), embroidery and conversation (the lady of the castle and her female attendants), lessons in etiquette, reading and writing Latin (the pages), archery and combat on horseback (the squires), fencing and tilting with lances (the knights) and filthy, backbreaking work (everybody else). The last category might involve cooking in a greasy kitchen, slaughtering and butchering animals, cleaning out stables, feeding livestock, washing sheets and towels in a caustic soda solution, emptying chamber pots, forging iron nails and implements by a hot fire and standing guard duty on the castle walls in all weather.

Medieval people ate two meals a day. Dinner, the day's main meal, began at 10 o'clock in the morning and usually lasted until noon.[18] This could be an elaborate affair, especially if the lord were entertaining guests. Meals were eaten in the main hall, the site of all the castle's indoor activities. Servants set up wooden sawhorses called *trestles* and placed board table tops (trestle boards) over them. They laid tablecloths over the boards and arranged benches or chairs around the table. A blast on a trumpet summoned everyone indoors. Washbasins with squirting jets of water were set up at the hall's entrance for the diners to wash their hands.

The lord, lady and their children ate at the head table at the end of the hall farthest from the drafty entrance doors. If the lord were entertaining important guests (bishops, other lords, the king) they would sit at the head table as well. Other people took their places on the lower tables that ran down the hall at right angles to the head table. Servants seated the diners according to social rank. The highest ranks sat nearest the head table, the lowest by the chilly entrance.

Social protocol obliged the castle's lord to serve a certain number of courses at dinner depending on whether or not he was entertaining guests and who his guests were. The king or a high-ranking church official such as a cardinal would expect no less than nine courses. A bishop or a count received at least seven courses. A low-ranking official like a messenger or tax collector rated just three or four courses, about what the lord would be having anyway. The Church, in an effort to curb gluttony, passed laws restricting the number and variety of dishes that the upper classes could serve at dinner. Everyone ignored them.

During the Middle Ages when a woman gave birth she was considered unclean and was obliged to undergo a rite of purification called "churching." In 1466 Lord Rozmital, a Bohemian noble, was entertained on his visit to London by the Yorkist king, Edward IV, at a banquet celebrating the churching of Edward's queen, Elizabeth of York.[19] According to Rozmital's Bohemian diarist, Gabriel Tetzel, the banquet took up four large rooms and consisted of 50 courses. Tetzel should know, because his noble rank earned him the privilege of standing with other nobles in a corner of the queen's dining room and watching her while she ate.

What did a knight eat? The medieval diet centered on meat and included beef, pork, lamb, mutton, chicken, goose and duck. Turkeys, native to North America, were unknown in Europe before 1500. Game such as venison, boar and crane supplemented the meat of domestic animals.

Fig. 53 King Arthur and his knights, illustrating a Medieval meal in a castle. Note that everyone has an eating knife on the table in front of him. The hermit on the left is about to introduce Galahad to the company. ©iStock.

Cooks pounded the meat of small game animals like squirrel and rabbit into a paste. They mixed it with spices and served it as a custard or mixed it with bread crumbs to make dumplings. If the lord were entertaining the king or if he were celebrating a wedding or a christening, the chefs might serve up a whole roasted calf stuffed with trout, or suckling pigs stuffed with crab meat or perhaps swans stuffed with carp. This might be accompanied by pickled ox-tongue, fish aspic, beef and eel pies, peacocks and cabbage and various fruits and cheeses. Sometimes cooks gilded the meats with a mixture of flour, saffron, egg yolk and real gold dust.[20]

Medieval diners even consumed farm draft animals. To court popularity with the common people, Richard Neville, Earl of Warwick, established a large townhouse in London in 1457. Whenever he was in residence he had six oxen roasted on spits for breakfast every morning. He maintained an open-house policy whereby any passer-by was welcome to stop in and help himself to as much meat as he could carry away impaled on the blade of his dagger.[21] Sales of extra long-bladed daggers must have gone up that year.

The most common vegetables served were peas, lentils, chickpeas, beans, onions, leeks and garlic. Maize (Indian corn), Lima beans, tomatoes and potatoes, all brought back by voyagers to the New World, would not be seen in Europe until after 1500.

Coffee, first grown in Ethiopia, would be unknown in Europe until introduced by Venetian traders in 1615. Fruits, in season, were apples, pears, plums, grapes and peaches. Cooks could go into town markets and purchase more exotic foods such as rice, dates, almonds, figs, oranges, pomegranates and sugar loaves. These were usually available at the fairs held on holy days such as the feasts of the Virgin Mary or local patron saints. Servants gathered nuts, mushrooms, berries and edible ferns from the nearby forest.

Food was usually sweetened with honey because table sugar, as we know it, was a rarity. Sugar cane, originally native to New Guinea, spread with Muslim traders through south Asia and along the Silk Route into Islamic lands. The use of sugar spread along with the conquests of Muslim rulers. Wealthy caliphs developed a taste for the white powder, especially when it was mixed with ground almonds into a concoction called *marzipan*. Crusaders returning from the Holy Land first brought cane sugar into Europe; its production at that time was still almost entirely in the hands of Muslims.[22]

The sugar cane plant, which requires a steady supply of sunshine mixed with frequent heavy tropical downpours, will not grow well in temperate zones, least of all in the harsh climate of northwestern Europe. The little supply of sugar from the Middle East was only affordable to the nobility and was a rarity even to them. Refined cane sugar would not become readily available in Europe until the second Columbus expedition (1493 – 1496) and its followers planted African sugar cane in the West Indies and began to produce lump sugar in large quantities. Since European colonists in the West Indian islands thought that only black Africans were capable of working in the cane fields under a tropical sun this also had the undesirable consequence of bringing the African slave trade to the New World.

(An interesting side note: The Spanish colonists thought that the local Arawak Indians were also capable of working in the cane fields but within a couple of decades all the Arawaks on the islands were dead, either from smallpox or killed by the Spaniards for their amusement. The only surviving Arawaks are now on the South American continent.)

The Church forbad the eating of meat on the many holy days of the year and during the seasons of Lent and Advent. Consequently cooks learned to serve up fish such as mackerel, cod, herring, pike, flounder, mullet, eel and shad in imaginative ways. They pounded fish into a paste and served it in a pie or as a custard eaten with spicy sauces. Crab, lobster and crayfish were boiled while oysters, clams and lampreys were eaten raw or jellied for preservation. Even whale meat (whales were thought to be fish at the time) occasionally made its way to the medieval table.

The diners could wash their food down with mugs of beer, ale, mead or wine. Before the introduction of corks, wine was drunk freshly made and unaged. In hot weather, it frequently turned sour before it got to table and the resulting flavor could make even a strong man gag.[23] The Arab art of distillation was just entering Europe and monks were beginning to distill wine into brandy, which kept much longer on the shelf. Also, monks were learning to fortify wine by adding distilled alcohol and aging the mix in barrels, producing port and sherry. This gave the wine a much longer and more dependable shelf life. Fortified wine soon took Europe by storm and drunkenness at meals by both men and women soon became commonplace.

Utensils were few and simple. Forks, a later invention of the Italian Renaissance, were at first used only in the kitchen and not at the table. Everyone commonly wore a sharp double-edged dagger called an "eating knife" on his or her belt. At mealtimes, people cut their meat with this knife and ate the meat with their fingers, washing their hands and their knives afterwards in a finger bowl. Soup was eaten with a spoon or sipped directly from the bowl. Salt was easily obtainable and was present on the table in large quantities. Pepper, cloves, ginger, cinnamon and saffron were harder to get and expensive. People used mustard, grown and produced locally, on everything in lavish amounts.[24]

There was little ceramic crockery on the table. Diners ate vegetables from wooden bowls. Meat was served on large square slabs of inferior, day-old bread called *trenchers*. Two people shared each trencher, one person of higher social rank than the other. The lower-ranking person cut the meat, ladled the sauce and in general waited upon the higher-ranked diner.[25] When the meal was over servants collected the trenchers, soaked through and dripping with gravy and sauces, and gave them to the poor. It was considered the height of gluttony and ill manners for a diner to eat his own trencher. A person who did so was called a "trencherman" and everyone looked down upon him as a *déclassé* oaf.

After dinner, jugglers acrobats or jesters provided entertainment. Those were rough times and life was short; the jesters were free to do just about anything they thought would get a laugh. They centered much of their humor on sex and they weren't subtle. For instance, if a widow had recently remarried she would be the butt of the evening's entertainment.[26] The jesters would cavort around behind her chair waving obscene phallic devices and mocking her imagined sexual voracity with orgiastic moans. A really good performance on this subject was a guaranteed laugh riot for both the men and women present. If her new husband was much younger than she was, the boys could bring the house down.

A more genteel form of entertainment was the singing of love ballads by professional musicians called troubadours. Many of these entertainers hailed from southern France and they sang their ballads in the romantic southern tongue of Provence known as Provençal or *langue d'oc*, ("The language of 'yes'"). The cruder versions of these ballads (popular with the peasantry) simply described male and female genitalia in the coarsest possible slang. The more courtly versions recounted one-sided love affairs between mismatched couples, usually a knight and a married woman. The ballads derived from Islamic love songs brought home from the Middle East by returning crusaders. These songs originally sprang from the theme of a man spending his entire life pursuing a veiled, unattainable woman confined in a Sultan's harem.[27]

Later in the afternoon the knight would accompany his lord as he rode around the estate on an inspection tour. When the lord rode to the hunt his knights would ride attendance on him and carry his weapons or his hawk. They also provided armed protection against any bandits or assassins that might be lurking in the forest.

Among the upper classes hunting was more than a pastime – it was a way of life.[28] It provided an opportunity for both men and women to demonstrate their horsemanship and skill with weapons against a quarry that (other than bears or wild boars) could not fight back. It was also an entertaining way to procure fresh meat for the table. Before the introduction of firearms, the only practical way to bring down a flying bird was to send another bird, a hawk or a falcon, after it. The training and use of these birds of prey achieved a cult-like status among medieval nobility and the art of falconry occupied the bulk of their spare time.[29]

Everyone in the upper classes, men and women, carried a falcon or a hawk around with them wherever they went, including church and dinner. Sometimes at dinner, the castle chefs would serve a large pie filled with live blackbirds. When the top crust was torn off, the birds would burst out of the pie and fly in a tight flock around the hall, looking for a way out. That was the signal for everyone to launch their birds of prey and cheer them on as they brought down the blackbirds and returned the mangled corpses to their owners.

A lord's favorite falcon sat on a perch behind its owner at mealtimes. The lord fed the bird with far choicer meats than any servant ever saw. In return, the falcon freely decorated the floor with its droppings. The lord extended the same privileges to his most productive hounds. To offset the stench of all the urine and fecal matter, servants covered the castle floor with straw heavily laced with herbs and flowers. Every evening they swept the straw up and replaced it with a fresh mixture. However, since — for reasons of security — the main hall rarely had any large open windows or anything else in the way of ventilation, the daily change of herbal straw, according to most contemporary accounts, had little effect on the hall's ambiance. Those who could afford them frequently wore tiny bottles of perfume around their necks to sniff every now and then for a brief change of atmosphere. (The same dodge would be used centuries later by the officers of slave ships to counter the stench of hundreds of Africans chained below decks with no toilet facilities.)

If our knight went into town, he could enjoy a hot bath in the town's public bathhouse or watch a mystery play put on by one of the town's guilds. The play would be about either the saint for that particular day or some event from the scriptures. Since few lay people could read or write, these plays formed the basis of their religious education. The knight could then visit the town's cathedral with its colorful frescoes and its statues of saints all painted in brilliant colors, another form of public religious education. The paint has long since worn away from the church walls and statues and today we see only the cathedrals' bare grey stone.

When he tired of gazing at the statues of saints, he could hire the services of a licensed prostitute, of which there were many. He could easily spot a prostitute by her red-striped dress. In some cities, by law, she had to wear her clothing turned inside out. The Church reluctantly sanctioned prostitution as a necessary evil. Prostitutes had their own guilds complete with mandatory fee schedules and restrictions governing work on holy days. In Milan (which boasted it had even more prostitutes than Paris) the girls had to pay a municipal tax used to maintain the city walls.[30] Sexually transmitted disease would not be a major problem until the first Columbus expedition returned in 1493 and introduced syphilis into Europe.

I have dwelt at length on the culture of medieval Europe and the training of knights because of the all-pervading militarism, and particularly the fascination with medieval knights, that characterizes the 14 degrees of the Consistory.

The original six "Americana" degrees all deal directly or indirectly with war. Aside from the 19th, 20th and 26th degrees, most deal with armed knights. Most of these knights belong to imaginary pseudo-Masonic orders having warfare as their *raison d'être*. Part of the allure of make-believe knighthood probably came from 18th-century France. There the *nouveau riche* merchant classes that were joining the higher degree bodies in Masonry longed for knightly titles, especially those that included the word "prince." These titles, when conferred in Charleston in 1801, almost certainly carried the same fascination for the largely small-town and rural denizens of the Old South.

The militaristic mystique, at least in the Northern Masonic Jurisdiction, blossomed during the period following the Civil War. It was the Golden Age of Fraternalism and everybody was joining something. Of course, every organization wanted to stand out as they marched down Main Street in the ubiquitous small-town holiday parades of the time. Once the Civil War was over and the danger had passed, everyone came to look upon the war as a glorious adventure. Both veterans and men who had not served wanted people to see them wearing a uniform. So the Odd Fellows and the Knights of Pythias and the Knights of Columbus and the Masonic Knights Templar designed dashing outfits modeled on Army and Navy uniforms of the period.

The Masonic Knights Templar adopted a Naval "Admiral Farragut" uniform complete with a sword and an admiral's hat that sported a large ostrich feather. Some bodies of the Scottish Rite adopted similar uniforms that, although still optional, are rarely worn today. The uniforms, along with military titles for officers such as Commander-in-Chief, 1st Lieutenant Commander, Captain of the Guard, Engineer and Sentinel reminded veterans of their days in the field and were felt to lend an air of military valor to the participants.

The 32nd Degree
of the Southern Jurisdiction:

MASTER OF THE ROYAL SECRET

The 32nd degree in the Southern Jurisdiction is beautiful, elaborate and laden with esoteric symbolism. There are triangles, seven-pointed stars, nine-pointed stars, lesser tetracts, greater tetracts, and pyramids of stars galore. There are connect-the-dots geometric figures honoring Hindus, Pythagoreans, Persian Zarathustrans, Babylonian Magi and Jewish Kabbalists. There is a beautiful seven-pointed star in the colors of the solar spectrum, which Pike may have derived from the Indian Vedic *chakra* system. There is a five-pointed Wiccan (witchcraft) pentagram in red. Finally, there is an enormous color diagram of an imaginary Masonic camp with banners and flags and pennants and tents, all representing the 33 degrees of the Scottish Rite Masonry combined. The ritual is colorful, impressive and mystical in the extreme. It combines almost everything Albert Pike unearthed in his researches and every symbol that he – rightly or wrongly, accurately or inaccurately – portrayed in his works. I would very much like to see this degree performed someday; it must be a beautiful and moving production.[31]

Appendix A

What is the Scottish Rite and Where Did It Come From? A Brief History.

To appreciate the history of the Scottish Rite we must have an idea of the history of Freemasonry in general. Today we in the Fraternity refer to working stone masons as "operative" masons and to modern Freemasons as "speculative" Masons. Masonry as a fraternity for purely speculative Masons is a British phenomenon dating from the 17th century. So we'll begin with the so-called Great Revival of 1717, the event that is generally accepted as the birth of the Fraternity.

1717

Great actions that champion ideas ahead of their times require brave men and women who are not afraid to make courageous decisions. In February of 1717 the members of four London mixed lodges are said to have made such a decision at the Apple Tree tavern on Charles Street in Covent Garden. Composed of both working ("operative") stone masons and "gentlemen" or "accepted" masons, the lodge members decided to form the first Grand Lodge of speculative or "philosophical" masonry. They met again on June 24th, St. John the Baptist's Day, and acted on their decision. Grand Lodge Freemasonry, the present-day form of the Masonic fraternity, was born.

What was momentous about these meetings was that a new form of Freemasonry, enshrining and perpetuating the ideals of the Enlightenment, was born. The Enlightenment was a major revolution in thought and attitude that had swept Europe in the previous decades and was taking root in the American colonies. The London Masons were especially intrigued by three particular Enlightenment ideals: The social equality of all men, civil rights stemming from political freedom and the ascendancy of science and reason over sectarian religious dogma. But most especially they treasured their own brand-new idea that reasonable men of all faiths, political persuasions and social status could meet on the level as social equals in fellowship and brotherhood. These ideals were the rough gems that, 59 years later, would become the polished Masonic jewels set in our Declaration of Independence and Constitution.

We Americans, like our founding fathers, hold these ideas to be true and self-evident. But they were by no means self-evident in the England of 1717. In fact, in the eyes of the Crown they were detested views, bordering on sedition and dangerous to the men who promoted them. The British government routinely fined, imprisoned or even executed men and women for espousing these ideas in public. The notion that religious or political differences ought not to hinder friendship and brotherhood among men of good will was anathema in 18th-century England.

Many of the Freemasons who gathered at the Apple Tree tavern could remember their childhood days when Anglican soldiers had shot or drowned Scottish Presbyterians who had refused to say "God save the king."[1] They all knew that the King's men had, only decades earlier, whipped Puritans and other Nonconformist Protestants through the streets, locked them in the pillory and cut their ears off. The public executioner had bored holes through the tongues of Quakers who spoke openly about the Inner Light. Thirty-seven years earlier, secret police had arrested a group of Jesuit priests on trumped-up charges of treason. The trial judge had not allowed them to present any evidence in their support. They were hanged, drawn and quartered, publicly butchered on the streets of London like animals in a slaughterhouse. (Some of the [imaginary] penalties of our degrees have been based on this practice.)

This attitude affected even the most venerable academic institutions. Cambridge University refused to promote no less a scholar than Sir Isaac Newton, the most lauded scientist of the day, to the position of Department Chairman. Why? He was a Unitarian and did not believe in the Holy Trinity. Therefore he could not be ordained a parson in the Church of England, a requirement for the chairmanship.

These were serious considerations, indeed. When the Freemasons published their constitutions (written by the Scottish Presbyterian minister James Anderson) in 1723 stating that Freemason need only profess "…that religion in which all men agree, leaving their particular opinions to themselves…" they weren't just being jolly good fellows. They were taking their lives in their hands. They were sticking their collective necks out, far out, in support of an idea whose time, for all they knew, had not yet come. With the safety of hindsight, we now know that the time *had* come and that their noble experiment was successful.

1741

The Scottish Rite and its system of "higher" degrees can be traced back to a single speech. The man who gave the speech was an expatriate Scotsman, the *Chevalier* Andrew Michael Ramsay.[2] If anyone deserves the title of "Father of the Scottish Rite," it is he.

Whether anyone had invented and worked a few higher degrees before a newspaper published his speech in 1741 is not Masonically significant, just as it is not historically significant that other European or Asian explorers may have made landfall in North America before Christopher Columbus arrived in the Bahamas. Columbus' voyages opened a new era in history and changed the world forever, the others did not.

There were others who suggested the need for higher degrees beyond the basic three. For instance, Dr. James Anderson, in the 1738 version of his Constitutions, had referred to Masons as "The Sons of Noah." This took the antecedents of the Craft far back before the time of Solomon into ancient Mesopotamian mythology. Anderson's theory formed the basis of several "Noachite" higher degrees, one of which a group called the Allied Masonic Degrees still works today. Even earlier, a Mr. Martin Clare (whom Ramsay respected and probably knew personally) wrote a defense of Freemasonry in 1730. There he traced Masonry's origins to the pagan mystery religions of Greece and Egypt, indicating that certain "lost" degrees may have existed that related to these religions.

A modern Masonic body, the Royal Order of Scotland, today confers two higher degrees: THE HEREDOM OF KILWINNING and THE KNIGHTS OF THE ROSY CROSS, claiming great antiquity for both. The Order maintains that crusaders established the first of these degrees in Palestine during the early Middle Ages and that Robert the Bruce created the second after the Battle of Bannockburn on June 24, 1314. However, the first documented reference to these degrees comes from a charter (no longer in existence) written in 1747, six years after Ramsay's talk was published. Whatever the case, it was Ramsay's dissertation that began an exciting new era in Freemasonry, one that continues to this day.

According to his own account, given to a friend and fellow tutor named Von Geusau who traveled with him throughout Europe near the end of his life, Ramsay was born around 1681 in the Scottish town of Ayr. His family was apparently well off, for they had been able to have him educated sufficiently in the liberal arts for the University of Edinburgh to accept him as an undergraduate at the tender age of 14. He left Edinburgh when he was 17 and, the next eight years, earned a living as a private tutor to the sons of Scottish nobility. He traveled to Flanders (present-day Belgium and northern France) around 1706 where he saw military service under the Duke of Marlborough in the War of the Spanish Succession (1701 – 1713).

In 1710, while still in Flanders, he met Francois Fenelon, a well-known author and intellectual of the period. Fenelon was the Roman Catholic Archbishop of the large and influential diocese of Cambrai in what is now the northern part of France. Ramsay adopted Fenelon as his mentor and studied under his tutelage for five years; he later wrote Fenelon's biography. Moved by Fenelon's charm and intellect, Ramsay converted from his native

Scottish Calvinism to Roman Catholicism and even adopted Fenelon's pet philosophy, Christian Quietism. This was a peculiar Buddhist-like doctrine current in the Catholic Church during the late 1600s that taught that, through meditation and asceticism, man could achieve a sinless Nirvana-like state and, eventually, unity with God. The Church condemned the movement and Fenelon got into a lot of trouble over his adherence to it.

Around 1715 Ramsay left Fenelon and found his way to Paris. There, as the tutor of an important young nobleman, he became friends with the King's Regent (deputy), Phillip of Orleans, who conferred the Order of St. Lazarus upon Ramsay. This was the equivalent of a British knighthood and gave Ramsay the title of *Chevalier*. With this calling-card he went to Rome and, for about 15 months, tutored no less a person than Charles Edward Stuart, the Young Pretender (in exile) to the throne of England. This was the young man who would later be known as Bonnie Prince Charlie to his Scottish supporters. Charles' father and grandfather (the Old Pretender) were both named James and, *Jacobus* being the Latin equivalent of James, people took to calling them and their supporters Jacobites. This brief interlude in Ramsay's life, together with his Scottish heritage and his adopted Catholic faith, has given rise to the notion that he was a covert Jacobite. Did some of the fanciful Masonic speculations in the famous speech he would later give denote sympathy for the Scottish House of Stuart and its claim to the English throne?

All evidence indicates that this was not the case. It now appears that, for his entire life, Ramsay remained loyal to George II and the House of Hanover. In deference to the English king's Protestant faith, the now Catholic Ramsay turned down an invitation to tutor George's son, the young Prince William Augustus, Duke of Cumberland.

This plump boy, 21 years later, would earn an ambiguous place in the history of Great Britain. If you were English you would regard him as the valiant general who crushed the Jacobite rebellion of 1745 at the Battle of Culloden on April 16, 1746. He was the "hero" to whom Handel dedicated his oratorio *Judas Maccabaeus* with its resounding movement "See, the Conquering Hero Comes." Legend has it that the English common folk were so grateful to Cumberland for defending them against the rapacious hordes of kilted, unwashed highlanders who were well on their way to sacking London that they named a common field flower "Sweet William" after the gallant duke.[3]

If you were a Scottish highlander you thought of Cumberland as the Butcher of Culloden, whose army committed unspeakable atrocities against men, women and children amidst the hills and heather of northern Scotland. The hill folk of the Scottish highlands now call a local weed "Stinking Billy." As they say in real estate, location is everything.

Ramsay spent the eight years from 1728 to 1736 back in England and Scotland. On March 17th, 1729, he became a Freemason at the Horn Lodge in the Palace yard of

Westminster in London. He received numerous other honors and awards such as election to Fellowship in the Royal Society and a Doctor of Law degree from Oxford, the first Roman Catholic the university had so honored since the English Reformation of 1535. As far as we can tell, Ramsay was an affable, intelligent and socially adroit man of the world. He was an accomplished linguist and a man of integrity whom people at all levels of society readily accepted. He seemed to regard Freemasonry as just another gentlemanly pursuit in which one could spend a few agreeable hours of good company and perhaps make some friendships further up the social ladder. He was not the ardent Freemason that Mozart was, nor was he an intellectual ferret in the mold of Elias Ashmole. Two aspects of his character are certain: he made friends easily and impressed everyone he met.

Ramsay returned to France in 1736 and, as an amusing sideline to his teaching duties, resumed his Masonic activities in Paris. By 1737 he had become the Grand Orator of some Masonic body in that city. The body was probably an ordinary blue lodge that the French had fancied up by giving ornate titles to its officers. On or about March 21st, 1737, the Master charged Ramsay with delivering a combined welcoming oration and instructional lecture to some new members the lodge was initiating that evening. A man of Ramsay's intelligence and experience had no difficulty in preparing such an address and he made the most of it.

He was well aware that, unlike the English, the French upper-classes despised the notion that Freemasonry had descended from the medieval guilds of common stone masons. The French nobility, in particular, chafed under the thought that they sullied their rose and apricot silk breeches by sitting in seats that low-class quarrymen and bricklayers had once occupied. In addition, the upper classes of pre-revolutionary France were decidedly anti-Semitic and longed to hear of a Christian, rather than an Old Testament, origin to Masonry. They were further put off by having access to only two degrees, Entered Apprentice and Fellowcraft. Even the introduction of a third degree, Master Mason, a few years previously hadn't satisfied them. They wanted more, and Ramsay knew it. He also knew that, with a little work, he could touch on all three problems and deliver a real crowd pleaser.

Whether or not Ramsay actually delivered his lecture to the candidates is uncertain. What is certain is that, for some reason, in 1741 an obscene Parisian newspaper (a forerunner of today's pornography magazines) called *The Cuckolds' Almanac* published the entire text under the title of *"Discourse pronounced at the reception of Freemasons by Monsieur de R, Grand Orator of the Order."* Here are excerpts from the lecture (not necessarily in their order of presentation) with discussions of their main points.

> "Our founders were not simple workmen in stone, nor yet curious geniuses;
> they were not only skilled architects, engaged in the construction of

material temples, but also religious and warrior princes who designed to enliven, edify and protect the living Temples of the Most High. The Crusaders vowed to restore the Temple of the Christians in the Holy Land. They agreed upon several ancient signs and symbolic words, and the promise to keep them secret was a bond to unite Christians of all nationalities in one fraternity."

This is the main point of the entire lecture: The true ancestors of later speculative Masons were not common laborers but noble warriors – Crusaders, no less. They also happened to be skilled architects and experienced stone masons (a romantic but unlikely combination in that time and place). According to Ramsay their purpose in going to the Holy Land was an idealistic and unselfish one: To rebuild and protect the shrines and churches at the many Christian pilgrimage sites there. While they were at it they also founded a secret society for European Christians using "ancient signs and symbolic words." This was a powerful concept that meant more to an audience of 18th-century Frenchmen than it probably does to 21st-century Americans. It meant that the ancestors of Freemasonry were not common laborers but were nobly-born members of the upper classes. In the rigid social class system of the time this was a potent notion and one that his listeners and readers readily accepted.

"Our Order then made union with the Knights of St. John of Jerusalem. Hence the name, Lodges of St. John. This union was made after the example of the Israelites in the erection of the Second Temple, who, while they handled the trowel and mortar with one hand, in the other, they held the sword and buckler."

Ramsay is saying that his warrior princes *cum* bricklayers decided to join forces with a semi-religious military order that had begun its existence in 1046 as the *Knights Hospitallers*. This group dedicated themselves to caring for knights wounded in combat and pilgrims who fell sick in the Holy Land. They changed their name to the Knights of St. John of Jerusalem in 1118. That was the same year in which Hughes de Payens arrived in Jerusalem with 8 other knights. He called his group the *Poor Fellow Soldiers of Christ.* They would shortly become known as the *Knights Templar.* Although the idea of Freemasons being descended from the Knights Templar is often traced back to Ramsay's speech, he never mentioned the Knights Templar by name.

Ramsay's romantic vision of upper-class armored knights sweating away with a sword in one hand and a trowel in the other proved attractive. It quickly found its way into several higher degrees in the York Rite having to do with Zerubbabel and other Jewish exiles returning from Babylon to build the second temple in Jerusalem. It especially appealed to upper-class French and British gentlemen who, never having worked a day in their lives, could not appreciate the unlikely picture that it presented.

> "Our Order, therefore, was founded in remote antiquity and renewed in the Holy Land. Returning from Palestine, the kings, princes, and lords, established lodges, first, in Germany, Italy, Spain, France, and, thence, in Scotland, because of the close alliance between the French and the Scotch. James, Lord Steward of Scotland, was Grand Master at Kilwinning in 1286."

Throughout the speech, Ramsay makes several references to a Masonic Lodge in Kilwinning, Scotland, which figures prominently in Masonic lore and lays claim to being the oldest blue lodge in the world.

It might be of interest here to pause a moment in our examination of Ramsay's speech and look at the claimed history of Freemasonry as put forth by Templarists, modern-day adherents of the theory that the Fraternity is directly descended from the Knights Templar. According to these theorists, a few days before the forces of King Phillip the Fair attacked the order on October 13th, 1307, a fleet of sixteen Templar ships set sail from the Templar seaport base at La Rochelle, a rich merchant city on the southwest coast of France. Legend has it that the ships were loaded with the treasures of the Templar fraternity and that the captains had orders to transport the treasures from France to Scotland, where they were to conceal them. In Templarist lore the cargos of the ships range from the possible (gold coins, silver bars, precious gems) to the fanciful (the Arc of the Covenant, the Holy Grail and, presumably, Aladdin's magic lamp). The legend maintains that these treasures are now buried buried under Kilwinning Abbey.

The Abbey, named for the Saxon St. Winning, was the home of the Tironensian Monks, an order founded by Bernard of Tiron, a Benedictine monk, around 1109. Tiron was the name of a forest near Chartes where Bernard had founded his first abbey. The Tironensian monks were master craftsmen in carpentry, wood carving, stone masonry, metal work and architecture. Those monks who were masons supposedly held work meetings (called "lodge" meetings by modern Templarists) in the Abbey's charterhouse. They are said to have welcomed the Templars and, according to some modern fringe theorists, our Masonic fraternity is descended from an amalgamation of the operative monk masons and the Templars. The lodge building of the modern-day Kilwinning Lodge No. 0, sometimes called the "Mother Lodge of all Freemasonry," appropriately abuts the ruins of Kilwinning Abbey.

There are more theories. Another one holds that the treasures lie in a crypt under Rosslyn Chapel, where they remain to this day. Still other theorists think that in 1398, before Rosslyn was built, the treasures were taken across the North Atlantic to Canada by Henry St. Clair, the 42nd Earl of Orkney, where he buried them in a famous "money pit" on Oak Island on the coast of Nova Scotia. Proponents of this theory point to carved stone images of New World plants that they say look like Indian corn (maize) and cactus. I have spent some time wandering around Rosslyn Chapel, inspecting the carvings, and I didn't see anything that looked to me much like either corn or cactus. But, then, my doctorate degree is in human anatomy and cell biology, not botany. You can take your pick of theories and govern yourselves accordingly.

Back to Ramsey's speech. Keeping in mind the audience to whom he's speaking, he has already taken care to point out "the close alliance between the French and the Scotch."

> "Prince Edward [Edward I], son of Henry III of England, brought his
>
> defeated troops back from the eighth and last Crusade and established them in a colony in England, and declared himself protector, whereupon, this Fraternity took the name, Freemasons. Since that time, England has been the seat of the Order, but the religious discord which tore Europe in the 16th century caused our Order to degenerate from the nobility of its origin. The rites are changed, disguised, and suppressed."

More revisionist history. According to Ramsay, our blue lodges were established not by common workmen but by "kings, princes and lords." He mentions rites that have been suppressed, a hint that they should be revived (or invented) and worked by the right kind of nobly-born, high-minded people like, for instance, his listeners. Ramsay himself, however, never actually established any higher degrees. He blames the loss of Masonry's noble pedigree on the Reformation together with the Thirty Years War and its aftermath of bitterness and hatred.

> "Our ancestors, the Crusaders, desired thus to unite in one Fraternity the individuals of all nations, and we owe it to them to carry out the project. Our ancestors, the Crusaders, desired to change a sad, savage, and misanthropic philosophy into one of innocent pleasures, agreeable music, pure joy, and moderate gaiety. Our secrets are the words of war which the Crusaders used to distinguish their companions and to detect Saracen foes."

Note how Ramsay harps on the idea that the Crusaders were "our ancestors." I'm not sure what the "sad, savage, and misanthropic philosophy" was that he claimed the Crusaders wanted to change, but he made it clear that they fully intended their military society to someday morph into the agreeable men's clubs familiar to his listeners. According to Ramsay, their military passwords became "our secrets." A very appealing notion to the colonizing, militaristic European upper classes of the time.

> "Yes, Sirs, the famous festivals of Ceres at Eleusis, of Isis in Egypt, of Minerva at Athens, of Urania amongst the Phoenicians, of Diana in Scythia, were connected with ours. In those places mysteries were celebrated which concealed many vestiges of the ancient religion of Noah and the Patriarchs."

Here Ramsay is paying tribute to Martin Clare and his theory of Masonry's descent from the ancient pagan mystery religions. Whether or not Ramsay himself believed it doesn't matter; his audience loved it. Note that he dragged Noah (whom Anderson also featured in his Constitutions of 1738) into the picture.

> "By degrees our Lodges and our rites were neglected in most places. This is why of so many historians, only those of Great Britain speak of our Order. Nevertheless it preserved its splendor among those Scotsmen to whom the Kings of France confided during many centuries the safeguard of their royal persons."

A recurrent feature of Ramsay's speech is the preeminent role played by Scotland in the development of Freemasonry. Whether this was due to nationalistic pride or to reinforce the idea of Scotland's friendship with France or for some other reason is not known. Whatever the case, this speech would eventually give birth to our *Scottish* Rite.

> "From the British Isles, the Royal Art is now repassing to France, which being one of the most spiritual [countries] in Europe will become the center of the Order. She will clothe our work, our statutes, and our customs with grace, delicacy, and good taste, essential qualities of the Order of which the basis is wisdom, strength, and beauty."

Finally Ramsay gives a flowery sop to the French, among whom he hoped to prosper. As Disraeli would later claim that he did with Queen Victoria, Ramsay applied his flattery not with a butter knife but a trowel.

On March 20, one day before his speech was scheduled to be given to the candidates, Ramsay sent a copy of it to one Cardinal Fleury, apparently for his approval. Fleury was a friend of his who happened also to be the Prime Minister of France. Ramsay seems to have postponed the speech's delivery as he waited on the Cardinal's verdict. On March 22, the day after the speech's scheduled delivery, Ramsay sent Fleury another letter, this time asking his support for the institution of Freemasonry in France, even hinting that Fleury should consider joining. Fleury sent that letter back with a terse note penciled in the margin: "The king does not wish it." Some scholars think that the Cardinal's disapproval caused Ramsay to cancel his appearance at the lodge indefinitely.

Another version of this incident has it that Fleury was an official government censor and that he had expressly forbidden Ramsay to give the oration from the start. Why Fleury, a powerful Cardinal and Prime Minister, would have considered a flowery, fictive Masonic lecture to constitute a threat to the state is unclear. Whatever the case, the politically astute Ramsay got the message immediately and never went near another Masonic lodge for the remaining six years of his life.

1754

In 1754, just 13 years after the publication of Ramsay's speech, a French nobleman named De Bonneville started a Masonic body he called the *Chapter of Clermont*, named to honor a Grand Master of France, the Duc de Clermont. It also may have been located in or near a Jesuit college named Clermont, where James II, the exiled Old Pretender to the throne of England, spent the last 13 years of his life. Whatever its location, the Chapter only lasted for a few years but it quickly became known as a place where a Mason could receive some of those new-fangled things called the *hauts grades* (higher degrees). At first the Chapter worked a rite consisting of only six degrees:

1° Entered Apprentice	4° Sublime Illustrious Knight
2° Fellowcraft	5° St John's Masonry
3° Illustrious Knight or Templar	6° Knight of the Eagle

There is some fanciful speculation that James II or his sons may have influenced the Chapter's creation of its degrees to promote the House of Stuart's claim to the English throne. Since James died in 1701 and the Chapter did not exist until 53 years later (fully eight years after the Duke of Cumberland's army brutally crushed the Jacobite cause forever at Culloden in 1746), this is highly improbable. At some point before 1760 one of the most prestigious and powerful Masonic bodies in France took over the short-lived Chapter of Clermont. This group bore the grandiose title of *The Emperors of the East and West*. The Emperors inherited the Chapter's multiple-degree rite and expanded it into something they called *The Rite of Perfection*. With 19 more degrees added to the original six, this Rite consisted of 25 degrees:

1. Apprentice
2. Companion
3. Master
4. Secret Master
5. Perfect Master
6. Intimate Secretary
7. Intendant of the Building
8. Provost and Judge
9. Elect of Nine
10. Elect of Fifteen
11. Illustrious Elect, Chief of the Twelve Tribes
12. Grand Master Architect
13. Royal Arch of Solomon
14. Grand Elect, Ancient Perfect Master
15. Knight of the Sword
16. Prince of Jerusalem
17. Knight of the East and West
18. Knight of the Eagle or Pelican, Perfect Master or Knight of Rose Croix
19. Grand Pontiff
20. Grand Patriarch
21. Grand Master of the Key of Masonry
22. Prince of Libanus [Lebanon]
23. Sovereign Prince Adept Chief of the Grand Consistory
24. Illustrious Knight Commander of the Black and White Eagle:
25. Most Illustrious Sovereign Prince of Masonry, Grand Knight, Sublime Commander of the Royal Secret.

The names of many of these degrees will be familiar to anyone in the modern Scottish Rite for a good reason. This *was* the Scottish Rite, circa 1760. It made up the ritualistic core from which our present-day Rite emerged. This is where we came from.

1761

The Emperors of the East and West lasted until around 1780, when they gradually faded out of existence. Because of their prestige and influence, the Rite of Perfection had become an instant hit, known and worked throughout Europe. It became so popular that the Grand Lodge of France (which had taken over control of the popular Rite) decided to export it.

On August 27, 1761, only a year after the Emperors of the East and West had worked out the other 19 degrees (or, as some think, had received them already written from the Chapter of Clermont), the Grand Lodge contacted a traveling Bordeaux wine merchant and Freemason named Etienne (Stephen) Morin. He had planned a trip to the West Indies to establish a commercial venue for his wines in Santo Domingo, in the present-day Dominican Republic. Since he was going there anyway (trans-Atlantic travel in those days was no cinch; you only did it if you really *had* to) the Grand Lodge commissioned him to spread the Rite there. They appointed him a "Grand Inspector General to all Parts of the New World," a newly-created title which sounds similar to our present-day 33rd degree. Perhaps it was an honorary "26th" degree of the 25-degree Rite of Perfection.

They issued a Masonic patent to Morin. This was a document that gave the bearer the right establish a lodge or other Masonic body and confer the degrees controlled by that body. The patent also allowed Morin to charge candidates an initiation fee for the degrees. Morin, a shrewd businessman, immediately realized that he was being offered a potential gold mine and humbly accepted the commission.

1762

Morin set sail for the New World, his lucrative patent in hand. But almost at once his luck changed for the worse. The Seven Years War (1756 – 1763, known in the American colonies as the French and Indian War) was raging and England and France were enemies. A British man o' war captured Morin's ship and the British interned him in England for a few months. Apparently they did not treat him too badly for he finally arrived in Santo Domingo fifteen months after he left France, later than expected but none the worse for wear. He set up his wine trade there and, later, in Jamaica. While in Jamaica he befriended a Dutch merchant, Henry Francken, and Morin used his newly-patented powers to make Francken a Deputy Inspector General, a degree that Morin seems to have invented. Perhaps Morin had conferred the 25 degrees of the Rite of Perfection on Francken beforehand.

1763 – 1766

Or perhaps not. Recent research indicates that, within a year after arriving in Santo Domingo, Morin had taken it upon himself to rework the original French 25-degree Rite of Perfection. He added a few new degrees and created a new rite that he called the Order of the Royal Secret (which he may have considered a more exotic – and marketable – name than Rite of Perfection; few men long to be perfect but many would like to be royal). The first 14 degrees of this rite constituted a body that Morin called the *Lodge* of Perfection. Morin then made himself the only Inspector General of that rite. Perhaps that's what he conferred upon Francken. Whatever the case, records show that it was the Order of the Royal Secret that spread throughout the American colonies in the following years.

1764

The first official appearance of the "High Degrees" in North America came with the creation of a French language Lodge of Perfection (*Parfaite Loge d'Ecosse*) in New Orleans, Louisiana. This followed the 1752 creation of a French craft lodge in New Orleans. Permission for the creation of the *Parfaite Loge d'Ecosse* had been requested from France as early as 1756.

1767

Francken sailed to the colony of New York and traveled to Albany, where he created an English language Lodge of Perfection, conferring the 4th to the 14th degrees. Soon, other 14-degree rites appeared in Philadelphia, Charleston, Baltimore, Savannah, Troy (NY), and New York City. There was no central governing body; the groups were completely independent of one another. Each "Lodge of Perfection" acknowledged that their charter had been authorized, however indirectly, by Stephen Morin in the West Indies. Other than that, they were on their own.

1783

Meanwhile, Francken was hard at work. He had gathered all of the original French-language degrees he could find, translated them into English and copied them into three notebooks. These notes describe a 25-degree system, the first three degrees being the three Symbolic degrees which Francken acknowledged could only properly be conferred under the jurisdiction of a Grand Lodge (Plate 23). These "Francken degrees" constitute the backbone of the American Scottish Rite of today. Throughout this book I have frequently refered to the earliest authentic version of a modern English language Scottish Rite degree as "the Francken version" or "the 1783 version," the year Francken published his notebooks.

1801

It was the Lodge of Perfection in Charleston, South Carolina, that finally formed our complete present-day 30-degree version of the Scottish Rite. Apparently there were, at the time, stray degrees of unknown origin that existed independently of any Masonic body. They were called "floating philosophic grades" and were probably given, for a fee, to any interested citizen. Some of them may not have been Masonic at all. In 1801, the Masons of Charleston selected eight of the most popular of these floating degrees and added them to their 25-degree Order of the Royal Secret to create a new ritual structure of thirty-three degrees. The senior members of Charleston's original Lodge of Perfection formed a new body that they called the Supreme Council of the Thirty-Third Degree, the Mother Council of the World.

As its motto, the Mother Council adopted the phrase "Order Out of Chaos," (Ordo ab Chao in Latin) which expressed what they hoped to accomplish. The "chaos" that the motto referred to was the result of quite a number of roving 25° "Deputy Inspectors" of the old Order of the Royal Secret who had been acting on their own as Masonic entrepreneurs, conferring higher degrees and establishing new bodies. They were also creating new Deputies - all for a fee. Many of these enterprising Masons were gradually moved over to the new 33° system of the Mother Supreme Council. In 1804, term "Ancient and Accepted" Scottish Rite began being used in France. It was not until the time of Albert Pike that the Southern Jurisdiction began using the term "Ancient and Accepted."[+]

In a surprise move, the founders of the first Supreme Council in 1801 produced a document that they claimed was their constitution. (They may also have been flaunting this document as their *charter*, a Masonic document that functions as a license for a lodge to come into being, operate and confer degrees). They said that this constitution had been written 15 years earlier, in 1786, by no less a Masonic luminary than Frederick the Great, King of Prussia. It declares that every country in the world, except the United States, may have no more than one Supreme Council. The United States may have two. Very considerate of the Prussian monarch to make this provision, especially since, in 1786, the U.S. consisted of a thin strip of land along the eastern seaboard of North America which Europe had only recognized as an independent country for three years.

1806

Three separate Scottish Rite bodies had sprung up in New York City around 1806. None of these bodies operated with the permission of Charleston's Supreme council so were considered, by modern standards, *clandestine* (Masonic parlance for illegitimate).

Antoine Bideaud, a resident of Santo Domingo who had been initiated on that island by the Second Supreme Council founded one of the bodies. He had fled to America when the above-mentioned slave revolt got the upper hand and vengeful ex-slaves destroyed the island's Council. In New York he established a "Consistory" (governing body) of 29 degrees. The highest, or 32nd degree, was "Sublime Prince of the Royal Secret." Bideaud initiated several men into his consistory, including one J.J.J. Gourgas, who would go on to become quite famous in American Freemasonry.

Joseph Cerneau, a Frenchman from Haiti, established the second council in New York. He fled to Cuba in 1802 to escape the slave rebellion and there met another French refugee, Antoine Du Potet, the Deputy Inspector General for a 25-degree "Lodge of Perfection" that had existed in Haiti before the revolt. This was probably the Chapter of Clermont's original Rite of Perfection that dated from around 1760. Du Potet appointed Cerneau the Deputy Inspector General for the northern part of Cuba. He gave Cerneau a "patent" that allowed him to confer all 25 degrees, but on only one candidate a year. In 1807 Cerneau left Cuba for New York and, once there, used his patent to establish a competing "Grand Consistory" that conferred the Lodge of Perfection's 25 degrees on as many men a year as were willing to come up with the price of admission.

A native New Yorker, Abraham Jacobs, started the third group. He had received the "Ineffable Degrees" of the Lodge of Perfection (a different degree system than Du Potet's Haitian "Lodge of Perfection") in Charlston, South Carolina and been advanced to the degree of Knight of the Sun in Kingston, Jamaica. Masons in Jamaica gave him a patent similar to Cerneanu's and he used it to found his own consistories (three of them, in fact) in New York.

1813

The Charleston group finally decided to flex their Masonic muscles (after all, they had that charter from Frederick the Great!) and sent their Grand Treasurer, a Mr. de la Motta, to New York to straighten out the situation. Or, de la Motta went there on his own without the permission or knowledge of the Charleston - we are not 100% sure. He adjudicated all three groups' positions and settled in favor of Bideaud's Consistory. Bideaud was glad to submit to the authority of the powerful southern organization and de la Motta declared his group to be the second Supreme Council of the 33rd Degree for the United States. Cerneau's group wandered in the Masonic wilderness for some 54 years until (probably forced by declining funds and membership) it yielded to the hegemony of the Northern Supreme Council in 1867 and ceased to exist as a separate organization. Jacob's groups peacefully submitted to the authority of Charleston and were also absorbed into the Supreme Council of the NMJ.

1815 – 1866

The five decades following were not happy ones for the Masonic fraternity in America. There were 15-year cycles of economic "boom and bust" during which families became impoverished when banks unexpectedly failed and their money vanished. In 1826 in Batavia, New York, a Mason (or a man claiming to be a Mason) named William Morgan disappeared after being released from jail on a charge of unpaid debt. He had threatened to publish a book exposing the ritual of his Blue lodge, and the word on the street maintained that his fellow Masons had kidnapped and murdered him. Although searchers never found his body the entire country lapsed into a mass convulsion of anti-Masonic hysteria. In the stacks of Princeton University's Firestone Library is a copy of the original edition of Morgan's book; I have read it and it is nothing less than a complete ritual cipher of the first three blue lodge degrees complete with passwords and illustrations of hand grips. It looks entirely accurate and seems to be much too extensive and detailed to have been written from the memory of one man. The Morgan hysteria endured for about 14 years until finally dying out around 1840. Then, from 1860 to 1865, the the Civil War tore the country in two.

1828

In March of 1828, the Northern and Southern Supreme Councils finally decided on a division of territory between them. The Southern Council agreed to cede jurisdiction of the 14 states north of the Mason-Dixon Line and east of the Mississippi River to the Northern Council. Later the North acquired the border state of Delaware to bring their total to 15. The North also tried to grab Washington D.C. but the South trumped them by moving their headquarters there. In 1828, the United States was a much smaller country than it has since become and the division between North and South was fairly even at the time. But, as time went on, the more powerful and better-organized Southern Council was able to seize every newly-admitted state and today controls all of the other 35 states.

1853

Albert Mackey inducted a frontier lawyer named Albert Pike into the Scottish Rite reportedly by the simple expedient of reading all the degrees aloud to him in one day. He was already a Blue lodge and York Rite Mason but had never heard of the Scottish Rite before. He was not impressed with what he heard on the day of his induction and later said: "The truth is that the [Scottish] Rite was nothing, and the Rituals almost naught, for the most part a lot of worthless trash…"

1855 – 1865

Within three years the Supreme Council appointed Pike to a committee charged with the task of rewriting the degrees. He seems to have done all the work himself; the committee may never have met. Until about 1855, most of the Southern Jurisdiction rituals were fragmentary and quite unimaginative; they consisted of little more than a title, a few words and signs, an obligation and a lecture in question-and-answer form. Pike, a brilliant and well-read man, was convinced that the material handed down from Francken contained hidden meanings and exotic mystical secrets that had been deliberately concealed under a blanket of uninspired drivel.

He researched all the knowledge then extant on ancient Egypt, mystery religions and the pagan past to compose colorful and interesting rituals with moral and philosophical content. From 1855 until 1865 he reinvigorated (and, for all purposes, probably reinvented) the rituals of all 33 degrees of the present-day Scottish Rite, Southern Jurisdiction. If the *Chevalier* Andrew Ramsay is the Father of the Scottish Rite, then Albert Pike is surely its Godfather.

1867

In the years following the Civil war, internal schisms had torn apart the Northern Masonic Jurisdiction. Two separate groups had split off, each claiming to be the Supreme Council of the North. The two sparring groups – the Hays-Raymond Body and the Van Rensselaer group – met in Boston on May 15, 1867 and agreed to merge, forming the Supreme Council of the Ancient Accepted Scottish Rite for the Northern Masonic Jurisdiction (NMJ) of the United States of America. Their newly formed Supreme Council was to consist of 66 voting members. This is what we have now – our present-day Scottish Rite, NMJ.

The Northern Masonic Jurisdiction, based in Lexington, Massachusetts, oversees the Scottish Rite bodies in the fifteen states east of the Mississippi and north of the Mason-Dixon Line. It uses the term *Valley* for its degree centers. Each Valley has up to four Scottish Rite bodies, and each body confers its own set of degrees.

The presiding officer for the entire Northern Jurisdiction is the Sovereign Grand Commander. The Supreme Council of the NMJ consists of the active (voting) members for the 15 states within its purview. All members of the Supreme Council are designated Sovereign Grand Inspectors General; each state is administered by the Sovereign Grand Commander's Deputy (the senior active member of that state).

1867 – PRESENT

With the revival of Freemasonry following the anti-Masonic hysteria of 1826 – 1840, many Scottish Rite Valleys in both the north and the south found themselves inundated with new members desiring to receive the "higher" degrees. There were too many candidates to handle in the old, traditional manner. So, over the next few decades, some bold Valleys hit upon a new method of conferring the degrees: The large group of candidates (the "class") would sit in a theater and watch each degree enacted in the form of a play. This way the Valley could initiate fifty or more men at once.

As this method of conferral spread and became popular, the degree rituals took on the character of costumed stage dramas. These stage presentations became more and more elaborate and by the 1870s an entire industry had grown up to supply costumes and stage props for the Biblical and medieval themes presented in the degrees. These programs of theatrical degree conferrals are called Reunions and, because they are so elaborate and labor-intensive, are usually put on no more than once or twice a year, generally in the spring and the fall.

STRUCTURE OF THE SCOTTISH RITE, NORTHERN MASONIC JURISDICTION

The Supreme Council of the Northern Jurisdiction oversees all of the Scottish Rite bodies in the following fifteen states: Maine, New Hampshire, Vermont, Massachusetts, Rhode Island, Connecticut, New York, New Jersey, Pennsylvania, Delaware, Ohio, Michigan, Indiana, Illinois and Wisconsin. As stated previously, each state is divided into several "Valleys." A Valley is the central headquarters for an area (a city or a group of counties) where an assembly of Scottish Rite bodies resides and operates under one roof. The Valley building where the Valley's bodies meet and operate is called either a "Temple" or a "Scottish Rite Cathedral."

A *body* is a named subunit of the Scottish Rite that has jurisdiction over certain degrees. Each Valley in the NMJ consists of up to four bodies: a Lodge of Perfection (4th – 14th degrees), a Council of Princes of Jerusalem (15th – 16th degrees), a Chapter of Rose Croix (17th - 18th degrees) and a Consistory (19th – 32nd degrees). Each body has a line of officers governed by that body's presiding officer: A Thrice Potent Master (Lodge of Perfection), a Sovereign Prince (Princes of Jerusalem), a Most Wise Master (Rose Croix) and a Commander-in-Chief (Consistory). Although the four bodies are held to be equal in rank and no presiding officer outranks any other, the Commander-in-Chief is considered the first among equals and usually presides over the Valley during his year in the chair.

ADMINISTRATION

The Ancient and Accepted Scottish Rite in each country is governed by a Supreme Council. There is no international governing body; the Supreme Council in each country is sovereign unto itself.

In the United States there are two Supreme Councils: one in Washington, DC, and one in Lexington, Massachusetts, which control the Southern Jurisdiction (SJ) and Northern Masonic Jurisdiction (NMJ), respectively. They each have particular characteristics that differentiate them. In the Northern Masonic Jurisdiction the Supreme Council consists of no more than 66 (2 x 33) active members. All members of the Supreme Council are designated Sovereign Grand Inspectors General, but the head of the Rite in each state of the Northern Jurisdiction is called a "Deputy of the Supreme Council."

The degrees of the Northern and Southern Jurisdictions differ in name and ritual content. They are:

Degree	Southern Jurisdiction	Northern Jurisdiction
4°	Secret Master	Master Traveler
5°	Perfect Master	
6°	Intimate Secretary	Master of the Brazen Serpent
7°	Provost and Judge	
8°	Intendant of the Building	
9°	Elu of the Nine	Master of the Temple
10°	Elu of the Fifteen	Master Elect
11°	Elu of the Twelve	Sublime Master Elected
12°	Master Architect	Master of Mercy
13°	Royal Arch of Solomon	Master of the Ninth Arch
14°	Perfect Elu	Grand Elect Mason
15°	Knight of the East, or Knight of the Sword	Knight of the East
16°	Prince of Jerusalem	
17°	Knight of the East and West	
18°	Knight Rose Croix	Knight of the Rose Croix of H.R.D.M.
19°	Grand Pontiff	Brothers of the Trail
20°	Grand Master of all Symbolic Lodges	Master ad Vitam "George Washington Degree"

Degree	Southern Jurisdiction	Northern Jurisdiction
21°	Noachite, or Prussian Knight	Patriarch Noachite
22°	Knight of the Royal Axe, or Prince of Libanus	Prince of Libanus (Lumberjack Degree)
23°	Chief of the Tabernacle	Knight of Valor "Four Immortal Chaplains Degree"
24°	Prince of the Tabernacle	Brother of the Forest "American Indian Degree"
25°	Knight of the Brazen Serpent	Master of Achievement "Benjamin Franklin Degree"
26°	Prince of Mercy, or Scottish Trinitarian	Friend and Brother Eternal "Civil War Degree"
27°	Knight Commander of the Temple	Knight of Jerusalem
28°	Knight of the Sun, or Prince Adept	Knight of the Sun
29°	Scottish Knight of Saint Andrew	Knight of Saint Andrew
30°	Knight Kadosh, or Knight of the White and Black Eagle	Grand Inspector
31°	Inspector Inquisitor	My Brother's Keeper
32°	Master of the Royal Secret	Sublime Prince of the Royal Secret
33°	Inspector General	

The 33rd Degree

In the United States, members of the Scottish Rite can be elected to receive the 33°. It is conferred on members who have made major contributions to society, to the Scottish Rite or to Masonry in general. In the Southern Jurisdiction, a member who has been a 32° Scottish Rite Mason for 46 months or more is eligible to be elected to receive the "rank and decoration" of Knight Commander of the Court of Honour (K.C.C.H.) in recognition of outstanding service. After 46 months as a K.C.C.H. he is then eligible to be elected to the 33°. In the Northern Jurisdiction, there is only one 46-month requirement for eligibility to receive the 33rd degree, and while there is a Meritorious Service Award (as well as a Distinguished Service Award), these awards are not required intermediate steps towards the 33°. A recipient of the 33° is an honorary member of the Supreme Council and is therefore called an "Inspector General Honorary." However, those who are appointed Deputies of the Supreme Council that are later elected to membership on the Supreme Council are then designated "Sovereign Grand Inspectors General."

Appendix B

History and Development of the Degrees

THE LODGE OF PERFECTION

Note: If you come across any peculiar spelling in any of the words you see in this section, just assume that the word sic (short for sic erat scriptum, "thus was it written") accompanies the word.

4th Degree: Master Traveler

For most of its history, from around 1783 until 2004, this was a completely different degree than the present one, that of SECRET MASTER. The ritual depicted a lodge of Secret Masters that had met to select a new guard to fill a vacancy among the guardians of the Temple's Holy of Holies. Most ritualists agreed that the SECRET MASTER degree (which included a long list of the various names of God that had to be memorized) was "Dead, dull and overloaded with symbolism." In its new form, that of MASTER TRAVELER, it is a response to the concern voiced by many Scottish Rite Masons to the "one day" reunions that have become prevalent over the last few years. In some of these shortened reunions a candidate is entered, passed and raised to Master Mason and then made a 32nd Degree Scottish Rite Mason in one day. The MASTER TRAVELER degree helps counter such abbreviated one-day events and provides a bridge from the Blue lodge degrees to the higher degrees of the Scottish Rite. So the Ritual Committee approved the MASTER TRAVELER Degree as the first degree every Scottish Rite candidate in the Northern Masonic Jurisdiction must see.

5th Degree: Perfect Master

The original 5th degree, PERFECT MASTER, was quite different from the present one in the NMJ. It described the elaborate funeral service for Hiram Abiff and hinted at plans for vengeance on his murderers. It also introduced the Lodge of Sorrow (that is, a memorial service for departed Masonic brothers). There was some criticism of the content of this ritual and the Committee on Rituals and Ritualistic Matters decided to make a change. The present version of the PERFECT MASTER degree started life as a degree called the CHIEF OF THE TABERNACLE, the 23rd degree of the Consistory. It dates back to the beginning of the nineteenth century and probably came over from France, perhaps with

Morin. Albert Pike wrote a long, elaborate ritual for it between 1855 and 1865, complete with a lecture from his *Morals and Dogma*. It remained as the 23rd degree of the Consistory until the Committee decided to move all Old Testament stories from the Consistory into the Lodge of Perfection.

In 2007 the Ritual Committee further revised the degree and deleted obscure references to the ancient Hebrew concept of the *Shekinah* (a kind of glowing plasma said to represent the presence of either a feminine version of Yahweh or of his wife, the goddess Asherah of the Sea). Also deleted were references to Hell (not a part of Hebrew belief at the time of Moses) and "Jehovah," a meaningless garbled word that came from a 17th-century mistranslation in the King James Bible of the Hebrew Tetragrammaton:

or YHWH, possibly pronounced "Yahweh."

6th Degree: Master of the Brazen Serpent

The KNIGHT OF THE BRAZEN SERPENT began life as MOSES IN THE WILDERNESS, the 25th degree of the Consistory. The original 6th degree in the Lodge of Perfection was called PERFECT MASTER BY CURIOSITY OF INTIMATE SECRETARY. It was based on a non-Biblical story in which Solomon, who owed King Hiram of Tyre a considerable sum of money, and Hiram are arguing over some worthless villages that Solomon, to pay his debt, had tried to palm off on Hiram as thriving cities. When Hiram makes an unexpected inspection tour of his new "cities," he realizes the scam and makes a beeline to Jerusalem to give Solomon a piece of his mind. While they are arguing in the Temple, a passer-by named Joabert overhears the ruckus and listens outside the door, thinking that he might have to come to Solomon's assistance if a fight breaks out. Hiram sees him and, thinking he is an assassin summoned by Solomon, attempts to kill him. Solomon intervenes and convinces Hiram that Joabert is really an innocent bystander. They shake hands all around and the two kings make Joabert their "intimate" (confidential) secretary.

When MOSES IN THE WILDERNESS was moved from the Consistory to become the new 6th degree, Scottish Rite rules decreed that it had to retain the old 6th degree's original name – INTIMATE SECRETARY – even though it no longer made any sense. Finally, in 2003, it received its present name. The Consistory's 25th degree then became the MASTER OF ACHIEVEMENT or the "Benjamin Franklin" degree.

7th Degree: Provost and Judge

This is one of the few degrees that have remained unchanged since it was rewritten into its present form some time before 1783. Before that time, this degree was called IRISH MASTER, because it was worked in France by a lodge that had received its charter from Ireland. In the original Rite of Perfection it was the eighth degree, number seven being INTENDANT OF THE BUILDING.

8th Degree: Intendant of the Building

The modern ritual is a direct descendant of the original French degree, INTENDANT DU BATIMENT. It may have also been called MASTER IN ISRAEL in reference to the so-called "Harodim" or Masters among the workmen, a group of over three thousand "Princes in Masonry" Solomon employed to oversee the work on the Temple (2 Chron. 2:2,18 - 1 Kings 5:16). Originally the action of the ritual took place in the Middle Chamber of the Temple following the murder of Hiram Abiff and concerned the search for five architects (one each for the five orders of architecture) to replace Hiram. Pike rewrote the original ritual into a much more elaborate form which was adopted by the Northern Masonic Jurisdiction in 1867. This was changed in minor ways through the 18th and 19th centuries and was not put into its present form until the revisions of 1981 and 2006, when the five architects disappeared, the time was moved to the end of David's reign and the scene was changed to the throne room of King David's palace.

INTENDANT OF THE BUILDING is also the name of a degree of Freemasonry once very popular in the north of England, especially in the county of Durham, and which was probably founded in Gateshead in 1681.

9th Degree: Master of the Temple

The original name of this degree in 1783 was CHAPTER OF MASTER ELECTED OF NINE and dealt with the murder of one of the assassins of Hiram Abiff by an over-enthusiastic pursuer. In 1801 its name was changed to CHAPTER OF ELECTED KNIGHTS and told of the "election" of nine workman-knights to hunt down and kill the assassin in his hiding place. Until quite recently (2003) its name was MASTER ELECT OF NINE and the plot, which had still centered on vengeance for Hiram's death, was replaced by the ritual that had been the 24ᵗʰ degree of the Consistory, PRINCE OF THE TABERNACLE, and it was given its present name. This reflected an effort on the part of the Committee on Rituals and Ritualistic Matters to move all Old Testament story lines into the Lodge of Perfection and to eliminate stories based on the Hiramic Legend.

10ᵗʰ Degree: Master Elect

This degree began life in 1783 as ILLUSTRIOUS ELECT OF FIFTEEN. Throughout the next 200 years it seems to have retained its Blue lodge Hiramic theme in which the assassins of Hiram are hunted down and brought to justice. A deputation is sent by King Solomon to the court of Maaka, King of Gath, to enlist his aid in apprehending the assassins. Subsequently the three murderers are discovered in a quarry. Solomon's deputation captures the murderers and takes them to King Solomon. The fifteen craftsmen who conducted the search are each rewarded by being created a "Master Elect of Fifteen."

By 1986 the Committee on Rituals and Ritualistic Matters had decided to begin moving all Old Testament story lines from the Consistory into the Lodge of Perfection. They also wished to de-emphasize the inordinate focus that had existed for almost two centuries on the theme of vengeance and retribution for the murder of Hiram Abiff. So the old 24ᵗʰ degree, PRINCE OF THE TABERNACLE was modified and moved to replace the original 9ᵗʰ degree and an entirely new play, dealing with Solomon's downfall through pride and disobedience and called MASTER ELECT OF FIFTEEN, was written for the 10ᵗʰ degree. In 2006 the name was shortened to MASTER ELECT.

11ᵗʰ Degree: Sublime Master Elected

This degree was first called, in 1783, SUBLIME KNIGHT ELECTED and had to do with Solomon appointing supervisors to oversee the workmen on the Temple. Originally, the Sublime Master Elected was a Master Mason elected by Solomon to oversee and report on all work being done on the Temple. In the Albert Pike version of 1855 – 1865 complaints regarding corruption and coercion in collecting taxes for the crown are heard. Fifteen *Elus* ("elu" means "elected one" and is an old French word for someone who has been elected or appointed to a position) are appointed to oversee and reform tax collection methods; the new version of the degree was thus established. In another version written around the same time it is stated that merely establishing a just and orderly tax collection method is not enough;

the Sublime Master Elected must also be what is called an *Emeth* ("True Man," probably the same as an *Ameth* in the SJ version) in order to be worthy of representing the people in the law courts.

In 1974 the ritual was elaborated somewhat. When Solomon's trusted emissary is found guilty of overtaxing the people and keeping the excess revenue for his personal gain, Solomon appoints twelve True Men (called, for some reason, the MASTERS ELECT OF *FIFTEEN*) to serve as governors of the twelve provinces of Israel (one province for each tribe) and to gather the taxes in their provinces. The degree was changed to its present form in 2004 and (as in most of the other degrees) the ceremonial section was deleted.

12th Degree: Master of Mercy

This degree, having the same theme – that of Joseph and his brothers – began as the 26th degree, PRINCE OF MERCY. In 1981 it was moved into the Lodge of Perfection, replacing the 12th degree, GRAND MASTER ARCHITECT, while retaining that degree's name. In 2005, the name was changed to MASTER OF MERCY. The ritual does not seem to have been altered very much over the years.

13th Degree: Master of the Ninth Arch

The original version of this degree in 1783 was called simply the ROYAL ARCH and took place in the underground vault where Enoch had deposited the gold plate. In the period 1855 - 1865 Albert Pike rewrote the ritual and called it KNIGHTS OF THE NINTH ARCH or ROYAL ARCH OF SOLOMON. Sometime around 1867 addition action concerning the search for and discovery of the gold plate was added. In addition, the three candidates are shown Moses' burning bush and given an explanation of its symbolism. At one point, the degree was called KNIGHTS OF THE NINTH ARCH. In 1871, a pledge of chastity (!) was added to the candidates' obligation. This was quickly omitted. By 1971 the degree was organized into its present form with a final revision in 2004.

14th Degree: Grand Elect Mason

This degree is very close to the original Francken ritual of 1838 when it was called PERFECTION – THE ULTIMATE DEGREE OF SYMBOLIC MASONRY. It was the longest and most elaborate of the 25 degrees of the original Rite of Perfection that Morin brought over from France. It has undergone some minor alterations over the years but is still a moving and solemn ceremony.

The Council of Princes of Jerusalem

15th Degree: Knight of the East

This is one of the "old" degrees that dates to the Francken rituals of 1783, when it was called COUNCIL OF KNIGHTS OF THE EAST, OR SWORD. Cyrus, attended by his coterie of Knights of the East is persuaded by a "Grand General" (not Daniel) to allow Zerubbabel to approach the throne and plead his case. There follows a story of the Jews returning to Jerusalem and fighting with Syrians over a passage across a bridge. The Jews win.

In the ritual of 1863 Cyrus is described as "the first precursor of Jesus of Nazareth." The ritual of 1878 introduced most of the elements we have in the present degree. In some of the early scripts, Zerubbabel has returned to Jerusalem on an inspection tour and has come back to Babylon. Daniel first makes an appearance in the ritual of 1873 where he interprets Cyrus' dream. The rest of the ritual is similar to the modern version, except that the struggle at the bridge is included. It was then called KNIGHT OF THE EAST, OR SWORD. The present ritual is that of 2005 in which both Zerubbabel's return to inspect the ruins and the struggle at the bridge is eliminated and the phrase "OR SWORD" was dropped from the title.

16th Degree: Prince of Jerusalem

The present degree is not so different from the original Francken ritual of 1783 where Babylon was represented as being in the west of the lodge-room and Jerusalem was in the east. The privileges and prerogatives of Princes of Jerusalem have certainly diminished, though. In the 18th-century they had exclusive control over Scottish Rite Freemasonry from the Fourth to the Fifteenth Degree inclusive. Grand Councils of Princes of Jerusalem could grant Charters to Lodges of Perfection, and also governed and controlled the Symbolic Degrees of the Scottish Rite in all countries where no regular Grand Lodge was established.

These days the Supreme Council of the 33° takes care of those things. In 1853 the debate over the Three Most Powerful Things (wine, women or the king) was introduced. By 1878 the degree had pretty much taken on its present form and has not been significantly revised (except for the Prologue) since 1992.

The Chapter of Rose Croix

17th Degree: Knight of the East and West

Apparently there had been a legend circulating in 18th-century Europe concerning a fictitious order of knighthood called the Knights of the East and West, Princes of Jerusalem. These warriors were supposed to have made their headquarters on the island of Malta in the year A.D. 1118 during one of the Crusades. Around 1750 this legend was incorporated into the Rite of Perfection as the 17th degree, KNIGHT OF THE EAST AND WEST. This early degree was completely different from the modern version and featured a collection of seven "seals" (actually symbols) such as a sword, a skull, a pot of incense, etc. In subsequent versions the ritual mentions the Lost Word, the island of Patmos and the Third Temple. In 1876 the Essenes are first mentioned.

The degree did not take on its present form until 1942 when Herod and the destruction of the Roman Eagle by the Pharisees were introduced. In the decades that followed there seemed to be disagreements among the ritual committees; the drama of Herod and the eagle was abandoned only to be brought back by popular demand in 1989. The present ritual was solidified in 2002. Recently the NMJ's Supreme Council has declared that the present 17th degree does not illustrate any of the Scottish Rite's Core Values and may be replaced.

18Th Degree: Knight of the Rose Croix of H.R.D.M.

The ritual of the Rose Croix degree looks to me as if it originated as some sort of a Church-sponsored ceremony unconnected with Freemasonry. It has the air of a surviving mystery play from the late Middle Ages, exactly the kind of play that a craft guild might have put on to celebrate a holy day. Historians have noted its first recorded appearances shortly after Pope Clement XII issued his anti-Masonic proclamation "In Eminenti" in 1738. You will recall that Ramsay had intended to deliver his oration on the noble origins of

Freemasonry in 1737 and the text of his speech (which he may never have delivered) wasn't published until 1741. Also remember that around 1754 the Chapter of Clermont, one of the first known bodies of higher degrees in France, was possibly connected to a Jesuit college.

The Jesuits are a highly intellectual order and, at that time in pre-Revolutionary France, could have had access to the scripts of medieval guild plays. The French nobleman, De Bonneville, a pioneer guru of the *Haute Grades* (Higher Degrees), founded the Chapter of Clermont. If he and his Chapter indeed collaborated with the Jesuit College of Clermont, he might have called upon the priests for source material to help in the writing of ritual for his new degrees. The Jesuits would have been very happy to oblige with approved Christian material that would dilute and subvert the patently Deistic, anti-clerical nature of the early French Masonic lodges.

The 4th, 5th and 6th degrees in De Bonneville's system were, respectively, KNIGHT OF THE EAGLE, ILLUSTRIOUS KNIGHT OR TEMPLAR and SUBLIME ILLUSTRIOUS KNIGHT. There are some indications that the degree now known as KNIGHT OF THE ROSE CROIX had something to do with a ritual used by an 18th-century Masonic Knights Templar system. This points to the Chapter of Clermont's 5th degree, ILLUSTRIOUS KNIGHT OR TEMPLAR, as a prime suspect for our present Rose Croix. Or possibly a conflation of that degree with KNIGHT OF THE EAGLE, because in 1763, when Stephen Morin brought his 25-degree Rite of Perfection over to the West Indies from France, the 18th degree in his system was called KNIGHT OF THE EAGLE OR PELICAN, PERFECT MASON OR KNIGHT OF ROSE CROIX. This, of course, was after 19 more degrees had been added to the Chapter of Clermont's original six.

So where did the name Rose Croix (French for "pink cross") come from? This subject has occasioned much dancing around an otherwise obvious answer. For some reason, Masonic writers have bent over backwards to disassociate Freemasonry from any hint of a connection to the Rosicrucian societies of the 17th- and 18th-century Europe. This amounts to a kind of pseudo-intellectual snobbery with no reasonable basis and is a favorite thesis of writers who know little about the Rosicrucians or their ideals.

In fact, the Rosicrucians were much like Freemasons. Seventeenth-century Rosicrucianism was a system of theosophy, a speculative religious philosophy based on mystical insights into the nature of Deity and the "hidden" meanings of sacred scriptures. The Rosicrucians were moral and social reformers. They used mystical studies combined with the metaphors of alchemy to illustrate their beliefs that the united efforts of intelligent men of good will should and would improve society. Despite the distaste with which most modern writers now regard alchemy, in the 17th century it was an honorable and legitimate pursuit. It attracted the efforts of such luminaries as Isaac Newton and Elias Ashmole, both members (Ashmole was a founder) of London's famed Royal Society.

The possible founder of Rosicrucianism was a Lutheran theologian and minister, Johann Valentin Andrea (1586-1654), of Würtemberg, Germany. As a logo for his new theosophical system, he adopted the coat-of-arms of Martin Luther, which featured a large open 5-petaled rose in the center of which was a red heart containing a black cross.

Rosicrucianism was very popular among the French intelligentsia and France was the last place that the system existed before it faded from history around 1840. Many French intellectuals of the educated classes were enthusiastic about joining secretive mystical religious systems; these were the same men who avidly joined and supported the higher degrees of Masonry.

By the time Morin got to the West Indies in 1762 with his 25-degree Rite of Perfection (or Order of the Royal Secret, as the case may be) the 18th degree in his system was called KNIGHT OF THE EAGLE OR PELICAN, PERFECT MASTER OR KNIGHT OF ROSE CROIX. The earliest English language written ritual of the degree, Francken's Ritual of 1783, featured three chambers, or "apartments."

Around 1865 Albert Pike fancied up the degree with elaborate stage props and long lectures. At one time the degree featured four apartments and a lurid Hell scene. Despite the strong Christian theme, the degree emphasized religious tolerance and universality to the extent that Masonic leaders could say: "Our door [to the higher degrees] can be thus unhesitatingly approached by the Unitarian as well as by the Jew."

Interestingly, Francken's original ritual of 1783 specifies "All the brethren that are admitted are to be Christians." This sentiment, while largely ignored for most of the Scottish Rite's history, has at times surfaced to become an issue of contention. For years Masonic integrationists have been at loggerheads with the exclusionists. The integrationists wanted to bring in all good men who wished to join into the Craft. The exclusionists wanted to keep Freemasonry the exclusive preserve of white Christians. For several decades the exclusionists won.

Not long after Anderson published his *Constitutions of 1723*, reaction against the inclusion of Jews and Non-Conformist Christians into Freemasonry began to develop in both England and Scotland. Sometime between 1741 and 1750 a Masonic group calling itself the Royal Order of Scotland appeared in London. By 1750, nine years after the publication of Ramsay's oration, the Order was conferring two degrees: HEREDOM OF KILWINNING and KNIGHT OF THE ROSY CROSS. The first degree deals with Blue lodge Masonry. The second degree, according to the Order's web site, "...deals more with the subject matter of the Rose Croix Degree of the Ancient and Accepted Scottish Rite than with that of Craft Masonry." The Royal Order of Scotland, which still exists today, is exclusionary and insists that its candidates not only be Christians but also must be "Trinitarians", that is they must believe in a triune Godhead. This excludes not only Jews but also Quakers who largely ignore the Father and the Son and mostly acknowledge the Holy Spirit, which they call the "Inner Light". Also left out are Unitarians who believe that God is one person only and that Jesus was just a great preacher.

All claims to "universality" evaporated with the ritual written by Enoch Terry Carson, 33° and introduced in 1870. Albert G. Mackey, a famous Masonic writer of the time, called it "an attempt to Christianize Freemasonry," and indeed, it was. Carson's ritual added an exclusively Christian emphasis. His ritual featured the Apostles' Creed, the Ascension of Christ and a Jewel Speech that included such phrases as: "The Cross, unto the Jew a stumbling block…No other foundation is laid…. The Son of God who died and was raised again … through faith in whom we are saved… The only Name given… whereby ye can be saved." In other words, no non-Christians need apply.

This situation went unchanged for 72 years, until 1942. During that whole time, integrationist Masons had deplored the vitriolic anti-Semitism of Carson's ritual and tried to substitute Pike's ritual from the Southern Jurisdiction, but to no avail. Finally, after several tentative experiments, the Scottish Rite adopted a new, less exclusionist ritual. They returned the setting to three apartments and dropped the Hell scene. They also substituted phrases like "A new law of love" in place of specific Trinitarian dogma. Most of the ritual we have today was formulated in 1964; in 1994 writers solidified the present ritual along with that of the present-day 17th degree.

The Consistory

19th Degree: Brothers of the Trail

The original 19th degree was found in the Francken rituals of 1783 under the cumbersome title of SUBLIME SCOTCH MASONRY CALLED BY THE NAME OF GRAND PONTIFF and consisted mostly of questions and answers on the topic of the mythical city of New Jerusalem described in the Apocalypse of St. John. Albert Pike elaborated the degree with a scene of twelve columns in a Chapter Room of adepts. The modern version of the ritual seems to have first taken shape in 1886. The central concept of the New Jerusalem (a sort of heaven-on-earth as envisioned by fundamentalist believers in the Apocalypse) was jettisoned in favor of the classical Mediterranean underworld journey of a mythical Hero. It was revised in 1934 and assumed its last most recent form under the title of Grand Pontiff in 1993 with final refinements in 2002. In 2011 it was replaced by the present Americana "degree" (to use a charitable name for a theatrical pratfall), BROTHERS OF THE TRAIL.

20th Degree: Master ad Vitam (George Washington/ Benedict Arnold Degree)

This started out in 1783 as MASTER OF ALL SYMBOLICK LODGES, SOVEREIGN PRINCE OF MASONRY, OR MASTER AD VITAM. "Ad Vitam" means "for life," as, in the 18th-century, Masters of a Blue lodge in France seemed to have held the office for life. The phrase as been kept as the title of the present degree although it no longer has any meaning. The original ritual consisted of a long lecture that had to be delivered by the candidate, the accomplishment of which ritualistically (but not in fact) qualified him to be Master of all blue lodges for the rest of his life. In 1865 Albert Pike rewrote the ritual to include an explanation of nine symbolic lights and a lecture on the qualities of effective leadership.

In 1896, the ritual was changed to recount a fictitious drama commemorating the 25th anniversary of the Masonic career of Frederick II of Prussia, using historical characters. The drama records a visit of Frederick, his entourage and distinguished guests, to a Lodge meeting in Europe on August 14, 1763. As a forerunner of the British spy story in our present ritual, a story was told of a spy who had gained entrance to a Masonic lodge with a patent which was, in fact, a map of the fortress. The spy escaped, but General Wallraven — a trusted Prussian engineer — was imprisoned for life for complicity in the plot. Wallraven, brought from his dungeon, exposed Prince de Kaunitz as the spy; Francis I of Austria, who had been a friend and sponsor of the Prince, renounced his friendship; the Prince was banished and Wallraven's sentence was commuted to expatriation.

Following World War I, all things German became unpopular and the ritual was rewritten in its present form with Washington and Benedict Arnold substituting for the European characters. It has continued to the present day with minor revisions reflecting recent discoveries concerning the history of the period.

21st Degree: Patriarch Noachite

There is not much recorded history about the origin of this rather un-Masonic ritual. It reads like something from Grimm's Fairy Tales. The degree's name, at least, has remained unchanged from Francken's ritual of 1783. The contents of the original 18th-century degree are unknown but, given the name, they must have been considerably different from what we have now. The modern ritual's text appears to have been first written in its present form in the Northern Jurisdiction in 1880 and there are no major recorded changes since. It looks to me as if it originated with Albert Pike after the Civil War years and was adopted whole cloth by the Northern Jurisdiction.

Pike was an idiosyncratic thinker who marched to his own drummer; he supported an armada of social causes, possessed a near-genius intellect, read every book he could get his hands on and remembered everything he read. An ex-Confederate, he may have admired and romanticized the exploits and atrocities of William Quantrill, a Confederate thug who led a loosely-controlled guerrilla band that massacred Union men, women and children during the Civil War.

Many historical and anthropological books of Pike's time were racially biased and inaccurate but he didn't care; anything was grist for his intellectual mill. He may have viewed the Vehmgericht as a kind of Robin Hood gang of armed do-gooders, reminiscent of the Ku Klux Klan (which he may have also romanticized), that went around the German countryside hanging bad guys (that is, anyone who might have disagreed with Pike's religious fantasies). The anti-German sentiment following WW I doesn't seem to have affected this degree as it did the previous one, although had it been written during or after World War II I think the hero would have been given a name other than Adolf.

22nd Degree: Prince of Libanus

The original Francken ritual of 1783 was titled "KNIGHTS OF THE ROYAL AXE — OR THE GRAND PATRIARCHS — BY THE NAME OF PRINCES OF LIBANON." There does not seem to have been much of a ritual script. Someone recited the legend of the Princes of Lebanon and rattled off a list of names of famous men; the candidate was expected to memorize the list.

As was the case with many of Francken's rituals, the documents contained a degree with an impressive title but no story. In 1867 Albert Pike presented a ritual that he had made up out of legends and inaccurate or fictitious historical romances. The script represented Pike's ahead-of-his-time social views on society, particularly on the dignity of the laboring man. It is highly unlikely that such a script would have found much acceptance in the aristocratic lodges of 18th-century France. Pikes script was adopted by the Northern Jurisdiction and was used almost unchanged until 1993 when the present-day musical operetta version was created. The following year a spoken version was also presented, using the identical text.

When I first saw the degree presented in 2007 I believe the locale was supposed to be somewhere on the slopes of a mountain in Lebanon, which gave the title some meaning. Due to the difficulty in finding nine or ten Scottish Rite Masons who could sing with professional talent the Supreme Council of the Northern Jurisdiction recently approved a video presentation in which the script was spoken rather than sung. The locale was changed to an American forest of the 19th century, and the actors represented American lumberjacks.

This spoken version was not received enthusiastically by the members and a new version was approved in which part of the script is once again sung. Rumor had it that the locale would be changed to a German beer hall, but this proved to be false. I have seen the new version and it is a lot of fun. The new locale is somewhere in the forests of the Pacific Northwest. Members are encouraged to come dressed as lumberjacks, the audience participates in some of the singing and there is even a break in the middle of the degree where beer and pretzels are served! Excellent! All the degrees should be like this.

23rd Degree: Knight of Valor (Four Chaplains Degree)

The original name of this degree was CHIEF OF THE TABERNACLE. This is because the original ritual for the 23rd degree was the story of Aaron's two sons, Nadab and Abihu, who tried to offer "strange fire" in the tabernacle in the Hebrew camp and were burned to death for their efforts. This story was moved from the Consistory into the Lodge of Perfection and is now the ritual for the 5th degree, PERFECT MASTER.

When the Old Testament Stories were taken out of the Consistory, the 23rd degree was left with a name but no ritual. In 1996, with the permission of the Four Chaplains Foundation of Philadelphia, the story of the Four Immortal Chaplains was offered as a tentative substitute. The ritual was modified into its present form in 1988. In 2007 the name was changed from the old title, CHIEF OF THE TABERNACLE, to the present more meaningful KNIGHT OF VALOR.

24th Degree: Brother of the Forest (American Indian Degree)

The original 24th Degree was called the PRINCE OF THE TABERNACLE (*Prince du Tabernacle*). It had no ritual story connected with it, consisting only of an obligation and some signs and words. It is thought to have been one of the eight "floating philosophical grades" that the Lodge of Perfection at Charleston added to the original 25 degrees of the French Lodge of Perfection that Francken had brought to America. In September of 1855 Albert Pike supplied a ritual in which a candidate is tested by the four elements – earth, fire, air and water – and then re-enacts the drama of the second part of the Master Mason Degree.

The Northern Masonic Jurisdiction adopted Pike's ritual and used it unchanged until 1909. Then the North substituted a new ritual in which Solomon convenes a religious congress in Jerusalem and invites priests of six or seven different religions from around the Mediterranean area to attend. A friendly discussion on comparative religion and the nature of the gods and goddesses takes place until a shouting skeptic interrupts the proceedings. By now you have probably recognized this as the present 9th Degree – MASTER OF THE TEMPLE – which was moved from the Consistory to the Lodge of Perfection in 1986 (when it was first called MASTER ELECT OF NINE). At the same time, the story of the petitioning Cherokee Indian was written and placed in the 24th Degree's empty slot and in 2003 the name was changed from PRINCE OF THE TABERNACLE to the more meaningful BROTHER OF THE FOREST.

25th Degree: Master of Achievement (Benjamin Franklin)

This degree began life as one of the "floating philosophical grades" of unknown origin that were added to the original 25-degree Lodge of Perfection in 1801. It was called the KNIGHT OF THE BRAZEN SERPENT (*Chevalier du Serpent D'Airain*) and was provided with a ritual in 1855 by Albert Pike. I'm not sure exactly what story line Pike pursued in his original ritual but the Northern Jurisdiction, with its penchant for the pre-teen Sunday school audience, seems to have preferred the story of Moses and the effigy of a bronze serpent on a pole as contained in Numbers 21: 4-9. For a while it was called MOSES IN THE WILDERNESS. Then, in 1951, the degree was renamed KNIGHT OF THE BRAZEN SERPENT and another completely unrelated scene that preceded the story of Moses was added.

In 1993 the KNIGHT OF THE BRAZEN SERPENT was removed as the 25th degree of the Consistory and reinstated as the 6th degree of the Lodge of Perfection, replacing the INTIMATE SECRETARY degree that had been there previously and which was discarded. The present Benjamin Franklin degree was then substituted as the 25th. The degree was modified in 2003 and renamed MASTER OF ACHIEVEMENT.

26th Degree: Friend and Brother Eternal (Gettysburg)

This degree was not a part of the original Francken rituals and it does not appear to have been one of the "floating philosophical grades." The title PRINCE OF MERCY had been around as the heading of a blank page in the DOSZEDARDSKI RITUAL OF 1805-1809 but there was no ritual text that could be found for it. A skeleton ritual of signs and handshakes first appeared sometime around 1845 and was placed as the 26th degree with the title "PRINCE OF MERCY." In 1856 the indefatigable Albert Pike, who seems to have been blessed with a lot of free time and an unending supply of ink, wrote a 53-page monster of a ritual that was adopted by the Northern Jurisdiction. This was called THE PRINCE OF MERCY OR SCOTTISH TRINITARIAN and refers not only to the Christian Blessed Trinity but to a tripartite covenant made with Noah, Abraham and "all the earth." The story takes place in the catacombs of Rome during the time of the Emperor Domitian.

The NMJ has always preferred easy-to-understand rituals more suitable to small children or illiterate farmers than to mature, educated adults. So in 1942 the NMJ substituted a more simple-minded ritual, the Biblical story of JOSEPH AND HIS BRETHREN. In

1981 JOSEPH AND HIS BRETHREN was moved from the Consistory to the Lodge of Perfection and became the 12th degree, MASTER OF MERCY.

A sentimental story of Abraham Lincoln, "The Perfect Tribute," had been written by a lady named Mary Raymond Shipman Andrews and published in 1906. In its original version the story had nothing to do with Masonry. It was rewritten as a public stage play by a Scottish Rite Mason in 1930. In the play, Lincoln visits a military hospital in Alexandria, Virginia and recites the Gettysburg Address to a dying Confederate soldier. In the late 1980s the play was revised, for some reason, to include Masonic references. In 1981 this new Lincoln ritual was substituted for the story of Joseph. But after numerous complaints from Civil War buffs over the story's historical inaccuracy, the ritual was withdrawn and replaced by the much better present ritual in 2006.

27th Degree: Knight of Jerusalem

The KNIGHT OF JERUSALEM degree was another of the "floating philosophical grades" that were added to Francken's original 25 degrees by the Supreme Council of Charleston, SC, in 1801. By the time of the Civil War it had become a simple initiation ceremony in which a 26° Prince of Mercy was inducted into an order of knighthood dedicated to the practice of five chivalric virtues: Humility, Temperance, Chastity, Generosity, and Honor. In 1896 a ritual of some sort was written for the degree and this was modified into a medieval 13th-century drama in 1944. This was further modified in 1983 but, by the beginning of the 21st century, the modified script was found to be undesirable. The greatly revised present-day ritual was written in 2003 and the name was changed from COMMANDER OF THE TEMPLE to its present form.

28th Degree: Knight of the Sun

This degree began as Francken's 23rd degree of the original Rite of Perfection, where it occupied no less than 35 closely written pages of script! This ritual, called either THE KEY OF MASONRY (English version) or KNIGHT OF THE SUN (original French version) gave rise to Frederick Dalcho's manuscript of 1801 called KNIGHT OF THE SUN OR PRINCE ADEPT. The ritual related the doings of an entity called Father Adam who is assisted in his work by another entity called Brother Truth and a bunch of either angels or some other kind of unspecified spiritual creatures.

Albert Pike expanded the already lengthy Dalcho ritual into 65 pages of long, incomprehensible, rambling lectures on esoteric and mystical topics with neither a common theme nor any discernible practical application. The Northern Jurisdiction adopted this monstrosity in 1867 and worked it for more than 40 years. A ritualist named Buchanan finally condensed it into 30 pages around 1911 but did not change the content. A committee of clergymen was appointed to come with a new ritual in 1938 but their amateur but well-researched efforts failed to oust Pike's work and instead became our present 17th degree (Herod's Temple and the Roman eagle), an introduction to the Rose Croix.

Finally, in 1980, Walker and Deutsch, acting on their own, submitted a ritual based on Elias Ashmole's reception into the Brotherhood of the Rosy Cross. It was adopted as the 28th degree ritual in 1984 and has remained so with only slight modifications made in 2006.

29th Degree: Knight of St. Andrew

The 29th degree was originally called KNIGHT OF SAINT ANDREW OR PATRIARCH OF THE CRUSADES. The French title is *GRAND ECOSSAIS DE SAINT ANDRE*. There are no old French Rituals of the 29° in the archives of the Supreme Council. A modern book of rituals gives only the outline of the Degree without ritual text. Decorations, signs and words are described without any suggestion as to content or meaning.

The Van Rensselaer Ritual of 1845 also has no ritual text. The sign and token are described; also signs of Fire, Air, Water and Earth. There is a Sign of Admiration and another of the Sun. These appear to suggest a relationship in the early rituals with the 28°, KNIGHT OF THE SUN, and its esoteric content. A ritual written by Albert Pike between 1855 and 1865 for the 29° was called GRAND SCOTTISH KNIGHT OF SAINT ANDREW. It describes the induction of a candidate into the Order in an old ruined Scottish castle.

Our present ritual is the Hays-Raymond Ritual of 1864. This ritual is a radical departure from that of Albert Pike. The time period is the 13th century. The scene is in the court of the Turkish Sultan. A group of captured European knights belonging to the Order of Saint Andrew appear before him loaded down with chains. The Sultan discusses ransom for the captives. He asks some questions concerning the Order of Saint Andrew and requests to be initiated. He is at first refused until the Knights learn from the Koran that the essentials of Islamic and Christian belief are the same. The Sultan and two Emirs (governors of Islamic states) are received into the Order. The Obligation follows the Pike ritual and investiture. The Sultan and Emirs pay the knights' ransom. Someone delivers a lengthy lecture on "Toleration" to conclude the Degree.

The last revision, in 2003, makes extensive changes in the dialogue and shortens the playing time considerably. These changes include modernization of the awkward "King James English" style, deletion of superfluous dialogue, and elimination of possibly offensive references to Islam.

30th Degree: Grand Inspector

This degree has a confused and cloudy history because there was nothing even remotely resembling it in the 25 degrees that made up the original Rite of Perfection from the *Council of Emperors of the East and West* in 1758. In the *Roi du Sanctuaire* by Doszedardski (1805-1809), there is a reference to a 31st degree under the title Le Vrai Macon, but there is no ritual text and the setting, investiture and secret work give no suggestion of our present 31st degree.

Albert Pike wrote a ritual around 1865 that was combined with something written by Van Rensselaer. Despite the anti-Catholic bigotry that Pike had included, his ritual was adopted by the Northern Masonic Jurisdiction in 1875. In 1938, the Supreme Council authorized a tentative ritual of the 31st degree based on a dramatic trial scene in an English Civil Court of the 14th century. This was withdrawn in 1941, but the trial scene was made optional. The ritual of 1949 retains the 1938 trial scene somewhat abridged.

The 1949 trial scene is said to follow the legal procedures in an English civil court of the 14th century. In 2004, the action was condensed to the essence of the trial scene, eliminating the "Sages and Lawgivers of the Past" and the admission of a new member to the judicial tribunal. The dialogue was extensively edited from archaic English and legal terms into more contemporary language. These modifications were intended to facilitate the presentation and comprehension of the ritual.

31st Degree: My Brother's Keeper

Please note: Again, the responsibility for this and for any other degree about which I have made critical comments is mine alone.

The 31st degree ritual was originally that of GRAND INSPECTOR INQUISITOR COMMANDER. When the degrees were revised in 2004, the GRAND INSPECTOR ritual was moved back to become the present-day 30th degree, which left the 31st degree as an empty space: a degree with a number but no ritual. The following degree - the 32^{nd,} – SUBLIME PRINCE OF THE ROYAL SECRET – had originally consisted of two parts; the first half of the degree was called "The Allegory of Constans." The allegory first appeared in the 32nd degree ritual in 1916 and told the tale of a young knight who sacrificed his life out of love for his people. In 2004 this allegory was split off from the 32nd degree and moved into the 31st degree's empty slot and the 31st degree was renamed KNIGHT ASPIRANT ("One who seeks advancement to knighthood"). The allegory of the young knight has now been restored to the 32nd degree (see the next section).

In 2011, when the Committee on Ritualistic Matters moved to reincorporate the 31° Ritual of 2008 into the 32°, a new 32° was introduced, on a test basis. This gave valleys the opportunity to confer the test 32° and communicate back to the Committee any suggestions for improvement before the new degree became official. Once the suggestions were reviewed and the test degree was modified to become the new 32° it would be necessary to produce a new 31°.

Thus was born the 31st degree of 2014. In 2014 the Committee on Ritualistic Matters submitted to the Supreme Council the final version of the 32° Ritual of 2014 and a new 31° Tentative Ritual of 2014. This tentative ritual is titled MY BROTHER'S KEEPER.

As I see it, there's a fundamental problem with both this particular degree - the 31st, the new 19th degree, and several others, a problem that has been endemic to the NMJ's degree system for decades: The ritual's concept is dull, juvenile and boring. It contains lots of teaching opportunities but all of them are sacrificed for the sake of delivering a sermon. We could have been given an intelligent, adult script showing a group of Masonic patriots debating and heatedly arguing over the dangerous ramifications of revolting against the British Empire and taking on the most powerful army and navy in the world. Instead we are presented with yet another childish NMJ "Sunday school" play based on, of all things, *The Good Samaritan*, a parable of Jesus that has nothing to do with the American Revolution.

I understand that the new 31st is being offered as a test degree allowing valleys to communicate constructive comments for improvement to the Committee on Ritualistic Matters. Well, here's one for starters: Perhaps our elder, more experienced Brothers who wear purple hats and run the Committee for Ritualistic Matters might, just a few times as an experiment, give the task of writing degree scripts to younger 33° and even 32° Brothers, secular college-educated men of the world, who would understand the kinds of degrees, dialogue and plots that would attract and keep the interest of other young adult men. Men who understand that Scottish Rite Masons are all grown-up and that our degrees do not have to feature plots and dialogue suitable for nine-year old children.

At the present time candidates who come to the Scottish Rite expecting to be presented with interesting esoteric degree work that their blue lodge doesn't offer - say, the Mysteries of Ancient Egypt or something from Grecian mythology - instead find themselves back in Sunday school in their church basement looking at amateur skits featuring Joseph and his brothers or old Solomon and his temple, stuff they grew bored with before they were ten years old. Many of them don't return after receiving their 32nd degree. Nobody wants to be stuck in church all day, yet that's where our candidates find themselves at a NMJ Reunion.

I'm a former medical person. In medicine, a blood transfusion is done as a lifesaving maneuver to replace blood lost through bleeding or depression of the bone marrow. Ritual writing in the Scottish Rite, NMJ, needs a transfusion of new blood, *stat* (hospital slang for "immediately!"). If you don't believe me, look at our declining membership numbers. How much longer must we sit through reworked versions of *Amahl and the Night Visitors* while the Southern Jurisdiction presents profound, adult, esoteric Masonic material to its members - material that teaches them things that they were perhaps unaware of before and that will enrich their lives?

32ⁿᵈ Degree: Sublime Prince of the Royal Secret

This degree, the 32ⁿᵈ, descends directly from the 25ᵗʰ and last degree of the original Rite of Perfection, where it was called "MOST ILLUSTRIOUS SOVEREIGN PRINCE OF MASONRY, GRAND KNIGHT, SUBLIME COMMANDER OF THE ROYAL SECRET." It took place in an 18ᵗʰ-century military encampment. All of the elements of the present degree – the symbolism of the camp, the signs and words, and the motto, "*Spes mea in Deo est*" [My hope is in God] – can be traced back to 1758. These things seem to have come down unaltered for over two centuries from the Emperors of the East and West. It was one of the degrees that Stephen Morin brought from France to San Domingo along with his barrels of wine in 1763. A few years later in Kingston, Jamaica, between 1767 and 1800, the original 25 degrees of the French Rite of Perfection were expanded into the 33-degree system that we now call the Ancient and Accepted Scottish Rite.

The earliest available ritual of this degree is in the manuscript archives of the Rite of Perfection which Henry Andrew Francken received from Stephen Morin and copied, in English, in 1783. The rather long-winded title of the 25ᵗʰ degree in the Francken ritual is "ROYAL SECRET, OR THE KNIGHTS OF ST. ANDREW AND THE FAITHFUL GUARDIANS OF THE SACRED TREASURE. *NE PLUS ULTRA* ('nothing more beyond this'"). Every member was called a "Sublime Prince of the Royal Secret" which, later, became the official title of our present 32ⁿᵈ degree. There was no ritual text, but the knights' camp is described in detail, with water-color drawings of the tents representing the preceding degrees. All of the signs, words and the motto are the same as used in the current 32ⁿᵈ degree.

A ritual written in 1916 is the one used until recently when the 32ⁿᵈ was rewritten. There is a ceremonial section with a condensed symbolism of the Camp that represents only the four Scottish Rite Bodies, not the individual degrees.

This had been followed by an allegory that portrayed the vigil of an aspirant for knighthood (the story of Constans and his tempters). In 2004 the allegory was removed from the 32° ritual to become the 31° degree Ritual of 2004. This change necessitated revisions to the Ceremonial Section, which became the 32° Ritual of 2004. In this ritual, the dubbing follows immediately after the investiture. The Degree concludes with the presentation of the flag and the Commander-in-Chief's dialogue on Patriotism and the triumph of "a worldwide brotherhood of man."

In 2012 the Supreme Council decided that the 32nd degree needed some added luster and it was decided to let one state experiment by recombining the 31st degree allegory, KNIGHT ASPIRANT, back into the old 32nd and designing a new 32nd degree, a new SUBLIME PRINCE OF THE ROYAL SECRET which would be put on only once a year for the entire state. The state chosen to be the guinea pig in the experiment was my own state of New Jersey and for two years we put on the combined degree each May. Since New Jersey is a small state we could easily accommodate all of the candidates in one valley and everything worked beautifully. At the Supreme Council's Membership Conference in Chicago the Council declared that this method henceforth would be obligatory in every one of the 15 states in the Northern Masonic Jurisdiction.

Epilogue

A scene from the play *"The Devil's Disciple"*
by George Bernard Shaw (1897)

The place is Saratoga, New York, the year is 1777. British General John Burgoyne is in his tent, talking with his second-in-command, Major Swindon. General William Howe is expected to arrive within hours from New York with several thousand more British troops. Swindon boasts that even though the Americans outnumber them at the moment, there is nothing to worry about; when Howe arrives from New York with reinforcements the British will wipe out the rebel American army in no time.

BURGOYNE [*enigmatically*] And will we wipe out our enemies in London, too?

SWINDON. In London? What enemies?

BURGOYNE [*forcibly*] Jobbery and snobbery, incompetence and red tape. [*He holds up a dispatch*] I have just heard that General Howe is still in New York.

SWINDON [*thunderstruck*] Good God! He has disobeyed orders!

BURGOYNE [*with sardonic calm*] He has received no orders. Some gentleman in Whitehall forgot to dispatch them; he was leaving town for his holiday, I believe. To avoid upsetting his arrangements, England will lose her American colonies.

SWINDON [appalled] Impossible!

BURGOYNE [coldly] I beg your pardon?

SWINDON. I can't believe it! What will History say?

BURGOYNE. History, Major, will tell lies... as usual.

Notes

Chapter 1 **The Lodge of Perfection**

1."History of the Usage of the Name." (2009). https://en.wikibooks.org/wiki/
Hebrew_Roots/Neglected_Commandments /Honouring_His_Name/History.

2. In the following pages you will come across many ideas with which you may be unfamiliar and which you may regard as strange and perhaps irreverent. Relax; there's nothing to worry about; you will be in good company. Most of these ideas are common currency among archeologists, anthropologists, historians and students of comparative religion. To get an idea of the sometimes violent disagreements among Israelis themselves you should check out the following web site. It's called The Mysteries Archive and it's at **http://hiddenmysteries.org/mysteries/history/ jehovah.html**. Start with the article on *The History of Jehovah* by someone called M-Theory. Here are some excerpts from that article's beginning:

"M-Theory. (1/13/2004). The Mysteries Archive; Hidden Mysteries: The History of Jehovah. http://www.hiddenmysteries.org/mysteries/history/jehova.html)

'All hell broke loose in Israel in November of that year [1999] when Prof. **Ze'ev Herzog** of Tel Aviv University announced: 'The Israelites were never in Egypt, did not wander the desert, did not conquer the land, and did not pass it on to the twelve tribes'.

Moreover, the Jewish God YHWH had a female consort - the goddess Asherah!

His conclusion that the kingdom of David and Solomon was at best a small tribal monarchy, at worst total myth, has made enemies for him in the camps of traditional Jewish and Christian belief systems. He asserts: all evidence demonstrates that the Jews did not adopt monotheism until the 7th Century BCE - a heresy according to the Biblical tradition dating it to Moses at Mount Sinai.

Herzog, moreover, states that Solomon and David are 'entirely absent in the archaeological record'. In addition, Herzog's colleague, **Israel Finkelstein**, claims the Jews were nothing more than nomadic Canaanites who bartered with the city dwellers."

These excerpts will give you some idea of the tenor of this book.

4° **Master Traveler**

1. Michael R. Poll. Personal communication.

2. I don't consider this to be an authentic Scottish Rite degree because it does not teach a character-building lesson (other, perhaps, than patience).

3. Hutchens, R. *A Bridge to Light.* p.17

5° Perfect Master

1. Barnes, I. The Historical Atlas of the Bible. p.69
2. Leviticus 9: 22-24 to 10: 1-5
3. Armstrong, K. *A History of God.* p.22
4. Hutchens, R. *A Bridge to Light.* p.24

6° Master of the Brazen Serpent

1. Draper, Robert. *Kings of Controversy* p.74
2. 2 Kings, 18:4
3. Patai, R. *The Hebrew Goddes*s p. 48
4. Hutchens, R. *A Bridge to Light.* p.32

7° Provost and Judge

1. Hutchens, R. *A Bridge to Light.* p.40

8° Intendant of the Building

1. 1 Kings 1: 5-53
2. 1 Kings 2: 12-25
3. Draper, Robert. *Kings of Controversy.* p73
4. Ibid., pp.79,83
5. 1 Kings 2: 46
6. 2 Samuel; 12:1-25
7. Weber, M. *Ancient Judaism.* p.267
8. 1 Kings 20: 38,41
9. 1 Samuel 10:10-13
10. Hutchens, R. *A Bridge to Light.* p.48

9° Master of the Temple

1. Archaeology ."Did Neanderthals Bury their Dead with Flowers?" http://www.archaeology.org/news/3788-151008-iraq-shanidar-cave. (2015).
2. Wolf, J. (1978). *The Dawn of Man.* New York: H. Abrams, Inc. p.98,99.
3. Mann, C. *The Birth of Religion.* p.48
4. John (4: 24)
5. Anderson, A. & Whitehouse, D. p.127
6. Smith, M. *The Early History of God* pp.191,192

7. Patai, R. *The Hebrew Goddess* p.53

8. Genesis 18: 1-15

9. Genesis 32: 25

10. Patai, R. *The Hebrew Goddess* p.60

11. Ibid., pp.41,58

12. Ibid., p.58

13. Ezekiel 8:14

14. Smith, M. The Early History of God p.34

15. Patai, R. *The Hebrew Goddess* p. 50

16. Jeremiah, 32: 34

17. Patai, R. *The Hebrew Goddess.* p.39

18. Ibid., p.65 Patai suggests that the women may have used molds to make whole-body figurines of Astarte instead of stars but I think that such molds would have been prohibitively expensive and would have used up too much cookie dough to have been very popular with the working class women of Israel. A cookie cutter in the shape of a six-pointed star would have been much more economical and easier to work with.

19. Ibid., p.65 Recent discoveries indicate that the Jews on Elephantine actually worshipped five gods but the exact identities of the last two are as yet uncertain. I suspect that one of them may have been Ashera, Yahweh's consort.

20. Ibid., p.285

21. Hutchens, R. *A Bridge to Light.* p.58

10° Master Elect

1. 1 Kings 1:38

2. Hutchens, R. *A Bridge to Light.* p.58 (essentially a continuation of the 9th degree)

11° Sublime Master Elected

1. Armstrong, K. *A History of God.* p.82 Armstrong opines that Jesus may have been guided in his ministry by the *bat qol.*

2. Hutchens, R. *A Bridge to Light.* p.70

12° Master of Mercy

1. Genesis: 37-45

2. Hutchens, R. *A Bridge to Light.* p.76

13° Master of the Ninth Arch

1. Genesis 5: 18-24

2. Genesis 5:24

3. Jude 1:14

4. Hutchens, R. *A Bridge to Light.* p.86

14° Grand Elect Mason

1. Hutchens, R. *A Bridge to Light.* p.94

Chapter 2. The Council of Princes of Jerusalem

1. I didn't mean to imply that the Babylonians were not good mathematicians. For instance, they were able to solve three-term quadratic equations. These are advanced algebraic expressions having the general form of $ax^2 + bx + c = 0$ in which the unknown (the first term in this form) must be raised to the exponent of 2 so that it can't be zero. Tricky things—especially when you come across them in an examination.

2. Ziggurat. Wikipedia, the free encyclopedia.https://en.wikipedia.org/wiki/Ziggurat.

3. Tobit 1:10

15° Knight of the East

1. Nehemiah 2, 2-4

2. Anglim, Simon et al. Fighting Techniques of the Ancient World 3000 BC -AD 500. p.14

3. Mark, J. (2014). Assyria. Ancient History Encyclopedia. *The Assyrian Deportation Policy.* http://www.ancient.eu/assyria/

4. 2 Kings 22:8

5. Bradford, A. With Arrow, Sword and Spear. p.44

6. 2 Kings 24: 17

7. 2 Chronicles 36:13; Ezekiel 17:13

8. Asimov, I. Asimov's Guide to the Bible. pp569-579

9. Lissner, I. *The Living Past.* pp.112-116

10. Hutchens, R. *A Bridge to Light.* p.113

16° Prince of Jerusalem

1. History of male circumcision. From Wikipedia, the free encyclopedia. (Sept. 2009). https://en.wikipedia.org/wiki/History_of_male_circumcision

2. Herodotus, on the other hand, claimed that Egyptians would not kiss Greeks on the mouth because Greeks ate *cows.* He thought that cows were sacred in Egypt because Hathor, a major Egyptian

goddess along with several other goddesses, were frequently represented as cows. Whatever the case, the prohibition on pig's flesh was only obligatory among the upper classes in Egypt; lower class Egyptians were not so fussy; they ate whatever meat they could get their hands on. In Cairo I have seen funerary murals from upper class Egyptian tombs and they show cows as one of the food sources to be enjoyed in the afterlife. But no pigs. Nor did the Jews or any of their Middle Eastern neighbors ever observe a ban on the consumption of beef. Draw your own conclusions.

3. Patai, R. *The Hebrew Goddess* p.255

4. Smith, M. The Early History of God p.187

5. Armstrong, K. *A History of God.* p.60

6. 1 Kings 12: 26-30; Tobit 1:5.

7. Smith, M. The Early History of God pp.83-85

8. 1 Kings 7:23-26

9. Jeremiah 32:35, 2 Chronicles 33: 6

10. Patai, R. *The Hebrew Goddess* p. 299, note 59 to Chapt. 1 Patai, like many scholars, believes that many of the Biblical condemnations of temple sacred prostitution only referred only to the male prostitutes who gave homosexual services to their customers, something the Jews condemned as unnatural.

11. Hancock, Graham. (2015). *Magicians of the Gods: The Forgotten Wisdom of Earth's Lost Civilization.* New York: St. Martin's Press. In his book, Hancock presents an interesting hypothesis on the possible cause of a flood that affected a good part of the northern hemisphere at the end of the last Ice Age. Some scientists think that fragments of a huge broken-up comet struck the two-mile thick North American ice cap around 10,800 B.C. The heat generated by the impacts melted the ice cap and raised the level of the Atlantic Ocean several hundred feet in a matter of weeks and flooded North America, Europe and the Middle East. The memory of these cataclysmic Ice Age floods is preserved in our scriptures as Noah's flood.

12. Wells, H.G. *The Outline of History.* p.266

13. Gardner, L. *The Shadow of Solomon.* p.185

14. Hutchens, R. *A Bridge to Light.* p.121

Chapter 3. The Chapter of Rose Croix

17 Knight of the East and West

1. Piñero, Antonio. (2016). Herod the Great: The Controversial King of Judea. *Nation Geographic History,*2 (No. 5): p. 44. Herod had already been declared king of Judea in Rome in 40 B.C. but it wasn't until 37 B.C. that Roman forces under Herod took Jerusalem and he could finally move his

capital to there from an old Sidonian city in Galilee named after the goddess Astarte (which Herod later rebuilt and renamed Caesarea). He felt that only in Jerusalem could he officially declare his claim to the throne.

2. Steinberg, Milton. (1947). *Basic Judaism.* New York: Harcourt, Brace & World, Inc. p.12

3. Piñero maintains that the Pharisees at the time of Jesus represented "the Establishment" and had become quite powerful in the Temple, holding high religious offices (Piñero, Herod the Great p.45)

4. Hutchens, R. *A Bridge to Light.* p.126

18° Knight of the Rose Croix of H.R.D.M.

1. Knight, C and Lomas, R. *Uriel's Machine.* p.127

2. Genesis 19: 38

3. 1 Kings 14:21,31 Rehoboam's Ammonite mother

4. 1 Kings 11:7

5. 2 Kings 23:10

6. 2 Kings 21:6. See also Patai, R. *The Hebrew Goddess* p.48

7. Hutchens, R. *A Bridge to Light.* p.136

Chapter 4. The Consistory

19° Brothers of the Trail (Oregon Trail)

1. Sandweiss, Martha A. (2017). Picturing United States History. *John Gast, American Progress, 1872.* http://picturinghistory.gc.cuny.edu/john-gast-american-progress-1872/

2. Cholera and the Thames. *Origins of Cholera.* (2017). http://www.choleraandthethames.co.uk/cholera-in-london/origins-of-cholera/

3. Ibid., *Cholera in London.* (2017).

4. BBC web site. Tchaikovsky & Stravinsky. *Tchaikovsky's Death.* (2014) http://www.bbc.co.uk/radio3/classical/tchaikovsky/atoz/tchaik_d_death.shtml You might want to look this web site up. The cause of the composer's death has been highly controversial and five versions are presented here.

5. Henahan, D. (1981) The New York Times: Arts. *Did Tchaikovsky Really Commit Suicide?* http://www.nytimes.com/1981/07/26/arts/did-tchaikovsky-really-commit-suicide.html?pagewanted=all. Mr. Henahan presents the view that the whole story of Tchaikovsky's suicide was just a fabrication.

6. Wikipedia, the free encyclopedia. *Grattan massacre.* https://en.wikipedia.org/wiki/Grattan_massacre

7. Wikipedia, the free encyclopedia. *Battle of Ash Hollow* [another name for the Battle of Blue Water Creek]. https://en.wikipedia.org/wiki/Battle_of_Ash_Hollow

8. Bray, K. Crazy Horse: *A Lakota Life.* pp.29ff

9. I came across many of the individual items in this essay in Dary, D. *The Oregon Trail*. and King, A. *Seven Trails West*. However, the many facts were so scattered throughout the pages of books that when I attempted to annotate the essay I found that the piece looked as if it had more end-note citations than words, a situation that I thought would prove distracting and annoying to the reader. So I will state here that, with the few exceptions that are indicated in these notes, all of the historical dates, facts and events in the essay must be credited to these two authors. I have made an earnest attempt neither to purloin their research (that is, to misrepresent their ideas as my own) nor to emulate their excellent writing styles. Hopefully, I have succeeded in accomplishing both of these endeavors.

10. Hutchens, R. *A Bridge to Light*. p.152

Interlude: Grand Pontiff, a Public Play

1. I here direct the reader who may be interested learning more about the mythological hero's journey to Joseph Campbell's excellent book, *The Hero with a Thousand Faces*. This book is slanted from the world-view of Jungian psychoanalysis and is a rich source of mythology taken from all the races of mankind.

20° Master ad Vitam (George Washington)

1. Nelson, J. Benedict Arnold's Navy. p.73

2. Ibid., p148

3. Miller, Bill. (2012). The Tea Party Papers, Vol. I, Second Edition. The American Spiritual Evolution Versus the French Political Revolution. https://books.google.com/books?id=V_A_jpVrmBIC&pg=PT152&lpg= PT152&dq=Guy+Carleton+prefabricated+ships+from+England&source=bl&ots=AWhDNXipV3&sig=goESE19pEtlW6w9eiRCKMFDr DiA&hl=en&sa=X&ved=0ahUKEwjUkviRrprUAhXFOyYKHVCeDp4Q6AEILzAC#v= onepage&q=Guy%20Carleton%20prefabricated%20ships%20from%20England&f=false

4. Nelson, J. *Benedict Arnold's Navy*. p.310-311

5. Ibid., p.337

6. Chadwick, B. *George Washington's War*. p.371

7. Ibid., p.372

8. Ibid., p.373

9. Milne, L. and Milne, M. *Franklin and Arnold*. The Philadelphia Inquirer, 23/9/2013. As a final point regarding Arnold's character, I would like to point out Chris Hodapp's note in the blog on his book, Freemasons for Dummies (August 5, 2010): "*Arnold was a proud but enigmatic character. Brother Mason Dr. Joseph Warren was widowed in 1773, leaving four children. After the death of Warren at Bunker Hill, his children were orphaned. Benedict Arnold came to their relief, true to his Masonic obligation. He had*

become friends with Brother Warren while in Massachusetts, and in April, 1778, Arnold contributed $500.00 towards their education. He also persuaded Congress to apply a pension to support them from the date of their father's death until the youngest child reached the age of consent. During the time he spent in Canada after the war, he went broke lending money to loyalists and Masons whom he knew would never repay him." Bro. Hodapp's note was sent to me by Bro. Mohamad Yatim, quoted in a paper that was submitted to the NJ Council of Deliberation Educational Comittee, written by Bro. Bill Morelli (April, 2017).

10. I should clear up two more points about Saratoga. First, all reports indicate that, at some point before his surrender, Burgoyne had received a dispatch from Howe indicating that Howe had tired of besieging New York and, instead of marching north to relieve Burgoyne, he intended to load his troops onto ships and sail up the Delaware River and attack Philadelphia. This would keep him busy for the rest of the year and was an indirect way of informing Burgoyne that he was now on his own. Second, I may have given the wrong impression of Lord Germain's position in the British government during the war. As Secretary of War (also called "The American Secretary" by Nelson) he was not just another bureaucrat warming a desk at Whitehall but exercised a great deal of command power in directing the administration of the war. For instance, he could tell Carlton weather to remain in Canada and direct all his forces to defending the Canadian border or to invade New England to provide a distraction to Washington who was operating further to the south. Howe was taking a chance when he sent his Whitehall friend a letter stating that he had no intention of helping Burgoyne, Germain's favorite. Howe had the authority to relieve him of his command, as he had done to Carleton.

11. Hutchens, R. *A Bridge to Light.* p.160

21° **Patriarch Noachite**

1. Daraul, Arkon. (1961) *A History of Secret Societies.* New York: The Citadel Press. p.202

2. Coil, Henry W. (Revised Ed. 1995 by Allen E. Roberts) *Coil's Masonic Encyclopedia.* Richmond, VA: Macoy Publishing and Masonic Supply Co., Inc. p.315. It is important to remember that both the story of Hiram Abiff and Noah are about exhumations, not resurrections. Nobody is brought back to life, and the frequent exhortations by Masonic officers to the effect that the Third Degree has some reference to the notion of life after death is nonsense. It's more closely akin to a biology lecture than to a sermon on eternal life. In both stories the principal character is dead and so thoroughly decayed when his body is taken from the earth that he can only be raised by a procedure that Masons call The Five Points of Fellowship, which apparently originated in the Noachite ritual. I can't help but believe that the authors of the rituals must have witnessed many such exhumations that were done by municipal workers to relieve the overcrowded conditions of graveyards in the walled Medieval cities of the time. Hence the grisly realism of the present-day Third Degree.

3. 1 Kings: 7, 13 and 2 Chronicles: 2,12

4. Coil, H. *Coil's Masonic Encyclopedia*. p.314

5. Genesis 11: 2,3

6. Hutchens, R. *A Bridge to Light*. p.170

22° Prince of Libanus (Lumberjacks)

1. Exodus 31: 1-6

2. Hutchens, R. *A Bridge to Light*. p.177

23° Knight of Valor (Four Chaplains)

1. Howard Kanowitz, Esq., 33°. Personal communication.

2. Hutchens, R. *A Bridge to Light*. p.182

24° Brother of the Forest (American Indian)

1. Indians.org (2017). *The History of the Cherokee Indians.* http://www.indians.org/articles/cherokee-indians.html

2. Wikipeia, the free encyclopedia. *Prince Hall.* https://en.wikipedia.org/wiki/Prince_Hall. Prince Hall's date and place of birth are unknown and have been given as Barbados, Boston and England, with dates ranging from 1735 to 1738. My story in this book is one of many versions.

3. Hutchens, R. *A Bridge to Light*. p.190

25° Master of Achievement (Benjamin Franklin)

1. Wkidedis, the free encyclopedia. *Benjamin Franklin.*https://en.wikipedia.org/wiki/Benjamin_Franklin

2. Stewart, M. *Nature's God*. p.188

3. Ibid., p.37

4. Ibid., p.31

5. Hutchens, R. *A Bridge to Light*. p.201(old ritual)/205(revised ritual)

26°Friend and Brother Eternal (Gettysburg)

1. McBee, Tresa et al. *Gettysburg*. p.14

2. Ibid., p.23 Years after the war, Heth wrote in a memoir that he hadn't entered Gettysburg with the intention of clashing with Yankees at all; he was really looking for a shoe factory that he had heard existed in the town. He said that he had intended to loot the factory to provide shoes for his men as their own shoes were worn out from marching on long, hard roads for the glory of the Confederacy.

The story was believed for decades and is still cited in some papers but it is now regarded as a fiction that Heth concocted to cover his butt. For one thing, in 1863 Gettysburg had no shoe factory.

3. Ibid., p. 43

4. Ibid., p. 43

5. Robertson, J. *For Us the Living.* p.121

6. Ibid., p.160

7. Ibid., p.160 One of Lee's generals, John B. Gordon, said later that Lee "died believing…that he lost Gettysburg at last by Longstreet's disobedience."

8. Ibid., p.160 Regarding Longstreet's delay on July 3rd, historian Douglas Freeman said: "He [Longstreet] should have obeyed orders, but the orders should not have been given."

9. Ibid., p.153 Barksdale's charge may have been an exercise in futility but it became the subject of one of Edwin Forbes' finest paintings (McBee, Tresa et al. *Gettysburg.* p.74-75).

10. Ibid., p.155

11. Ibid., p.157 Chamberlain was awarded the Medal of Honor (sometimes erroneously referred to as the *Congressional* Medal of Honor) for his defense of Little Round Top. The medal is presented to its recipient by the President of the United States in the name of Congress but the Congress doesn't decide who gets it. Created in 1861, the medal's recipient is decided upon by a complex procedure within the Office of the Secretary of Defense, an appointed Cabinet minister in the administration.

12. . Ibid., p.158 General Heth's statement.

13. Ibid., p.158 Lee wrote in his official report: "The movements of the army preceding the battle of Gettysburg had been much embarrassed by the absence of cavalry."

14. Wolfe, Brendan (4 Jun. 2012). Encyclopedia Virginia. Culp's Hill and Wesley Culp (1839–1863) Accessed 5 July 2014. https://www.encyclopediavirginia.org/Culp_s_Hill_and_Wesley_Culp_1839-1863#

15. McBee, Tresa et al. *Gettysburg.* p.105 Custer had many faults but false modesty was not one of them. After the battle he declared: "I challenge the annals of war to produce a more brilliant charge."

16. Fowler, W. et al. *The Illustrated Encyclopedia of Guns.* p.281 The 7-round Spencer lever-action repeating rifle was patented and first produced in 1860 as a percussion rifle. Soon it could accommodate self-igniting brass-cased ammunition that was loaded into a tubular magazine in the rifle's butt stock. In operation each round was pushed into the firing chamber by working the trigger guard which doubled as a loading lever. This lever also extracted the spent cartridge case of the previous round. It fired a .52 caliber bullet (slightly smaller than the .58 caliber of both Union Springfield and Confederate Enfield rifles) accurately up to a range of 800 yards and could be reloaded in a fraction of the time it would take to reload a percussion revolver of the period. The only drawback

of the weapon was that, when subjected to rapid fire for a prolonged period of time, the rifle became too hot for the shooter to hold and valuable time was lost waiting for the barrel to cool.

17. Ibid., p.126-128 The Civil War was the first major American conflict that saw the universal use of mass-produced revolvers. These pistols, perfected by Samuel Colt (1814-1862) had rifled barrels, were accurate up to forty yards and held six rounds. The revolving cylinder was rotated by cocking the hammer. The .36 caliber Colt Navy 1851 was Colt's masterpiece, a model of perfection; more than 250,000 were turned out in Colt's factory in Hartford, CT. in the 23 years of its production. Within 30 years the pistol would render the use of swords in combat obsolete. Just before the battle of Omduran, during the Boer War in 1898, a forward-thinking young British officer named Winston Churchill replaced his officer's saber with a newly-invented semi-automatic pistol, the ten-round 7.63 mm Mauser C96 *Selbstladen* (self-loading) "Broomhandle". After 1914 the Broomhandle's caliber was raised to the more powerful 9mm Parabellum cartridge (with a muzzle velocity of 1,420 feet per second and accuracy up to 200 feet) and, despite its awkward design, the gun proved so popular among military officers and civilians that it remained in production until 1937. In 1983 the sci-fi movie *Star Wars: Episode VI – Return of the Jedi* featured the character Han Solo using a Mauser Broomhandle as a blaster! Apparently Mauser even has a factory in a galaxy far, far away.

18. Robertson, J. *For Us the Living.* p.159 Alexander has also introduced Maj. Albert Myers' "wig-wag" system of sending messages on the battlefield by waving signal banners. On July 3, 1863 he had 150 cannon under his command. On that day he wrote that he thought everything was going to "come out right because Gen. Lee had planned it."

19. Ibid., p.135

20. Fowler, W. et al. *The Illustrated Encyclopedia of Guns.* p281. One reason for the tremendous number of casualties in the Civil War was the recent advances in firearm technology. A deadly innovation of the Civil War was the use by both North and South of the recently-invented Minié bullet. Introduced around 1850, the conical bullet had a hollow base. Slightly smaller than the diameter of the rifle, the round could be easily dropped or rammed down the rifle barrel, enabling a trained soldier to load and fire his rifle three times a minute. When the gunpowder was ignited, the gases caused the hollow base of the bullet to expand and fit tightly into the grooves of the barrel's rifling, giving it tremendous muzzle velocity, deadly accuracy and a killing range of up to 1000 yards, the same as the author's semi-automatic M1 Garand rifle that was issued to him as a recruit in the U.S. Marines at Paris Island.

21. Armistead is usually portrayed as running out in front of his troops twirling his hat on the tip of his sword all the way across the field. I have used the version given by Dale Carnegie in his classic book *How to Win Friends and Influence People* (p.132) only because it was the first time I had ever read about the incident and the description has stayed with me over many years. Armistead was a 46-year old widower who was revered by his men. As young man he had been expelled from West Point

for hitting another cadet, Jubal Early, who would later become a fellow Confederate general, on the head with a dinner plate. His closest friend in the Army was fellow Freemason and Union general Winfield Scott Hancock. I'm certain that, in his weakened state, the news of Hancock's severe wounds hastened Armistead's decline and death.

22. As with Lord Germain in the 20th degree, I don't want to minimize Hancock's role at Gettysburg. Gen. John Reynolds, the Corps Commander of the entire field, was killed when the battle began early on July 1. When the news reached Gen. Meade, who had not yet arrived at Gettsyburg, Meade sent Hancock, who had been promoted to Major General the previous December, on ahead to be temporary Corps Commander. Before Hancock could assume his duties he had to argue with another Maj. Gen., Oliver Howard, who ranked him in seniority and thought that *he* should be Corps Commander. Hancock won the argument and commanded the field until an even more senior Maj. Gen., Henry Slocum, arrived that evening and assumed command until Meade arrived around midnight.

23. Gerard, Philip (2012) Our State: Celebrating North Carolina. https://www.ourstate.com/kinston-hangings-part-2/

24. Hutchens, R. *A Bridge to Light*. p.215

27° Knight of Jerusalem

1. Wikipedia, the free encyclopedia.

https://en.wikipedia.org/wiki/ Treatise_of_the_Three_Impostors.

2. Gardner, L. *Realm of the Ring Lords*. pp.21-23

3. Norwich, J. *Absolute Monarchs*. p.54

4. Ibid., p.17

5. Hutchens, R. *A Bridge to Light*. p.227

28° Knight of the Sun

1. Revelation 21: 9-27

2. McNab. A History of the World in 100 Weapons. pp.85-87

3. Fowler, W. et al. The Illustrated Encyclopedia of Guns.pp.24-25

4. Weapon: A Visual History of Arms and Armor. (2006) London: DK. pp.164-165

5. Forged In Fire: Cutting Deeper; S1 Ep 13 – *The Zweihander*. Recorded 4/2. 7:59p on 875 HISHD 61 min. TV-PG HD CC.

6. Wikipedia, the free encyclopedia. Elias Ashmole. https://en.wikipedia.org/wiki/Elias_Ashmole#Solicitor.2C_royalist_and_freemason.

7. Hutchens, R. *A Bridge to Light*. p.255

29° Knight of St. Andrew

1. Tuchman, B. *A Distant Mirror.* p. 543

2. Ibid., p. 540 This action was customary in many Asian cultures of the time. See the actions of Cambyses in the 16th degree.,

3. Ibid., p. 541

4. Ibid., p.545 The European class system was rampant in the Middle Ages; all knights and officers were from the nobility and the upper classes.

5. Ibid., p. 546

6. Ibid., p. 546 DeCoucy is the principal character in Tuchman's book; she follows his life history throughout.

7. In an age before refrigeration the only ways to insure a supply of fresh meat were either to drive your own cattle with you or steal animals from the lands you passed through. Most bands of Crusaders did both.

8. Bennett, M. et al. *Fighting Techniques of the Medieval World.* A ballista was a giant crossbow that shot a bolt the size of a spear. Mangonels and trebuchets were stone-hurling machines like catapults.

9. Tuchman, B. *A Distant Mirror.* p. 553

10. Ibid., p. 552

11. Ibid., pp. 554-555

12. Ibid., p. 556 Nicopolis actually consisted of two adjoined walled cities, both well prepared to withstand a long siege.

13. Ibid., p. 557

14. Ibid., p. 559

15. Singman, J. *The Middle Ages.* p.139

16. Tuchman, B. *A Distant Mirror.* p. 559

17. Ibid., p. 560 A dismounted knight in full armor, although not nearly as fearsome as when mounted on a charger, was still quite deadly, at least until he tired from the weight of his armor (which he was unable to remove unaided while in the field).

18. Ibid., p. 562

19. Ibid., p. 562

20. Ibid., p. 571 Also spelled Brusa in some accounts.

21. Ibid., p. 582

22. Ibid., p. 585

23. Hutchens, R. *A Bridge to Light.* p.264

30° Grand Inspector

1. Hutchens, R. *A Bridge to Light.* p.272

31° My Brother's Keeper (Paul Revere)

1. Boston Massacre Historical Society. *Captain Preston's Unknown Biography.* http://www.bostonmassacre.net/players/preston-biography.htm Very little today is known about Captain Preston other than the facts that he was an officer in the 29th Regiment of Foot and that he commanded the relief detail that came to back up Pvt. White on the evening of March 5, 1770. There is a disagreement over whether Preston was 40 or 48 years old at the time of the Massacre. Either age would seem rather advanced for someone holding the rank of Captain. However, historian Michael P. Quinlan noted that: "...the average man in the twenty-ninth was over thirty, medium tall and Irish". Perhaps promotion was infrequent in that regiment. After his acquittal Preston resigned his commission and is thought to have lived the rest of his life in Ireland. There is even disagreement over his severance pay that he received upon retirement, ranging from a one-time payment of £200 to an annual payment of £200.

2. This is only one of several versions of the colonial "Triangle of Trade" that I have seen. This one was taught in my undergraduate college U.S. History course. All of the versions, however, include a stop on the west coast of Africa to trade for slaves.

3. Perhaps the men had already loaded their musket barrels with powder and shot while still at their barracks. Then they would need only to prime their frizzen pans with a small charge of powder to render them fully ready to fire when given the order.

4. Boston Massacre Historical Society. *The Boston Massacre Trial.* http://www.bostonmassacre.net/players/preston-biography.htm

5. See Plate 20 at https://www.facebook.com/highdegrees/

6. Hutchens, R. *A Bridge to Light.* p.289

32° Sublime Prince of the Royal Secret

1. Graves, R. *The White Goddess.* p.478

2. Alcock, L. *Arthur's Britain.* pp.87-91

3. Churchill, W. *The Birth of Britain.* p.43

4. Tuchman, B. *A Distant Mirror.* p.52

5. Singman, J. *The Middle Ages.* p.140

6. Wikipedia, the free encyclopedia. *Geoffrey II, Duke of Brittany.* https://en.wikipedia.org/ wiki/Geoffrey_II,_Duke_of_Brittany

7. Cavendish, R. (2009). History Today. *Henry II Dies of Tournament Wounds.* http://www.historytoday.com/richard-cavendish/henry-ii-france-dies-tournament-wounds. Catherine was also an ardent disciple of the French astrologer Nostradamus who is said to have prophesized the event.

8. E-ssortment. (2011) Medieval History: *The Vigil Of Arms.* http://www.essortment.com/medieval-history-vigil-arms-21329.html

9. Yamamoto, T. *Hagakure; the Book of the Samurai.* The author of the book, a samurai living in the year 1679, tells us that, seven times in his career, he was ordered to fight on foot as a *ronin* (a masterless samurai who didn't rate a horse). At last he was restored permanently to a mounted status again. The saying among samurai was "If one has not been a *ronin* at least seven times he will not be a true retainer. Seven times down, eight times up." p.48

10. Sumptuary Laws of the Middle Ages. http://www.lordsandladies.org/sumptuary-laws-middle-ages.htm.

11. Wikipedia, the free encyclopedia. *Sumptuary Law.* https://en.wikipedia .org/wiki/Sumptuary_law# Medieval_ and_Renaissance_Europe

12. Singman, J. *The Middle Ages.* p.56

13. Ibid. p.150

14. . Gies, J. & F., *Life In a Medieval Castle.* P.107

15. Singman, J. The Middle Ages. p.192

16. Ibid., p.269

17. Ibid., p.151

18. Gies, J. & F., *Life In a Medieval Castle.* p.116

19. Weir, A. *The Wars of the Roses.*

20. Gies, J. & F., *Life In a Medieval Castle.* pp. 112-114

21. Weir, A. *The Wars of the Roses*

22. Cohen, R. *Sugar Love.* p. 86. A 15th-century caliph had an full-sized mosque built, made entirely of marzipan. Poor people were allowed to pray in it and then eat some of it on the way out. It didn't last long.

23. Gies, J. & F., *Life In a Medieval Castle* p.115

24. Ibid., p.113

25. Ibid., p.116

26. Tuchman, B. *A Distant Mirror* p.503

27. Gies, J. & F., *Life In a Medieval Castle* p.118

28. Ibid., p.125

29. Ibid., pp.128-134

30. Tuchman, B. *A Distant Mirror* p.242

31. Hutchens, R. *A Bridge to Light.* p.301

Appendix A. A Brief History of the Scottish Rite

1. The soldiers tied the recalcitrant Scotsmen, kneeling or lying prone, to short stakes driven into the ground between high and low tide. When the tide came in, the victim slowly drowned. This is said to have formed the basis of the mournful Scottish song, Loch Lomond. The woman takes the safer, patrolled highway but the man, to avoid capture, takes the lesser-used low roads that ran along the coast. He is apprehended by British soldiers, and on his refusal to acknowledge the hegemony of the English king, is drowned in the sea. Another theory holds that the song is a lament for clansmen killed in the Battle of Culloden (1746).

2. McGregor, Martin I. (2007) *A Biographical Sketch of Chevalier Andrew Michael Ramsay.* http://www.freemasons-freemasonry.com/ramsay_biography_ oration.html This web site gives a detailed biography of Ramsay plus the complete text of his speech and is well worth a look. The analysis of Ramsay's speech is, of course, entirely my own and I am responsible for any errors or awkward writing in the analytical paragraphs. Any differences of opinion a reader may hold regarding this material will be with me, not Brother McGregor.

3. Prebble, John. (1967). *Culloden.* Harmondsworth, Middlesex: Penguin Books. p.227

4. Michael R. Poll. Personal communication.

5. Ridley, J. *The Freemasons.* p.267

Appendix B. History and Development of the Degrees

1. The contents of this appendix are the intellectual property of the Supreme Council of the Scottish Rite, Northern Masonic Jurisdiction of the United States of America and, as proprietary information, are not in the public domain. They cannot lawfully be reproduced or published without the express permission of the Supreme Council's Committee for Ritualistic Matters. The manuscript of this book, including the contents of Appendix B, has been reviewed carefully (twice) by the Committee for Ritualistic Matters of the Northern Masonic Jurisdiction's Supreme Council and in accordance with Article 602 of the Scottish Rite's Constitution the Committee has given the author both written and verbal authorization to publish the contents thereof in this book.

Due to the scattered nature and variety of the information presented in this section Appendix B is not annotated. The credit for the informational sources are:

Trexler, DeForrest. (2008). *The Degree Rituals of the Supreme Council, 33°, AASR for the Northern Masonic Jurisdiction.* Supreme Council, 33°, AASR, NMJ.

Scripts of the degrees on several CD ROMS issued to Scottish Rite Masons by the Supreme Council of the Scottish Rite, Northern Masonic Jurisdiction of the United States of America.

Epilogue

1. Shaw gives the first version of the story: that Howe's orders had been delayed and he never received them. Perhaps, as an Englishman, Shaw didn't want to acknowledge Howe's disregard for a fellow British officer. Actually, Howe would have been in Philadelphia rather than in New York by the time Burgoyne received the dispatch if he had not already been forced to evacuate the city, since reports say that Howe, in the dispatch, had told Burgoyne of his plans to invade Philadelphia.

Bibliography

Alcock, Leslie. (1973). *Arthur's Britain.* New York: Penguin Books.

Anglim, Simon et al. (2002). *Fighting Techniques of the Ancient World 3000 BC –AD 500: Equipment, Combat Skills, and Tactics.* New York: Metro/Amber Books, Ltd.

Anthony, David W. (2007). *The Horse, the Wheel and Language: How Bronze-Age Riders from the Eurasian Steppes Shaped the Modern World.* Princeton and Oxford: Princeton University Press.

Armstrong, Karen. (1993). *A History of God: The 4000-Year Quest of Judaism, Christianity and Islam.* New York: Alfred E. Knopf.

Asimov, Isaac. (1988). *Asimov's Guide to the Bible: The Old and New Testaments.* New York: Avenel Books.

Aslan, Reza. (2013). *Zealot: The Life and Times of Jesus of Nazareth.* New York: Random House.

Baigent, Michael, Leigh, Richard and Lincoln, Henry. (1982). *Holy Blood, Holy Grail.* New York: Delacorte Press.

Baigent, Michael and Leigh, Richard. (1989). *The Temple and the Lodge.* New York: Arcade.

Barnes, Ian. (2006). *The Historical Atlas of the Bible: A Visual Guide from Ancient times to the New Testament.* New York: Chartwell Books, Inc.

Barrett, David V. (2007). *A Brief History of Secret Societies.* Philadelphia: Running Press.

Barrett, William (Ed.). (1956). *Zen Buddhism: Selected Writings of T. D. Suzuki.* New York: Doubleday Anchor Books.

Beaderstadt, Jan L. (2004, 2005). *On the Wings of the Double Eagle: A Commentary of the Degrees of the Ancient Accepted Scottish Rite Northern Masonic Jurisdiction.* Vol. I, II, III. Turner, MI: Coffee Time Press.

Beitzel, Barry J. (1985). *The Moody Atlas of Bible Lands.* Chicago: Moody Press

Bennett, Mathew et al. (2006). *Fighting Techniques of the Medieval World AD 500 – 1500: Equipment, Combat Skills, and Tactics.* New York: Metro/Amber Books, Ltd.

Bradford, Alfred S. (2001, Fall River Press Ed. 2007). *With Arrow, Sword and Spear: A History of Warfare in the Ancient World.* New York: Fall River Press.

Bray, Kingsley M. (2006). *Crazy Horse: A Lakota Life.* Norman, OK: U. of Oklahoma Press.

Bronowski, Jacob. (1973). *The Ascent of Man.* Boston: Little, Brown and Company.

Brown, William M.; Cummings, William L. and Voorhis, H.V.B. (Editors) (1996). *Coil's Masonic Encyclopedia.* Richmond: Macoy.

Budge, E. A. Wallis. (1904, Dover ed. 1969). *The Gods of the Egyptians.* Vols. I and II. Dover Publications, Inc.: New York.

Butler, Alan. (2004). *The Goddess, the Grail, and the Lodge: Tracing the Origins of Religion.* New York: Barnes & Noble.

Campbell, Joseph. (1949, Princeton U. Ed. 1973). *The Hero with a Thousand Faces.* Princeton: Princeton University Press.

Campbell, Joseph. (1959). *The Masks of God: Primitive Mythology.* New York: Penguin Books.

Campbell, Joseph. (1962). *The Masks of God: Oriental Mythology.* New York: Penguin Books.

Campbell, Joseph. (1964). *The Masks of God: Occidental Mythology.* New York: Penguin Books.

Campbell, Joseph. (1968). *The Masks of God: Creative Mythology.* New York: Penguin Books.

Cantor, Norman F. (1993). *The Civilization of the Middle Ages.* New York: Harper Perennial.

Chadwick, Bruce. (2004). *George Washington's War: The Forging of a Revolutionary Leader and the American Presidency.* Naperville, IL: Sourcebooks, Inc.

Churchill, Winston S. (1956, Bantam ed. 1963). *A History of the English-Speaking Peoples: Vol. 1. The Birth of Britain.* New York: Bantam Books, Inc.

Cohen, Rich. (2013). Sugar Love (A Not So Sweet Story). *National Geographic,* 224 (No. 2): 78 – 97.

Cornfeld, Gaalya (General Editor) (1982). *Josephus: The Jewish War.* Grand Rapids: Zondervan.

Cooper, Robert L. D. (2006). *Cracking the Freemasons' Code: The Truth about Solomon's Key and the Brotherhood.* Toronto: Atria Books.

Cross, Frank Moore. (1973). *Canaanite Myth and Hebrew Epic: Essays in the History of the Religion of Israel.* Cambridge: Harvard University Press.

Dary, David. (2004). *The Oregon Trail.* New York: Alfred A. Knopf.

DeLuca, Allan. (2015). Prince Hall – The First Negro Freemason. *The Square,* 41 (No.1): 45 – 46.

Dever, W.G. (2003). *Who Were the Early Israelites and Where Did They Come From?* Grand Rapids: Wm. B. Eerdmans.

Dever, W.G. (2005). *Did God Have a Wife? Archeology and Folk Religion in Ancient Israel.* Grand Rapids: Wm. R. Eerdmans.

Draper, Robert. (2010). Kings of Controversy. *National Geographic,* 218 (No. 6): 66 – 91.

Ehrman, Bart D. (2014). *How Jesus Became God: The Exaltation of a Jewish Preacher from Galilee.* New York: Harper Collins.

Erlande-Brandenburg, Alain. (2000). *The Cathedral Builders of the Middle Ages.* (Transl. R. Stonehewer). London: Thames & Hudson.

Fagan, Brian. (2015). Did Akhenaten's Monotheism Influence Moses? *Biblical Archeology Review,* 41 (No. 4): 42 – 49.

Ferling, John. (2009). *Almost a Miracle: The American Victory in the War of Independence.* New York: Oxford University Press.

Fernández-Armestro, Felipe. (2002). *Near a Thousand Tables: A History of Food.* New York: Free Press.

Frank, Harry Thomas. (1975). *Discovering the Biblical World.* Maplewood, NJ: Hammond Incorporated.

Franklin, Benjamin. (1793, Spencer ed. 1936). *Autobiography.* New York: The Spencer Press.

Frazer, Sir James G. (1900, Touchstone abridged ed. 1996). *The Golden Bough: A Study in Magic and Religion.* New York: Touchstone.

Freud, Sigmund. (1939). *Moses and Monotheism.* New York: Knopf

Friedman, Richard E. (1989). *Who Wrote the Bible?* New York: Harper One.

Gardner, Joseph L. (Ed.). (1981). *Atlas of the Bible: An Illustrated Guide to the Holy Land.* New York: Reader's Digest Assoc.

Gardner, Laurence. (2000). Bloodline of the Holy Grail. The Hidden Lineage of Jesus Revealed. New York: Barnes & Noble Books.

Gardner, Laurence. (2002). *Genesis of the Grail Kings: The Explosive Story of Genetic Cloning and the Ancient Bloodline of Jesus.* Gloucester, MA: Fair Winds Press.

Gardner, Laurence. (2002). *Realm of the Ring Lords: The Myth and Magic of the Grail Quest*. Gloucester, MA: Fair Winds Press.

Gardner, Laurence. (2005). *The Shadow of Solomon: The Lost Secret of the Freemasons Revealed*. London: HarperElement.

Gies, Joseph and Gies, Frances. (1974). *Life in a Medieval Castle*. New York: Perennial.

Gimbutas, Marija. (1982). *The Goddesses and Gods of Old Europe: Myths and Cult Images*. Berkeley and Los Angeles: U. of California Press.

Ginzberg, Louis. (2005). *Legends of the Jews*. New York: Standard Publications, Inc.

Graves, Robert. (1948, Farrar, Straus and Giroux ed. 1966). *The White Goddess: A Historical Grammar of Poetic Myth*. Amended and enlarged edition. New York: Farrar, Straus and Giroux.

Halley, Henry H. (1965). *Halley's Bible Handbook: An Abbreviated Bible Commentary*. Grand Rapids: Zondervan.

Heller, Julek and Headon, Deirdre. (1982). *Knights*. New York: Shocken Books.

Herd, Robert. (2012). *The Initiatic Experience: Ancient Pathways that Led to Your Initiation Into Freemasonry*. Colorado Springs, CO: Starr Publishing, LLC.

Hodapp, Christopher. (2005). *Freemasons for Dummies*. Hoboken, NJ: Wiley.

Hodapp, Christopher and Von Kannon, Alice. (2008). *Conspiracy Theories & Secret Societies for Dummies*. Hoboken, N.J: Wiley

Hoebel, E. Adamson. (1958). *Man in the Primitive World; An Introduction to Anthropology*. 2nd Ed. New York: McGraw-Hill.

Howarth, Stephen. (1982). *The Knights Templar*. New York: Barnes & noble.

Hughan, W.J. and Hawkins, E.L. (Eds). (1920). Albert G. Mackey's *An Encyclopedia of Freemasonry and Its Kindred Sciences*. Vols. I & II. New York and London: the Masonic History Company.

Hutchens, Rex R. (2006). *A Bridge to Light: The Revised Standard Pike Ritual.* Louisville, KY: V.G. Reed & Sons.

Jacob, Margaret C. (2006). *The Origins of Freemasonry: Facts & Fictions*. Philadelphia: University of Pennsylvania Press.

Johnson, Paul. (1987). *A History of the Jews*. New York: Harper Perennial.

King, Francis. (1975). *Magic: The Western Tradition*. Thames and Hudson: London.

Knight, Christopher and Lomas, Robert. (1996). *The Hiram Key: Pharaohs, Freemasons and the Discovery of the Secret Scrolls of Jesus*. New York: Barnes & Noble.

Knight, Christopher and Lomas, Robert. (2001). *Uriel's Machine: Uncovering the Secrets of Stonehenge, Noah's Flood, and the Dawn of Civilization*. Gloucester: Fair Winds Press.

Knight, Christopher and Lomas, Robert. (2005). *The Book of Hiram: Freemasonry, Venus, and the Secret Key to the Life of Jesus*. USA: Element.

Koch, G. Adolf. (1933, Apollo ed. 1968). *Religion of the American Enlightenment*. New York: Thomas Y. Crowell.

Lissner, Ivar. (1957). *The Living Past: 7000 Years of Civilization*. (Transl. J. Maxwell Brownjohn). New York: Capricorn Books.

Mackey, Albert G. (1898, Dover ed. 2008). *The History of Freemasonry: Its Legendary Origins*. Mineola, New York: Dover Publications.

Mann, Charles C. (2011). The Birth of Religion. *National Geographic*, 219 (No. 6):34-59.

McBee, Tresa; McPherson, James M., et al. (2013). *Gettysburg: A Day-by-Day Account of the Greatest Battle of the Civil War*. Time Books: New York.

Milne, Larissa and Milne, Michael. (2013). *Franklin and Arnold, hero and villain in London*. The Philadelphia Inquirer, Sunday edition, September 23, 2013.

Morris, S. Brent. (2006). *The Complete Idiot's Guide to Freemasonry*. New York: Alpha Books.

Nelson, James L. (2007). *Benedict Arnold's Navy: The Ragtag Fleet That Lost the Battle for Lake Champlain but Won the American Revolution*. Camden, ME: McGraw-Hill

Nemet-Nejat, Karen Rhea. (1998). *Daily Life in Ancient Mesopotamia*. Peabody, MA: Hendrickson.

Newell, Aimee E. (2010). Joseph Cerneau's Supreme Council: Misunderstanding or Malice? *The Northern Light*, 41(No. 2): 4-7.

Norwich, John Julius. (2011). *Absolute Monarchs: A History of the Papacy*. New York: Random House.

Pagels, Elaine. (1989). *The Gnostic Gospels*. New York: Random House Vintage.

Patai, Raphael. (1990). *The Hebrew Goddess*. 3rd Ed. Detroit: Wayne State U. Press.

Peters, Arthur King. (1996). *Seven Trails West*. New York: Abbeville Press.

Piatigorsky, Alexander. (1997). *Freemasonry: The Study of a Phenomenon*. London: Harvill Press.

Pike, Albert. (1871, NuVision ed. 2007). *Morals and Dogma of the Ancient and Accepted Scottish Rite of Freemasonry*. Digital Publication: Nu Vision.

Porter, Cliff. (2011). *The Secret Psychology of Freemasonry: Alchemy, Gnosis, and the Science of the Craft*. Colorado Springs, CO: Starr Publishing, LLC.

Ralls, Karen. (2003). *The Templars and the Grail: Knights of the Quest*. Wheaton, IL: Quest Books.

Ridley, Jasper. (2001). *The Freemasons: A History of the World's Most Powerful Secret Society.* New York: Arcade.

Roberts, Allen E. (1985). *Freemasonry in American History.* Richmond: Macoy.

Robertson, James L. (2010). *For Us the Living: The Civil War in Paintings and Eyewitness Accounts.* New York: Sterling.

Robinson, John J. (1989). *Born in Blood: The Lost Secrets of Freemasonry.* New York: M. Evans & Co.

Schonfield, Hugh J. (1965). *The Passover Plot: A New Interpretation of the Life and Death of Jesus.* New York: Bantum Books

Segovia, Carlos A. (2015). The Dead Sea Scrolls, Hidden Jewish Archives. *National Geographic History,* 1: 30-39.

Singman, Jeffrey L. (1999). *The Middle Ages: Everyday Life In Medieval Europe.* New York: Sterling.

Smith, Mark S. (2002). *The Early History of God: Yahweh and the Other Deities in Ancient Israel.* 2nd Ed. Grand Rapids: Wm. B. Eerdmans.

Stewart, Matthew. (2014). Nature's God: The Heretical Origins of the American Republic. New York: W. W. Norton & Company.

Strong, James. (1984). *The New Strong's Exhaustive Concordance of the Bible.* New York: Thomas Nelson Publishers.

Tannahill, Reay. (1988). *Food in History.* New York: Three Rivers Press.

Trexler, DeForrest. (2008). *The Degree Rituals of the Supreme Council, 33°, AASR for the Northern Masonic Jurisdiction.* Supreme Council, 33°, AASR, NMJ.

Tsunetomo, Yamamoto. (1979). *Hagakure; The Book of the Samurai.* (Transl. William Scott Wilson). New York: Avon Books.

Tuchman, Barbara W. (1978). *A Distant Mirror: The Calamitous 14th Century.* New York: Ballantine Books.

Wallace-Murphy, Tim and Hopkins, Marilyn. (2000) *Rosslyn: Guardian of the Secrets of the Holy Grail.* New York: Barnes & Noble.

Wallace-Murphy, Tim and Hopkins, Marilyn. (2004) *Templars in America: From the Crusades to the New World.* San Francisco: Red Wheel/Weiser, LLC.

Weber, Max. (1952). *Ancient Judaism.* (Transl. Gerth, H. H. and Martindale, D.) New York: The Free Press.

Weir, Alison. (1995). *The Wars of the Roses.* Random House: London.

Wells, H. G. (1920, Doubleday ed. 1949). *The Outline of History.* New York: Country Life Press.

White, T.H. (1958, Ace ed. 1987). *The Once and Future King.* New York: Ace Books.

Scriptural Sources

Berlin, A. and Brettler, M. Z. (Eds.) (2003). *The Jewish Study Bible: Torah, Nevi'im, Kethuvim. Tanakh Translation from the Traditional Masoretic Text.* Oxford University Press.

Fox, Everett. (1997). *The Five Books of Moses: Genesis, Exodus, Leviticus, Numbers and Deuteronomy.* New York: Schocken.

Moffatt, James. (1954). *A New Translation of the Bible Containing the Old and the New Testaments.* New York: Harper & Row.

The Comparative Study Bible: King James Version; Amplified Bible: New American Standard Bible; New International Version. (1984). Grand Rapids: Zondervan.

The Holy Bible; King James Version. (No date of publication). Denver: Life for Laymen, Inc.

Jones, Alexander (Ed.) (1968). *The Jerusalem Bible; Reader's Edition.* Garden City, NY: Doubleday & Company, Inc.

The New American Bible. St. Joseph Ed. (1970). New York: Catholic Book Publishing Co.

New Orleans Scottish Rite College
http://www.youtube.com/c/NewOrleansScottishRiteCollege

Clear, Easy to Watch
Scottish Rite and Craft Lodge
Video Education

Made in the USA
Columbia, SC
17 June 2018